TONGUE OF THE PROPHETS

ROBERT ST. JOHN

Eliezer Ben Yehuda, the Jewish scholar who almost unaided revived the Hebrew language and helped to lay the cornerstone for the new state of Israel, was born in a small town in Lithuania, educated in Russia and France. It was in Paris that he conceived the idea to which he was to devote his life, for even as a young man he realized that Jews could never have any country of their own, or any national entity, unless they had a common language. He determined to revive ancient Hebrew and make it the common language of a new Jewish state.

In 1881, with practically no money and in the worst possible health—the doctors told him he had only a few months to live—he set out for Palestine. Shortly after his arrival he sent for Deborah, the daughter of one of his benefactors, but before he married her he made her promise to speak nothing but Hebrew to him or to any children they might have. Thus, with the birth of their first child, Deborah Ben Yehuda became "the first Hebrew mother in nearly two thousand years."

In Jerusalem, Ben Yehuda taught school, published a newspaper, the *Deer*, which became a fighting spokesman for Jewish independence and a testing ground for the words which he was constantly adding to the Hebrew language. At the same time he began work on his great Hebrew dictionary.

Deborah died, but the crusade went on. The *Deer* became the center of controversy both inside and outside Palestine, and the Turks finally banned it for almost two years. Ben Yehuda married his wife's sister, who in 1909 found a German publisher for the first volumes of the dictionary.

gr
m
his dictionary ... was spoken freely in Palestine, and Zionism had become firmly established in the political thinking of the world. While he was alive, he had been attacked on all sides, but in death he was mourned by all factions as a truly great man.

This biography of Ben Yehuda is the touching and inspiring story of a frail scholar burning with an inner fire, whose fanatical devotion to a single idea triumphed against overwhelming odds.

During World War II, Robert St. John doubled as a top-flight foreign correspondent and radio commentator broadcasting to the United States from London, Paris, and the fighting fronts. From his personal observations as an Associated Press reporter in the Balkans, he wrote his first book, *From the Land of Silent People*, an unforgettable story of the brutal Nazi conquest of Yugoslavia. A few years later, he authored *The Silent People Speak*, covering Yugoslavia during the early post-war period. In this latter book he forecast an early break between Tito and Moscow, and three months after publication his prediction came true.

Turning his attention to Palestine, Mr. St. John wrote *Shalom Means Peace*, a dramatic eyewitness report of the birth of the new state of Israel. With the co-operation of the Ben Yehuda family, he then commenced research on TONGUE OF THE PROPHETS, and he has worked on this biography for the past three years.

Mr. St. John currently resides in France, returning to the United States for periodic lecture tours. In addition to his non-fiction works, he is also the author of a novel, *It's Always Tomorrow*.

Hemda and Eliezer Ben-Yehuda in Jerusalem, 1893

„הילד העברי הראשון" בגיל 4

Ben Zion Ben Yehuda, the first *modern* Hebrew speaking child.

Hemda, Deborah's sister and second wife of Eliezer Ben-Yehuda.

Shlomoh Yonas, father of Deborah and Hemda.

דוד ילין

[illegible] הירושלמי

למלך שכעס על עבדו,
והרגו בבית קלון וכו׳

ר׳ נחמן [illegible]
ר׳ אחא

[illegible]

[illegible]

מצוות הנהרגים היו מתיזין את
ראשו בסיף כדרך שהמלכות עושה
ר׳ יהודה אומר ניוול הוא (זה)
אלא מניחין את ראשו על הסדן
וקוצץ בקופיץ אמרו לו אין מיתה מנוולת
מזו

Handwritten notes of Eliezer Ben-Yehuda.

Some early members of the Hebrew Language Committee in 1912—from right to left: (seated) E. Ben-Yehuda, Y. Klausner, D. Yellin, E. M. Lipschütz; (standing) H. A. Zuta, Q. Silmann, A. Z. Idelsohn, A. Y. Brawer (the latter three were not members, but close to the Committee's work).

יום הששי ה' חשון . אלף ושמנה מאות ושש עשרה לחרבן . Jaffa (Palestine)

שנה ראשנה

הצבי

גליון א

מחיר כל גליון בארץ ישראל
בחשבון הסלך .

מחיר מודעות חצי גרוש
בעד שורה קטנה .

יבשר פעם בשבוע חדשות ... יום יום ומעניני היהודים בכל מקומותם

נערך על ידי ... עסק ירושלם ת"ו .

דברי ימים להסריעת .

ארץ מצרים ר תה עתה להממשלות שנית ענין לעסוק בו . כי חרל חדלה ממשלת מצרים משלם תשלו' תוצותיה , כי ..ן כסף לה להוצאותיה יום ... ותודיע כי ששה שבועות ג תשלם עד אם ירוח לה מעט , ותגדל מבוכה בין נושיה כי יראים הם פן יהיה ליהם לחכות ימים רבים עד אשר ירוח לה . צוינה כל הממשלות לציריהן להודיע את משלת מצרים כי לא בצדק עשתה את הדבר הזה , ויתר מכלן תתמרמר צרפת על הדבר וכלן יחד מרשיעות את ממשלת אנגליה כי בעצתה עשתה ממשלת מצרים את מעשיה .

— בסודן נהפך הגלגל לטובת גרדן מעט . כי פעמים נגפו לפניו נדודי המהדי , והמצור הורם מעל העיר תרטום. שר הצבא ולסלי הולך בצבא אנגליה לעזור לגרדן וקרוב היום אשר צבא המהדי ינגף כלו .

— גם בארץ הזולים (באפריקה) אין שלום ועל האנגלים לשום עיניהם שם לבלתי יבלע להם בארצות ממשלתם הגובלות בארץ הזאת. כי שבטי הזולים נלחמים איש ברעהו יום יום , ועתה נגף אחד מראשיהם אשר שמה אנגליה בארץ הזאת אחרי מלחמתה איתה וימלט אל ארץ ממשלת אנגליה ומבקש ממנה כי תעזור לו אנגליה במלחמתו את הזולים אויביו .

— ובין צרפת וארץ הסינים עוד אין שלום ואולי מהרה תחדש המלחמה ביתר עז . בימים האחרונים בא ציר ממשלת אמריקה לטינטשין ויודיע את לי הונג שנג משנה המלך כי צרפת שאלה מממשלת אמריקה כי תהיה היא המפשרת בין צרפת ובין הסינים , וכשמוע לי הונג שנג כי אין חפץ צרפת לותר דבר מכל אשר שאלה עד עתה ויחר אפו מאד , ויאמר כי שמר לא תשמר צרפת את חקי המלחמות, וכורבה שר האניות בא למבוא הנהר מין כאיש שלום ולא הודיע כי להלחם בא , ויהרוס את המבצר בעת שלום והסינים לא ידעו ולא יכלו להלחם כמשפט , ועתה תעשה ממשלת הסינים כל אשר בכחה לעמוד על נפשה והממשלה והעם נכונים לזה . כן דבר לי הונג שנג וציר אמריקה לא יכל להשיב לו דבר וישב למקומו .

אניות רוסיה רבות תעמדנה עתה אצל חוף ארץ הסינים ויש חושדים כי נכרתה ברית עזרה בין רוסיה ובין צרפת לחלק להן את ארץ הסינים ולרשת אותה ,

— באונגריה נפתח בית בחירי העם , ויבא קסר אוסטריה לפסט לדבר לפני הבחירים דברים אחדים על עניני הממלכה , כמשפטו בכל שנה , ויאמר כי את ארץ אשכנז הוא בידידות רבה ובשלום אמת את כל יתר הממשלות , ובתוך יתר דבריו רמז גם על תעלולי אויבי בני שם , ויאמר כי תקותו חזקה כי בחירי העם יעשלו לעשות שלום בין כל העמים ובני הדתות אשר בארץ אנגריה .

First issue of the Jerusalem newspaper, Hatzvi (1886), edited by Eliezer Ben-Yehuda

ספר

טהרת הקודש

פסק דין בענין איסור נוסח בביהכ"נ אשר ערכתי אני הצעיר
לפני גדולי רבותינו שבגולה אשר מפיהם אנו חיים הי"ו לשאול מהם
תורה והלכה למעשה ועידה בזמן הבריאה ק"ק חסידים פעיה"ק צפת ת"ו

הק' שמואל העליר :

ציור ציון התנא האלקי רשב"י ור"א בנו ור"י

נדפס פעיה"ק 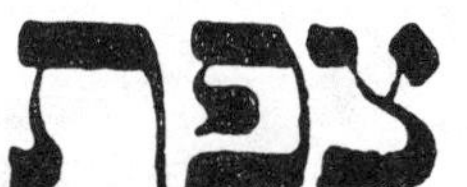 צפת תובב"א

בדפוס הרב החכם מו"ה דובער ק"מ

בשנת יזכרו וישבו אל יהוה

Title-page of one of the first books to be printed (1864) in modern Safad in Galilee

An Ancient Language in a Modern Context

Tel Aviv street scene. Most young people read only Hebrew.

The Jewish National and Hebrew University Library in Jerusalem has more than one and a half million volumes. *Overleaf: Main reading room at the Library.*

CLASSICAL HEBREW	ת	ש	ר	ק	צ	פ	ע	ס	נ	מ	ל	כ	י	ט	ח	ז	ו			ה	ד	ג	ב	א
CLASSICAL ROMAN	T	S	R	Q		P	O		N	M	L	K	I		H	Z	V	Y	F	E	D	C	B	A

SQUARE HEBREW
- AIN-DUK 200 CE
- PAPYRUS NASH 100 CE
- DEAD SEA SCROLLS 100 BCE
- KFAR BARAM 200 BCE
- OSSUARIES 200-100 BCE

ARAMAIC
- ELEPHANTINE 450 BCE
- TAIMA 600 BCE
- NERAB 700 BCE
- SHAMAL 800 BCE

HEBREO PHOENICIAN 1100 BCE

OLD GREEK
- CYPRUS 900 BCE
- LYDIAN 800 BCE
- THERA 700 BCE
- CRETE 600 BCE
- CLASSIC GREEK 500-400 BCE

OLD ITALIC
- ETRUSCAN 400 BCE
- OLD LATIN 300—200 BCE

THE DEVELOPMENT OF HEBREW AND LATIN WRITING FROM A COMMON SOURCE

In 1958 the state of Israel honored the memory of Eliezer Ben-Yehuda, the pioneer of modern Hebrew, with a 250 pruta stamp to commemorate the centenary of his birth.

Books by Robert St. John

TONGUE OF THE PROPHETS

SHALOM MEANS PEACE

THE SILENT PEOPLE SPEAK

IT'S ALWAYS TOMORROW

FROM THE LAND OF SILENT PEOPLE

tongue of the prophets

The Life Story of Eliezer Ben Yehuda

ROBERT ST. JOHN

Melvin Powers
Wilshire Book Company

12015 Sherman Road, No. Hollywood, CA 91605

PRINTED IN THE UNITED STATES
AT THE COUNTRY LIFE PRESS, GARDEN CITY, N.Y.
FIRST EDITION

LIBRARY OF CONGRESS CATALOG CARD NUMBER 52-5233

ISBN 0-87980-166-2

To the memory of the two women
in the career of Eliezer Ben Yehuda:
DEBORAH,
who gave her life for him and his dream, and
HEMDA,
who lived for that dream until she saw "his" language spoken in the gathering places of the mighty and in the byways of ordinary Jews everywhere,

THIS BOOK IS HUMBLY DEDICATED

Tongue of the Prophets

Prologue

ONLY A FEW HOURS BEFORE THE ARAB LEGION BEGAN its siege of Jerusalem in 1948, I went down Ben Yehuda Street to look at the still unrepaired buildings which had been wrecked by an explosion set off by British "irregulars" in the dying days of the mandate.

At that time there was nothing ironical to me that dozens of innocent Jews had been killed by this act of terrorism, for "Ben Yehuda" then was merely a name I had seen on street signs in Jerusalem, in Tel Aviv, and in other Israeli communities.

I was unaware, then, that these streets honored a man who had written and argued for almost half a century that Britain was the Jews' best friend. I knew as little about Ben Yehuda, the man, as most Americans, including most American Jews.

In Israel that year I saw Jews from sixty or seventy different oriental and occidental countries creating a nation; people with different customs and costumes, different religious attitudes and levels of culture, different languages and dialects. I kept asking myself what the one thing was that they had in common. Was it religion? No, because many were agnostics and freethinkers. Was it that they had all been victims of vicious anti-Semitism and had a common experience of persecution? No, because some had come from places like Australia, Canada, and the United States, where the worst experiences they had ever had were perhaps being denied membership in a restricted country club. Neither was it a common cultural or intellectual bond, for it would be difficult to find two individuals as dissimilar as a Reform New York Jew and a Yemenite.

Before I left Israel I decided that, in addition to a burning desire for a land of their own, the great coagulating agent holding together these diverse elements was their common language.

As I wandered around Israel during that cataclysmic summer I saw signs everywhere:

HEBREW
TEACHER

I heard on the streets of the cities, in trenches along the frontiers, in air-force camps, and on Israeli ships at sea men and women of all ages speaking a soft, melodious language, but I had no idea that Hebrew had been revived, after a slumber of nearly two thousand years, largely through the efforts of one man.

Then I went back to New York and at a cocktail party met a slim, vivacious woman, Mrs. Max Wittmann, who told me she was the daughter of Ben Yehuda. I blinked several times. Ben Yehuda was still a street to me.

Several days later the daughter took me to a hospital on upper Fifth Avenue to see her mother, Hemda Ben Yehuda, who had recently been flown over from Jerusalem, as she put it, "to have my hip nailed together." Hemda Ben Yehuda was nearly eighty years old and the operation had been a serious one, but she was propped up in bed scribbling words on a pad of paper.

"My memoirs!" she explained, her bright eyes twinkling in a coquettish manner.

I made many visits to that hospital. I learned much about the man after whom the streets had been named. I read the sketchy memoirs, which were being written in English.

Years ago Hemda Ben Yehuda had written, in Hebrew, a biography of her husband which had been published in Jerusalem. Mrs.

Prologue

Max Wittmann (the Shlomit or Dola of *Tongue of the Prophets*) translated that book into English for me, and the facts it contained are incorporated in the following pages.

I also had access to Ben Yehuda's own writings, including a very short autobiography covering his early years.

As the story of his life took form it seemed unique. Here was the only man in history, as far as I could discover, who almost single-handed had revived an ancient language and popularized it, in the face of intense opposition from the very people who were to benefit, many of them convinced that God would destroy this "infidel" for tampering with a holy tongue.

After I had the family's version of the man I began to search for a more objective picture. I worked for nearly a year in the libraries in the United States and Europe. On two continents I talked with men who had known him, scholars who had worked with him. But although Ben Yehuda had had more enemies than friends during most of his life, it was difficult to get any "critical" viewpoint, so I employed a professional researcher, who was also a Hebrew scholar, to hunt out exclusively derogatory matter. She worked for weeks. Still I had nothing that cast doubt on his accomplishment.

I talked with Jerusalem neighbors who spoke slightingly of the Ben Yehudas, but they offered no biographical material which changed the story. It was just that they did not like the hats that Hemda wore or the conduct of some of the children.

Finally I got on the trail of a Jerusalem journalist who had been one of Ben Yehuda's chief latter-day critics. He agreed to send me a file of his own articles which would give me "the other side." What I finally received were two eulogies which said, in effect, "I once disagreed with him, but . . ."

Ben Yehuda's critics are either literally dead or have been silenced by the ultimate success of his dual campaign, to help create a Jewish state in which Hebrew would be the generally accepted language.

This is a story about a Jew written by a non-Jew for non-Jews as well as Jews to read; therefore it is not assumed the reader knows even the difference between a *seder* and a *kibbutz*. It might better have been written by a Hebrew scholar, but no Hebrew scholar had done it. Besides, it then would have been a book interesting only to other Hebrew scholars. The story is too pulsating with human struggle to be written exclusively for students of philology.

It is the story of a man who made it possible for several million people to order groceries, drive cattle, make love, and curse out their neighbors in a language which until his day had been fit only for Talmudic argument and prayer.

It is the story of a faithful fanatic who had two great love affairs, made enemies of his best friends, went to prison for his beliefs, was always on the verge of death from tuberculosis, yet fathered eleven children, gathered the material for a sixteen-volume dictionary unlike any other philological work ever conceived, authored plays, a geography, and two of the most urgent "appeals" ever addressed to his own people, and died while working on the word for "soul."

The story will please few Jews, because during his lifetime Ben Yehuda made enemies in every camp. He was brutal in his criticisms. Being a fanatic, he never allowed even personal friendships to deviate him from the course he had charted. His life was one long running feud. Many times he was undoubtedly wrong in the stands he took, but I have nowhere in this book passed judgment on him or his views. The story is told as factually as possible.

The conversations which sprinkle these pages are not from stenographic recordings, but I believe they are in the spirit of the characters. Some few were actually written out by Ben Yehuda himself before he died.

Once in a public lecture, attempting to explain the traditional spirit of Jewish freedom of thought, I said that if three Jews were in a room there would be three opinions on any subject that arose. Whereupon a Jewish heckler in the back of the hall shouted:

"You are obviously a *goy* [non-Jew]. Otherwise you would know that if there were three Jews in the room there would be four opinions on any subject!"

In Hebrew there are sounds for which we have no letters or combinations of letters in the Roman alphabet. The result is that there are at least three or four ways of spelling many Hebrew words in English.

In the library of the University of Geneva, in Switzerland, I found Eliezer Ben Yehuda's name spelled five different ways.

Prologue

The rule followed in these pages is that proper names are spelled the way the owners of the names spelled them when they wrote them in Roman characters, even though this results in the confusion of the same name often being spelled in several different ways. (Some men named Jacob spell it that way; some spell it "Yakov.")

Otherwise, all Hebrew and Arabic words are spelled as they appear in the Universal Jewish Encyclopedia, whose editors, in transliterating, have attempted to give the phonetic spelling of words for the benefit of readers not acquainted with Semitic languages. The Hebrew pronunciation used, although Ben Yehuda himself might disagree with it, is the pronunciation with which most American Jews are acquainted.

Problems also arose on the matter of dates. Most Palestinian Jews under the Turks used the Hebraic calendar. When it became necessary, under the British, to translate dates into the Roman calendar, many were not converted correctly. Some of the Ben Yehuda children, for example, are not even sure today of the exact year of their birth by the Roman calendar.

Gratitude is expressed to Mrs. Dola Ben Yehuda Wittmann for her translations and the supplying of factual material, and to Dr. Alexander Safran, once Grand Rabbi of six hundred thousand Jews in Rumania and now Grand Rabbi in Geneva, Switzerland, for his help on technical problems.

It is too late to thank Hemda Ben Yehuda for her hospital-bed conferences and all her memory searching. After being flown back to Jerusalem from New York, she died in the summer of 1951. She lived long enough, however, to read in final manuscript form, and to approve, this story of her husband's life. She died happy in the knowledge that a definitive account of his struggle to revive a language would soon be published.

With these explanations and acknowledgments I give you the story of a man who had a dream.

Robert St. John

Geneva, Switzerland
October 1, 1951

1

Thy Will Be Done

ONE ICY DAY DURING THE WINTER OF 1858 A CROWD gathered around two men engaged in an argument in a narrow street in the Jewish quarter of the small town of Luzhky, Lithuania, which then was part of the Russian Empire ruled over by Czar Alexander II.

A newcomer pushed his way through the throng.

"And why do they argue?" he asked.

"He with the fur hat says it is colder in Minsk than in St. Petersburg. The one with the green cap says it is colder nowhere else in the world than in St. Petersburg. His grandfather told him. They have been at it for thirty minutes and we are all freezing. Oih yoi yoi! If they do not settle it soon we shall all die of how cold it is in Luzhky!"

"Why don't they let Reb Perlman decide which one is right?"

"Yes, yes! Reb Perlman! He knows everything!"

"He can settle an argument quicker than anyone in Luzhky!"

So the crowd started for the street in which the learned man of Luzhky lived. Even before they reached the house they began shouting his name. But when he came to the door there was a frown on his face and he held a finger to his lips. The crowd instantly grew silent.

"Feygeh, my wife, has just delivered a child. Our fourth, as you know. It is a frail child. We did not have money for a doctor. My Feygeh is ill. I beg of you, let someone else settle your arguments to-day. Begone, my friends, and pray for our child."

With Jewish respect for the mystery of birth, the men forgot their interest in comparative meteorology and dispersed.

Leib Perlman closed the door and turned toward the bed on which his wife lay. She was tossing restlessly. He bent down on one knee to try to make out what she was saying.

"Leybaleh, my husband, I hear voices!"

"Yes, Feygaleh, it is the villagers in the street."

"No! I hear the voice of the Evil One. You told me yourself, Leybaleh, that until the ceremony of the circumcision he will try to steal our little one from us. Promise you will stay close to us! Guard us, Leybaleh! Pray for us! Protect our child from the Evil One!"

The young husband reached down to stroke her hot forehead, then suddenly drew his hand back. He had almost forgotten the Orthodox law that for six weeks, until the woman who has borne a child goes to the temple for the purification ceremony known as the *Mikveh,* it is not permitted that she be touched by a man. So Leib Perlman drew back his hand and caressed her merely with his eyes and his voice. In a whisper as reassuring as the touch of his fingers on her forehead might have been he said:

"Feygaleh, my dear one, while you were sleeping I cut up many small pieces of paper. On them I wrote words from the Great Book. I have hung the pieces of paper around the crib, in accordance with ancient custom. Now, my Feygaleh, close your eyes and sleep, for the Evil One will not be able to harm our child. Thus it is written!"

The young mother gave a deep sigh, then smiled slightly.

"I hear other voices now. I hear Rachel. Hers is a sweet voice. Rachel will protect us, won't she, Leybaleh?"

It was quiet in the Perlman home now, except for the swishing sound the wind made as it blew through the bits of paper that festooned the crib suspended from the ceiling by ropes.

Leib Perlman tiptoed to a chair by the window that looked out on the road. For the fourth time God had seen fit to bless him. God's will be done. Then he dozed off to sleep.

Leib Perlman was not a rabbi. He had been given the title of "Reb" by the townspeople according to a custom then prevalent among Jews in Russia of thus distinguishing a man wiser than the average. They also referred to him as *Talmid Haham,* "Learned Man." Those who knew him well put the diminutive ending on his name and affectionately called him Leybaleh, as did his wife. He was handsome and blond, with the soft eyes of an aesthete.

Leib Perlman was one of the most impractical men the parents of Feygeh Wolfson could have picked to be her husband. It bothered Feygeh that for the first three years they had to be supported entirely by money contributed by her family and his. But after the birth of her first child, Esther, and a son, Shalom David, she found a way to a degree of financial independence. It was a good way because it left Leybaleh free to pore over his books. She opened a miniature grocery store in a corner of the wooden shack which by then was housing two adults and two children.

At first patronage came from townspeople who hoped that along with flour and wax candles they might also get a little free advice on ethical matters from the man of the family. But gradually they came to shop here because of the pleasing personality of Feygeh herself.

So it was that gradually the womenfolk of Luzhky began to ask Feygeh for advice. If it were a deep philosophical problem the decision must be made by Reb Perlman. But in intimate, personal matters Feygeh's word was taken. And so her small business prospered, and her customers began adding an extra syllable to her name and she became known to everyone as Feygaleh: Little Feygeh; Feygeh the Sweet One.

Existence was tolerable, although not very happy, for the average Jew in Russia in 1858, the year Eliezer was born.

Resignation was part of the creed of the majority of Jews. They took the fatalistic attitude that, as long as the Exile continued, they had no right to expect anything better than a life of poverty and squalor; a life symbolized by an absence of even the beauty which nature can bestow on those denied material riches. This attitude was common in ghettos everywhere in the Diaspora, as the Jews still call those areas of the world through which they were scattered after their forced flight from the Middle East nearly twenty centuries ago.

But in 1858 a new spirit was abroad in Russia. The contagion of it found its way into many Jewish quarters. The young of Russia, especially those who had spent any time in the university, were beginning to rebel against the tyranny of the Cossacks.

Many Jewish parents became distressed over the activities of their young. They feared that their young would forget their Jewishness, neglect their religion, and become so obsessed with their fight for a free life that they would end up as victims of agnosticism or infidelism.

When their young brought home the rebellious ideas and progressive thoughts they had picked up at the university or in their secret meetings, the parents would wring their hands and cry to God to save them from listening to such blasphemy.

Czar Alexander II was not the only one whose sleep was troubled by what was happening in Russia in 1858, the year Eliezer Perlman was born in a small cottage on a side street in the Jewish quarter of Luzhky.

2

Czar Alexander Outwitted

ALL THE ORTHODOX CUSTOMS WERE SCRUPULOUSLY observed in the Perlman home. So it was that on one Passover eve the mother called two of her sons to her side and handed them a package of herring.

"Take them to the river and wash them carefully so they will be kosher for our Passover tomorrow."

Hayim Maeer, being several years the senior of Eliezer and much less reticent, grabbed the package and started on the run for the river. His younger brother trailed behind.

An hour later Feygeh began to worry because they had not returned. She was pacing the roadway when Eliezer appeared. His face was pale and his right hand trembled as he pushed the hair from his eyes.

"Where is Hayim Maeer and where are the herring?" Feygeh demanded.

"Hayim Maeer is all right, my mother, but——"

"Where are the herring for Passover?"

"They have gone to their homes where they belong," the boy stammered.

"What nonsense do you talk!"

"It was all my fault. We washed them so clean you would have been pleased with us. But as we started for home the package slipped from my hands and the fish fell into the river. The current was swift and took them away. You may beat me for it, but they went so fast I am sure they are more happy than we would be eating them!"

For an instant Feygeh hesitated between anger and amusement at her son's reasoning. If one of the others had done it she would not have been so lenient. But it was always difficult to be stern with Eliezer. She patted his head reassuringly and said:

"Perhaps it is best. We shall let this be an atonement for our sins. But where is Hayim Maeer? Did he go down the river with the fish?"

Eliezer pretended not to hear and rounded a corner out of sight.

As Feygeh sighed and started back into the house she suddenly stopped and looked toward the river.

"Something tells me it was Hayim Maeer who dropped the herring into the water and sent Eliezer home to take the blame. And I let them get away with it! *Dummkopf* that I am!"

The three-to-one ratio of boys to girls in the family caused Feygeh great concern. During the long hours that she was alone she brooded about it. Sometimes she would confide her fears to her more intimate customers.

"It is fine to have three such good sons," she would say, "but I can never forget what happened to Leib Beer, my brother. When he was only seven years old the Cossacks took him. It was the Czar's order. As you know, that is the way they get soldiers for the army. So he disappeared and we never saw him again. Now I have three sons. How short a time will I have them before they, too, are taken for the army?"

The intimate shop customers all agreed that the matter should be discussed with the Wise Man, her husband. So one night, after the children were asleep, Feygeh told Leybaleh of her worry.

With his genius for solving problems, the husband found a solution. The rule in Russia in those days was that one son in each family was exempt. That meant Shalom David, the first-born, would never be conscripted. They need be concerned only about

Hayim Maeer and Eliezer. But, Leib Perlman reminded his wife, the births of these two boys had never been duly recorded.

"So," he said, "we need only find two families who are childless and who will co-öperate with us. Then we give their names to our sons and register the births. So you see, Feygaleh, as with Shalom David, they, too, shall be exempt from service."

Thus it was that Eliezer, although born a Perlman, acquired in his youth the surname Elyanof, while his older brother became, for purposes of evading military service, the son of the family Seydel.

It was obvious from Eliezer's interest in books that he was going to be the intellectual of the family, so Feygeh and her husband, despite their often impecunious condition, put his education in the hands of a good secondary teacher who one day confidentially told the mother:

"He has a fine mind, but it needs cultivation, just as a garden with soil that is rich but unworked needs cultivation. You must sacrifice to make a good education possible for him."

The advice worried Feygeh. There was no use talking to Leybaleh about it. He had no understanding of financial matters. But one night, sitting alone while her husband was at a gathering of Luzhky's intellectuals, she thought of her brother, David Wolfson. He was the one member of the family who had prospered. Besides, he was deeply religious, which was important, because Feygeh made no secret of her hope that Eliezer would one day be a great rabbi. Also, Uncle David's estate was not far from Luzhky.

So it was that Eliezer went to live with Feygeh's brother and began to study rabbinical law.

Feygeh was still young when Leybaleh died after an illness. He left her not four children to care for, but five, because a few months after his death another boy was born. After several years she married again. But it was a mistake. She was never able to avoid comparisons.

"Leybaleh would not have done that."

"Leybaleh was so much wiser!"

So her second marriage ended in divorce. So did her third. From then on she was vehement in expressing the opinion that only stupid women ever tried to replace a great love with a substitute. To those who came into her shop she would say:

"Everything that any of my children ever make of themselves they will owe to Leybaleh. He was a learned and a great man. May his sweet soul rest in peace!"

3

Thanks to Robinson Crusoe

FOR ONE YEAR ELIEZER WAS HAPPY AND COMFORTable, living in the great home of his uncle, enjoying food such as he had never known before, a room of his own, good clothes like those worn by gentlemen's sons, and the instruction of able teachers.

"There is only one thing I demand of you," Uncle David had said; "that you have a serious attitude toward your education."

The repetition of this admonition was unnecessary. Eliezer had a sincere interest in learning. His childhood was therefore devoid of frivolity both by choice and by compulsion.

When he became thirteen life took a new turn. At thirteen, by Jewish custom, a boy celebrates his *Bar Mitzvah,* which, next to birth and death, is the most important event in his life, for on this occasion a Jewish boy becomes a man and henceforth has the duties, the privileges, and the responsibilities of manhood.

Eliezer remembered his Bar Mitzvah for the rest of his life principally because it was then that his uncle announced that his year of ease and comfort was over.

"You go now to the Yeshiva, to the rabbinical college in the city of Polotzk. From now on all my assistance to you ends. In Polotzk you shall make your own way, just as the others do. I have ordered it thus because truth, learning, and wisdom are never acquired in comfort. It comes only with pain. You will sometimes go hungry. You will often be cold. You may suffer. But that is as it should be, for you will grow in intellectual stature and someday, if the great God wills it, you will become the fine rabbi that your mother hopes you to be."

Eliezer was tired the night he arrived in Polotzk after an entire day on the road. His small bones ached. The blood was pounding in his head. There were sharp pains in his chest. By comparison with Lushky, Polotzk was a large place and frightened him.

Soon after his arrival he met David, a fellow student who changed the course of his life. They were walking to classes one day when David stopped short and looked intently at Eliezer.

"Shall I tell you a secret? I am leaving the great Yeshiva!"

"Why? Have you decided not to become a rabbi?"

"It's not that. It's really because of Rabbi Joseph Blucker. Wait until you meet him! When he talks I could sit and listen all day and all night without sleep! And he has a house so beautiful! And books! Eliezer, you have never seen so many books! He knows everything in them! If I ask him to let me bring you to see him, will you promise to go?"

The next Friday evening, after attending prayers at their own school, the two boys went to the home of Rabbi Blucker. A servant ushered them into the library. Eliezer stood in the doorway, gaping. It was the largest room he had ever seen.

But it was not the room itself which most attracted him. It was the figure of a man. He was about thirty-five years old, tall, fair, dressed in well-tailored clothes unlike any garments Eliezer had ever seen a rabbi wearing. He was walking quietly back and forth over the thick carpets. He was so intent on the book in his hand that he was unaware of his visitors. He was humming softly the words of a Jewish hymn:

"The prophet Elijah will come to us with the Messiah, the son of David."

Still ignoring his guests, the rabbi then began singing the *Zmeerot*. Now his voice filled the book-lined room. It also filled the heart of the boy from Luzhky, who, telling about it later, said:

"Religion until then was something in books; something abstract; something without any human qualities to it. But during the half hour I stood in the doorway I felt the power of something above and beyond, as I had never felt it before. It was almost as if I were in the presence of the Almighty."

Finally the private service ended and the rabbi turned toward the door. When he saw his visitors he greeted them warmly. But Eliezer was still in a trance.

It was David who did the talking, explaining that he and Eliezer wanted to leave the larger school and study under him.

"You must appear at ten o'clock in the morning for an entrance examination," the rabbi was saying. "Now let's talk of other things."

Both boys passed the examination. In a short time Eliezer became one of the favorites of Rabbi Blucker, who appointed him tutor to a wealthy student. To justify this faith in him, Eliezer studied with a burning intensity and also made a practice of attending early-morning services seven days a week.

One Friday evening when Eliezer went to the rabbi's study, his host took from under the cushion of the chair in which he sat a strange small volume and handed it to the boy.

"Tonight you and I shall read from this one."

It was a translation into Hebrew of the story of Robinson Crusoe.

Eliezer was fascinated at the idea that the language of the Holy Books could be used to tell the tale of a shipwrecked sailor. He was excitedly reading aloud when there was a knock at the door. Quickly the rabbi grabbed *Robinson Crusoe,* put it back in its hiding place, thrust the Torah into the boy's hands, and only then went to the door.

It was Rabbi Blucker, with his personal magnetism and his books, who was responsible for creating within this child from a small Lithuanian town an interest in culture and learning; in scholarship and general education. He did it by making the acquisition of knowledge exciting, as all great teachers do.

But more important, from posterity's point of view, it was Rabbi Blucker who kindled a spark which grew into a scorching flame that only death would someday extinguish. This spark was a love of the

Hebrew language, not only as a vehicle for preserving the words of great Jewish religious leaders and the conveyance of them from generation to generation, but also as a secular language.

It was Rabbi Joseph Blucker and *Robinson Crusoe* who started the boy then known as Eliezer Elyanof on a career which was to have a profound effect on the future history of the Lost People of Israel.

Eliezer had been studying under Rabbi Blucker for almost a year when his uncle one day arrived in Polotzk.

"Pack your clothes. You are leaving here," the uncle summarily announced.

There was no explanation until they were well along the road that led out of Polotzk. Then the uncle delivered a speech to the frail young man who sat in the carriage beside him.

"I have been hearing tales about you. They cast you in the role of a young devil. There are reports you have been blaspheming the holy language, neglecting your studies, reading what they call 'philosophy.' It is good that I have heard these reports, for perhaps I have saved you in time from the evil ways into which you have fallen. From now on you will walk in the path of righteousness and confine your reading to the holy books."

Eliezer was unhappy in the days that followed. His forced separation from the life and people he had grown to love in Polotzk was as painful as the sudden yanking of an arm from its socket. He now looked on his uncle as an enemy rather than as a benefactor. The only place he found serenity was in the local synagogue. There, after services, when the others had left, he would take from under his coat one of the Hebrew books he had smuggled out of Polotzk and stand in a corner reading by the light of the flickering candles.

One early evening, leaning against a column in the synagogue, he was absorbed in his book when suddenly all the candles went out. In the semi-darkness he saw half a dozen figures in long white robes converging on him. They made an unearthly noise. His knees trembled. He dropped the book. The Angels of Destruction must have come to drag him away to their kingdom! In panic he ran screaming from the building.

After he had left, the "Angels of Destruction" took off their white robes and removed the masks from their lanterns. David Wolfson turned to the others.

"Thank you, my friends. You see, it was just as I told you. He comes into this holy place and profanes it. He hides here, and when he thinks he is alone he reads the evil books instead of studying the Torah."

Another man turned his lantern on the base of the pillar and exclaimed:

"Look! He has left behind the evidence of his sin. There is the book he was reading!"

They all bent over and peered at the volume on the floor.

"Don't anyone touch it!" Wolfson commanded. "Let not a single man of us be contaminated, for it is an unclean thing!"

As he spoke Wolfson took his cane and flicked the book in the direction of the door. Finally, without touching it with his hands, he got it into the roadway. It landed in a mud puddle, open to the title page. One of the men turned his lantern on it and suddenly exclaimed:

"David, you are not entirely correct. Observe! It is written by a Bible student and defends the holiness of God!"

Wolfson looked. For a moment he was silent. Finally he said:

"It is still a profane book. Is it written by one of the great rabbis? Is it a book they study in the Yeshiva? No! The writer is some Dummkopf from western Europe. It is blasphemy for such a one to write of God. He defends God. God needs no defense. The book is poison, and my nephew is a victim of the devil!"

That night Eliezer was sent to his room without supper. Hours later he was lying in bed reading, oblivious to how late it was, when he heard footsteps. He slipped the book under the mattress, snuffed out the candle, and pretended sleep. His uncle opened the door without knocking and turned his lantern on the boy.

"So, you would like me to think I have disturbed your slumber! On top of all your other sins you lie in this manner to your uncle. But you are stupid as well as evil. You forget that by touching the tip of the candle I can feel that it is still warm. Get out of that bed I have provided for you in my kindness! Now, where is the book you were reading?"

Eliezer cringed in a corner of the room, saying nothing, while his uncle conducted a search. Finally, from underneath the mattress, he pulled a slim volume, flashed his lantern on the cover, and read the Hebrew characters which spelled out the title:

ROBINSON
CRUSOE

The halls of the manor house echoed with Wolfson's bellows as he berated the boy from Luzhky. Finally sentence was imposed.

"Get into your clothes! Not for another hour will I allow my house to be polluted by an infidel. If you go home to Feygeh, tell her I wish no further dealings with the Perlmans. Here! Take your *tefillin*. You will need them! You will need to pray the rest of your life for eternal forgiveness!"

Eliezer left his uncle's home with no baggage except the prayer devices known collectively as tefillin, a miniature wooden box shaped like a derby hat which is worn on the front of the head and a similar boxlike object which is fastened by leather thongs to the left arm during prayer.

But Eliezer did not go home to Luzhky. He was afraid of his mother's anger.

That night, as he plodded in the dark down the road to the nearby city of Glubokiah, the boy felt himself the victim of a gross injustice. What evil thing had he done? Rabbi Blucker read books written in Hebrew which were not about religion. He was not a bad man. Why should a beautiful language like Hebrew not be used to tell a story like *Robinson Crusoe?*

It was still dark when Eliezer reached Glubokiah. He was tired, cold, hungry, and very sleepy. He knew no one in Glubokiah. But he remembered that by Jewish custom no synagogue is ever locked at night. So he began to tramp the streets in search of a synagogue.

The next morning those people of Glubokiah who answered the call of the *shammash* to morning prayer found, on the first bench inside the door, a small dark figure dressed in the long frock coat which rabbinical students were required to wear, and with a long blond curl hanging down over each travel-stained cheek.

The caretaker had to shake Eliezer by the shoulder before the boy could escape from the hold which a sleep of exhaustion had on him.

Many of the people in the synagogue stared at Eliezer, but one man seemed to be looking with more than mere curiosity. He was exceedingly tall and straight, well dressed and very dignified-looking. His hair was gray, but his eyes were young. In them Eliezer thought he saw kindness. While Eliezer was taking off his tefillin, the tall figure approached.

"Shalom and good morning, young man. You are a stranger amongst us. What brings you to Glubokiah?"

Eliezer blurted out his entire story. Some instinct made him realize he was speaking to sympathetic ears. When he finished, he looked up to see that the man was smiling.

"I am Shlomoh Naftaly Hirtz Yonas and I would like to be a friend to you. I have a large family, and one more will only increase my pleasure. Will you accompany me home?"

Shlomoh Yonas was the owner of a distillery situated in a large courtyard. The family home was in an adjacent garden.

It might have been merely by chance that the host left his fourteen-year-old guest in the library while he went to alert the rest of the family. If it were, it was a happy chance for Eliezer. This was a room such as he had never even dreamed about. There were cases and cases of books. There were pictures on the walls in frames, pots full of flowers, deep rugs, comfortable armchairs, and a sofa piled with embroidered pillows. Here there was none of the drabness of his own home in Luzhky, none of the austerity of Uncle Wolfson's manor house, and by comparison with Rabbi Blucker's study it was warm and livable, not just a room for study and prayer.

The tired young man drank in the beauty with eager eyes, turning his head slowly from side to side. The palace of the Czars could not possibly be grander! And he, Eliezer, who an hour ago had felt himself without a friend in the world, was actually a guest here. He walked over to one of the bookcases.

When Shlomoh Yonas returned he found Eliezer's face clouded.

"What troubles you now, my boy?"

"These books, sir! The words are so strange. I cannot read them. They must be in languages I do not know. They are not in Yiddish or Hebrew either!"

Shlomoh Yonas laughed heartily.

"This case, Eliezer, is full of the works of the great philosophers, Mendelssohn, Spinoza, and many others; men with great thoughts and big ideas. The books are in German, French, Russian; languages which you will someday read and also speak. But now you must meet someone who is going to feed your body, just as these men will someday feed your mind. This is my wife, Rivkah."

Eliezer decided that Mrs. Yonas was as kind as her husband. She smiled warmly at him and put her arm around his shoulder.

"The books will wait, Eliezer, but the food will not."

There were six children in the Yonas family, four girls, two boys. Eliezer was placed next to the oldest, Deborah, who was eighteen. Across from him sat Pola, who was a mere infant.

They sat long around the table that morning as the mother served cup after cup of tea from a great brass samovar. Pola, the baby, never took her eyes from the face of the boy with the strange curls. Deborah was the one who asked him all the leading questions, encouraging him to tell of his life in Luzhky and Polotzk.

"Father says you wish to learn French and German and Russian. Would you like me to be your teacher?"

Eliezer blushed and nodded.

"I think we should start at once, don't you? If the others will excuse us, let's go into the library now."

After they had left, Shlomoh Yonas turned to his wife.

"Did you hear, Rivkah, how intelligently he talks? Even little Pola was impressed!"

"It was just his curls that fascinated her!"

4

Two Curls + Two Girls

THE RUSSIAN WINTERS ARE LONG, BUT THE DAYS are short. The days that first winter were much too short for all the studying Eliezer wished to do. Deborah often lighted the oil lamps and then returned to the boy's side to help him in his struggle with his new languages.

The library was their study hall. Day after day they sat at the great table in the same two chairs placed close together. Deborah would pronounce the words aloud, explaining their meaning, drilling her pupil in their use, correcting his enunciation.

It went on all winter with few interruptions except the occasional visits from Pola, which were not really interruptions because the child rarely made a sound. She often spent as much as an hour sitting on the floor, silently looking into Eliezer's face. The only time she caused a scene was the day Eliezer, at Deborah's suggestion, cut off the two curls which had marked him as a student at the Yeshiva.

That day Pola burst out crying.

"Curls gone! Curls gone!"

For days she treated Eliezer as a stranger. It was several weeks before she returned to the library.

When spring arrived Father Yonas found an excuse to get fresh air and exercise for his protégé. Several afternoons each week he took the boy on a long walk through the woods, giving him lessons in natural history. On one such walk he said:

"Deborah tells me you are making considerable progress with your French and German. That is good, but I hope, Eliezer, that you will never forget your Hebrew. It is a language of beauty. The tragedy is that Hebrew is like Latin. Today it is a language only for prayer and the preservation of our old Jewish literature. But we must keep Hebrew alive, always. It has a melody of its own, like some of the deep sounds of the forest which we have been hearing on these walks. So promise me, my boy, that you will repay what I am trying to do for you by always keeping Hebrew alive in your mind and your heart."

Eliezer solemnly promised.

For almost two years, with few interruptions, Deborah and Eliezer worked together. Finally the pupil was almost as proficient as his teacher, and Father Yonas decided it was time for Eliezer to make plans to enter the nearest *Gymnasium,* at Dünaburg.

They all knew when the last day came that it was going to be difficult. Father Yonas kept insisting to his wife that it was not the end of anything; that the ties would never be broken. But Mother Yonas started crying even before breakfast was over that last day.

"It's going to be like losing one of our own, Shlomoh! He has been such a sweet boy! I hate to think how lost Deborah will be without him. Yet it's little Pola who really worries me. Lately she has even been talking in her sleep about him. It will be an empty house after today. The two of them sitting there with their books! I shall miss that picture!"

Eliezer behaved as if it were just another day of lessons. As impersonally as if his teacher were a rabbi in the Yeshiva, he was reciting to Deborah the words he had practiced in bed the night before. Suddenly the young woman beside him slammed the book shut with a bang.

"Eliezer, do you realize—does it mean nothing to you that this is the last day?"

The boy smiled.

"Thanks to you, Deborah, I can say that it is the last day in five different languages."

"There are things I wish you would say in any language!"

"I guess you mean I should say how grateful I am to all of you. I say it now. I shall never stop saying it!"

"But, Eliezer, isn't there anything—anything personal you wish to say while we are alone this last time?"

Eliezer blushed and looked away toward the window.

"You know I am going to miss you, Deborah."

"I am glad you finally said it. But 'miss' is a very poor word in any language for the feelings which I am going to have. My life ends, in a way, when you go off down the road. I love you, Eliezer. There, I have said it! And in your own strange way I think you love me. Promise me one thing. Promise you will always remember me!"

In his embarrassment the boy reverted to the language he had first learned as a child. In Yiddish he said:

"Yes, I promise!"

"No, Eliezer, I would like to hear you say it in Hebrew, the sacred language, for it is a sacred oath we are taking. I shall say the words with you. And someday——"

She was interrupted by her mother bustling in, red of face and short of breath.

"Come, come! Eliezer must have food before starting, and someone must settle the matter of the valise. Father and I do not agree. He keeps taking clothes out to make room for books and papers, while I keep taking out books and papers to make room for clothes. But before I forget, promise me, Eliezer, that you will do one small favor for me?"

The boy looked at the woman who for two years had treated him in as motherly a manner as if she had actually given birth to him herself.

"I have made a promise to Father Yonas and just today I made a promise to Deborah, so it is only fair that I make one to you. I promise. . . . But what is it that I must promise?"

"It's your cough, Eliezer. If it gets worse you must see a doctor in Dünaburg."

Just then Deborah, who had left the room, came back holding something behind her.

"Eliezer, you must close your eyes and count ten. Do not be so embarrassed! It will be quite painless."

While he counted she put around his neck a white wool scarf she had been secretly knitting for him.

"It is to keep you from coughing, but it is also to keep you remembering the promise you made to me just now, Eliezer!"

5

Growing Pains

DAVID WITTINSKY WAS THE SON OF A SIMPLE JEWish family, yet he had a brilliant mind. Soon after he entered the Gymnasium at Dünaburg he became a convert to Christianity. He made the move coldly and deliberately. Looking around, he decided that there were too many paths along which a Jew could never travel. Some of his fellow Jews might criticize him. The ultra-religious ones might even spit on him. But most non-Jews would respect him and no paths would be blocked. So David Wittinsky remained a Jew in name only.

Eliezer met him quite by chance. He was a friend of the son of the family in Dünaburg from which Eliezer rented a room. Wittinsky took the younger boy under his wing and coached him for the entrance examinations. When Eliezer passed with high marks, Wittinsky said:

"You owe me nothing. You have already repaid me by proving that my judgment is good."

When the principal sent Eliezer a note announcing that he would receive a scholarship of twenty rubles per month, Wittinsky said:

"You need me no longer. You are well launched. Only I hope you will not forget me."

Eliezer made many friends in Dünaburg. The other Jewish students decided that this frail newcomer would probably become one of their leaders, so they vied with each other to be gracious to him. Many who were "day students" invited him to their homes and Eliezer accepted. It was of great economic advantage to be such a frequent guest for dinner. Twenty rubles a month was little on which to try to exist and buy books. But Eliezer found most of the other Jewish students dull by comparison with Wittinsky.

David Wittinsky was typical of his times. He was one of those young Russian intellectuals who in that period were aflame with the idea of freedom.

"Our goal," he once told Eliezer, "must be to play leading roles in the liberation of Russia from her masters."

"Do you mean 'we' as Jews?" Eliezer asked.

"Naturally not! We must forget we are Jews. What difference does religion make? We are all freethinkers here, and if you remain long you, too, will become a freethinker."

Another time Wittinsky said:

"It is quite proper that we should no longer be hemmed in by the customs of our religion. Those things are outdated. You must renounce your religion, Eliezer, as I have done, in order to take part in the great movement beginning to sweep Russia!"

At first Eliezer was stunned by Wittinsky's talk. But the ideal of freedom was one with which he instinctively agreed and so he was able to throw up few defenses against his friend's arguments. Yet for more than a year he refused to be rushed into a decision.

"Think, Eliezer, of the great men you have read about who have changed the course of history. How many were bound by the shackles of an outdated religion? We must become free, as they were, if we are to help lead the world to new heights."

Day after day, month after month, Wittinsky prodded him. Eliezer listened and was impressed.

"After you make the great decision, Eliezer, you must then be willing to suffer for your convictions. Some of us may be arrested, imprisoned, sent to Siberia, or even put to death. But strong men have no fears."

Eliezer was wavering when an event occurred which finally, like a great ray of light thrown into a murky scene, illuminated the road down which he really wanted to travel.

Russia went to war, among other things for the liberation of Bulgaria. This gave the young Russian intellectuals a concrete focal point for their enthusiasms. Now they became ardent supporters of the czarist battle for freedom for those whom the Turks for so long a time had kept enslaved. But if the Bulgars could be liberated, why, Eliezer asked himself, not also the Jews? Why could not Jews have their own land, their own language, their own way of life? How were Jews inferior to Bulgars? Is liberty something only for a race down in the Balkans? The Bulgars had suffered oppression for a few generations, but for nearly twenty centuries the Jews had been kept a dispersed and homeless people! If freedom for the oppressed was so important to men like Wittinsky, why did they not show some concern for those who had been oppressed for so much longer than any others?

Then Eliezer remembered his mother saying that the liberation of the Jews could come only with the arrival of the Messiah. But why? If the Bulgars could be liberated now, why must Jews wait indefinitely?

All these questions were answered to Eliezer's own satisfaction by a clear strong voice which rang constantly in his ears. It drowned out the arguments of the Wittinskys. It put to rout the indecisions Eliezer himself had. He knew now which battle he wanted to fight. He would consecrate his life to the liberation of his own people and the establishment of Jews in the land of their forefathers.

But he must have allies. And all his studying from now on must be directed toward a single end. He must learn about politics, about the customs of various lands through which the Jews had been dispersed. He must fit himself for some profession by which he could earn a living.

As the day of his graduation from the high school in Dünaburg drew near, the boy from Luzhky finally decided to continue his education in Paris, because Paris was the center of the political and diplomatic life of Europe. He also decided to take up the study of medicine, a profession which would give him a certain social standing wherever he went and place him in contact with people in a position to help in the realization of his dream.

6

Convert No. 1

"Dear Deborah:

"This is to inform you that I have arrived in the wonderful city of Paris. The first thing which astonished me was the discovery that everyone here can speak French better than I can. Even the coachmen, the janitors, and the men who clean the streets. Somehow I had thought that, with your instruction and the work I did at Dünaburg, I was more perfect in the language than anyone except French scholars.

"It is wonderful to be living in the great world center of wisdom and learning, where there is complete freedom of thought, of expression, of action.

"My immediate object is to reach a certain *niveau* which will enable me to come into intimate contact with the great Jewish personalities of our time, in order to interest them in my plan for the reestablishment of the Jewish people on the soil of our ancestors. I am desirous of learning all that I am able about the history of our own people. I hope to find everything in the university called the Sorbonne.

"Tell your father and mother I think often of them and please bear my greetings to all, including little Pola.

"Eliezer"

"Dear Deborah:

"I have received your letter in which you ask me intimate questions about my life here. The matter of existence does not very much bother me. I need only a small room, which I have found, and a slice of bread and some sausage each day, which is enough.

"I read as many newspapers as possible. From time to time I go to the lectures of Gambetta on the political situation in the world at large. I often attend sessions of the French Parliament.

"It is now my great desire to meet important men and to talk to them about my idea and ascertain how they are going to react. Will they lend me their ears, or will they ridicule me? If they advise me to dismiss the whole matter and concentrate on my medical studies, I shall be bitterly disappointed.

"In the Russian reading room at the library I have met a very cultured and famous journalist, a descendant of Polish nobility, who is the Paris correspondent for a liberal Russian newspaper, the *Russian World*. His name is Tshashnikov. He has been as kind to me as Wittinsky in Dünaburg. But there is one queer difference. Wittinsky was a Jew, but was unsympathetic to all that I had in my mind. Tshashnikov is not a Jew, yet he has an understanding of the problem and the solution. He says that his own people, the Poles, have begun to be reconciled to their loss of liberty and he had thought until now the same was even more true of the Jews. He encourages me because he says it is refreshing to find someone interested in freedom and liberty. We often meet in the Café de la Source, where we discuss politics and literature over coffee.

"One evening I revealed to him my idea for a revival of the Hebrew nation. He seemed very much impressed and said he would do anything to aid me because of his feelings for freedom. Therefore, my first convert to The Idea is this man who is a Polish aristocrat and not a Jew at all.

"I shall write to you from time to time of my progress.

"Eliezer"

"Dear Deborah:

"Life has become exciting for me in Paris. Through the kind offices of my Polish friend I have been meeting many important people and have been entertained in some of the great homes of Paris which are the meeting places of a circle of artists, literary figures, and diplomatic personalities such as Gambetta, Victor Hugo, Emile de Girardin, and Sarah Bernhardt. I have also met such Jewish figures as Adolphe Crémieux and others. In these circles one hears interesting topics of the day and some 'evil language' from and about the intellectuals.

"There was a big wedding in the Panthéon at which most of the important personalities of our time were present. Victor Hugo and an actor from the Comédie Française spent the time walking around and around the Panthéon while the wedding was in progress discussing the café gossip about the morals of the bride, which I am sorry to say were very shocking. I know the story is true because I was present, having been taken by my friend Tshashnikov. The story may offend you, but I tell it because it amuses me that even such great men should indulge in the evil tongue. It is good, at least, to know that they are human.

"I wish, Deborah, that you could be here to enjoy the experiences which I am having. I often think how it all started in Glubokiah, thanks to your father.

"I regret to say that the cough troubles me and I have begun to spit blood, which Tshashnikov says is a bad symptom. I have an appointment soon with Dr. Charles Netter, the founder of the Mikveh Israel colony in Palestine. I shall take his advice, whatever it is.

"Shalom!

"Eliezer"

"Dear Deborah:

"I must inform you that I have seen Dr. Netter and his diagnosis is not good. He says I have tuberculosis, that my lungs are badly affected, and has ordered me to stop my studies immediately. He has recommended a climate such as Algiers.

"The news has very much frightened me because I have the feeling that I have not much longer to live. If I should find the means to go to North Africa it is likely that I would never be able to return to Paris to continue my studies. What is distressing is that I am on the threshold of success in my plan. It has taken me two years in

Paris to prepare the ground. Now, just as I am ready to make the appeal to our people, the ground is to be cut from under me. I have worked hard, gaining the knowledge which I needed, but what good will it be if I die before I can put it to use?

"I have the feeling of a person condemned to death and I so much wish to find a way to utter my last words. For this reason I work now without sleep to put onto paper the reasons why it is so important for the Jewish world to become inflamed with the idea of returning to the land of our forefathers and working for the freedom to which we are entitled.

"I have decided that in order to have our own land and political life it is also necessary that we have a language to hold us together. That language is Hebrew, but not the Hebrew of the rabbis and scholars. We must have a Hebrew language in which we can conduct the business of life. It will not be easy to revive a language dead for so long a time.

"The day is so short; the work to be done so great.

"I wonder often, since receiving the report of the doctor, who is going to be the trustee of this great mission. My friend Tshashnikov has the enthusiasm and interest, but is not a Jew, which would make it impossible for him to carry on my plan.

"For all these reasons I am working like a man with but a few hours to live. I cover hundreds of pieces of paper with arguments, reasons, and proofs. If I can write something which is convincing and get it into a publication where it will command attention, then possibly someone will be found to put the plan into action.

"I beg you and your family to give me the benefit of your good wishes for my success at this critical time.

"Eliezer"

"Dear Deborah:

"I write with great excitement, for I have completed my appeal. It is not exactly as I wish it to be, but the day is so short, the work to be done so great, that I cannot delay longer.

"I have sent the article to a Hebrew paper in Warsaw, *Hamaggid,* which means 'The Teller.' Since the article has been posted I have not slept a single hour. My cough is worse, the spitting of blood goes on all the time, and the doctor insists I must go quickly to Algiers, but I cannot leave, even if I find the means, until I know that my appeal has been accepted for publication.

"I shall inform you when I hear from the editor in Warsaw.

"Ben Yehuda"

"P.S. Do not be surprised that I sign a new name to my letter. This is the name which will appear over my article. Someday I shall find the way to make it my own."

7
Cognac Celebration

TSHASHNIKOV KNOCKED REPEATEDLY ON THE DOOR. There was no answer. Finally, alarmed that Eliezer might have died during one of his coughing spells, he ran down four flights of stairs to the quarters of the *concierge* and reported his fear.

The white-haired concierge put on his coat, picked up a circle of wire strung with keys, and said:

"*Alors!* Let us go and see. It is possible that something serious has happened, but I think not. I think it is the letter. For days *notre triste jeune homme* (that's what we call him) has been so nervous he neither eats nor sleeps. For days he comes to my room every few hours asking, 'Has a letter come?'

"Finally today it arrives. I climb all the stairs to deliver it to him. When he takes it, his hand shakes like a leaf on a tree in winter.

"It must have been a small letter, because he reads it in one minute, then throws it onto the floor. Then he walks back and forth. Then he picks it up and reads again.

"What happened after that I do not know, because then I heard the noise of the bell on the street door, so I had to go down to let someone in.

"But anyway, here is his room. I shall open the door and you can go in. If there is any need for the doctor I shall send my son. May the Blessed Virgin protect notre triste jeune homme!"

Eliezer was face down on his bed, the letter beside him on the floor. After Eliezer had read the letter to him Tshashnikov understood. It was one of the briefest rejections he had ever heard of. Except for the formal salutation and conventional ending, it merely said:

> We find the article signed Ben Yehuda not good enough for publication.

Tshashnikov was perplexed.

"One thing I do not understand," he said. "This letter is addressed to you, but it concerns an article written by some 'Ben Yehuda.' Perhaps there has been an error!"

Eliezer, after several deep coughs, replied:

"No, Tshashnikov, there is no mistake. 'Ben Yehuda' is the name I signed. It is my article which is not good enough for them; the article I worked on for so many months. I must admit now that I am finished. The world is against me and God is against me. God gave me this disease and the world now gives me a negative answer to my plan. . . ."

Eliezer punctuated almost every sentence with a cough. He spoke more with resignation than bitterness. When he finished Tshashnikov said quietly:

"Wash your face, Eliezer. I received some unexpected money today and I think we both need a good meal. How many times have I told you the mind cannot function unless the body is fed? We shall talk about the article later, but tell me now, where did this pen name come from? Ben Yehuda! What does it mean?"

"It is a name I have always liked. My father was Leib. That's Yiddish. Translated into Hebrew, it's Yehuda. Ben is Hebrew for 'son.' So Ben Yehuda means 'Son of Yehuda,' which is what I am. But there is a deeper significance. Yehuda is also the Hebrew word for 'Judea,' so I now have a name I like. Ben Yehuda, the Son of Judea!

"Someday I wish to find a way to drop the name of Perlman, my own family's name, and also Elyanof, which I acquired for nonmilitary purposes. Neither has any meaning to me. But Ben Yehuda is a good name. It has a good sound. How do you like it?"

Tshashnikov smiled. This was Eliezer again. The color had begun to return to his face.

Only after they had finished a good meal and were having coffee did the Pole allow the article to be discussed. Then he introduced the subject himself, saying:

"I understand your feelings about the rejection, Eliezer, but surely there is some other Jewish weekly or monthly besides this one in Warsaw. Think now. Name me another!"

"There is an important monthly in Vienna called *Hashahar,* which means 'The Dawn,' but its articles are all by famous literary people and big politicians. I am a nobody. Whoever heard of Ben Yehuda?"

"Send it anyway! What have you to lose? Sometimes you surprise me, Eliezer! You have such burning convictions, such energy, such enthusiasm, yet you allow one insignificant editor to wreck your entire dream. If *Hashahar* rejects it, we shall try somewhere else."

The reply from *Hashahar* was only a postal card, but if it had been on the finest of parchment, engraved in letters of gold, it could hardly have brought more happiness to the tubercular student from Luzhky.

"We are pleased to announce that we are publishing your article in an early issue. We have changed the title from 'A Burning Problem' to 'A Worthy Question.' You possess a talent for writing. May your pen be blessed!"

That was all, but it breathed new life into the twenty-two-year-old boy now known to himself, to an editor in Vienna, and to two friends as Ben Yehuda. That night as Tshashnikov approached the table in the Café de la Source for their evening rendezvous he saw the transformation immediately.

"I can read in your face that the article has been accepted, yes?"

They sat long that night in the café drinking cognac. Before they separated Tshashnikov gave Eliezer two pieces of advice.

"First you must obey the doctor's order and go to Algiers. Then, when your health returns, you must use your pen to keep the issue burning. You must convince others, as you have convinced me."

"But how am I to get to Algiers? It costs money to travel that far!"

"It shall be arranged. I have a few friends, thank God. Tomorrow I shall speak to some of them. Now, let us have one more cognac before we go."

It was only a few days later that a copy of *Hashahar* arrived with Eliezer's new name in print for the first time. Sitting again in his favorite café, he spread the paper out on the table and with trembling hands displayed it to Tshashnikov.

Eliezer had read and reread the article to his friend in manuscript, but now he went through it again, translating passages he had revised.

> "If, in truth, each and every nation is entitled to defend its nationality and protect itself from extinction, then logically we, the Hebrews, also must needs have that same right. Why should our lot be meaner than that of all others?
>
> "Why should we choke the hope to return and become a nation in our deserted country which is still mourning its lost children, driven away to remote lands two thousand years ago? Why should we not follow the example of all nations, big and small, and do something to protect our nationality against extermination?"

Tshashnikov liked that passage and said:

"It is compelling logic, Eliezer, and I see no possible argument against it!"

Eliezer went on translating:

> "Why should we not lift ourselves up and look into the future? Why do we sit cross-handed and do nothing which would serve as a basis upon which to build the salvation of our people? If we care at all that the name of Israel should not disappear from this earth, we must create a center for the whole of our people, like a heart from which blood would run into the arteries of the whole, and animate the whole. Only the settlement of Eretz Israel can serve this purpose."

"You improved that passage since you last read it to me. It is a good argument, plainly stated."

Then they skipped to paragraphs which read:

> "Today, as in ancient times, this is a blessed land in which we shall eat our bread not meanly; a fertile land upon which nature has bestowed glory and beauty; a land in which only hard-working hands are needed to make it the happiest of all countries. All tourists to that place state such facts unanimously.
>
> "And now the time has come for us, the Hebrews, to do something positive. Let us create a society for the purchase of land in Eretz Israel; for the acquisition of everything necessary for agriculture; for the division of the land among Jews already present and those desiring to emigrate there, and for the provision of the funds necessary for those who cannot establish themselves independently."

When he put down the article, Tshashnikov looked into Eliezer's pale face and said:

"Remember your promise to go to Algiers? Well, I have found the means. I talked today to Baron Edmond James de Rothschild, the great French banker, and——"

"Surely you did not ask him for charity for me?"

"Not charity, Eliezer. The baron is a good man, and you are one of his own people because you are both Jews. He is a man of great wealth; one of the few I know who consider the acquisition and possession of money a responsibility, not just a right. I think that someday you may be able to win him to your big idea. In the meantime I have persuaded him to finance your trip to Algiers."

"What did you tell him?"

"Nothing about the nature of your writings. I merely advertised you to him as a young Jew of ability."

8

Detective, Scholar, Magician, Midwife

ELIEZER BEN YEHUDA, SELF-STYLED "SON OF Judea," stayed many months in Algiers. During the winter Tshashnikov came to visit him. He found his friend greatly improved in health and full of enthusiasm.

The first night, as they sat down to dinner, Eliezer gave the Polish journalist a long dissertation on languages. He explained that Hebrew began to die out as a commonly spoken language at the time of the Maccabees, almost two hundred years before the start of the Christian Era. In one period Greek was the common language of many Jews. Later, as Jews settled in various parts of the world, they began to use the tongue of the countries in which they found themselves.

In Germany in the Middle Ages the Jews spoke the language of those around them, medieval German, only they wrote it in Hebraic characters. When vast numbers of them were forced to leave Germany and settled in Poland and Russia they took medieval German with them as their language. But gradually their talk became unintelligible to a German, even to a German Jew, for several reasons.

Back in Germany, medieval German underwent many changes, until modern German finally developed. But in their ghettos in the East the Jews were isolated from such changes. Also, they grafted many Hebrew words to their language. And then they often distorted words on purpose, in order to be able to say things among themselves without their non-Jewish neighbors being able to understand. Thus Yiddish was born.

The same thing happened with medieval Spanish, which came to be known as Ladino.

At this point Tshashnikov laughed and interrupted.

"I already know some of this, Eliezer, but I wonder if you know that the Cockney which is spoken in the East End of London developed because the charwomen, the costermongers, the pub keepers wanted to be able to say things that the bobbies wouldn't be able to understand."

Eliezer nodded, then, even more intent, he expounded his theory that if Jews were ever to be unified they must be given a common language again.

"I read somewhere that we Jews speak seventy different languages, yet not one of us speaks our own language! Today the languages of the ghetto cling to us like leprosy. We can never aspire to be free men, Tshashnikov, as long as we use those ghetto dialects.

"They argue with me that Hebrew is a bookish language, lacks vitality. I ask them, when the prophets spoke to the people, did they speak only in the temples? Wasn't Hebrew, then, a language spoken in the streets, a language of the masses?

"It's just that Hebrew needs to be modernized. I agree that it is equally important to have words for tools and dishes as words for philosophical concepts. Hebrew once had those words, but they have become lost. They entered Arabic and Greek and other languages as immigrants and remained as citizens. Now we must bring them back home again.

"Listen to the people around us. They are all Sephardic Jews. Listen to the depth of tone, the beauty of the way they talk. When they pray in Hebrew they make the words sound so melodious.

"When the Ashkenazim (that's what we call the people who

speak Yiddish), when they talk Hebrew they give it a distinctly Yiddish or Ashkenazim accent, but the Sephardic or Spanish Jews pronounce the words quite differently, and with what I am sure is almost the sound that Hebrew had in ancient days."

For a long time Tshashnikov listened. Finally he said:

"I am no expert at languages, but I agree with you."

"And don't you think, Tshashnikov, if we are going to have a common language for all the Jews of the world we should settle on one pronunciation?"

"Certainly, but I imagine you will have a job getting your people from the north to give up their pronunciation. You are mapping out a big job for yourself, my frail friend. As far as I know, never before in history did any one man set out to 'create' a language. But how exciting! It will be like building a modern nineteenth-century structure on a solid foundation thousands of years old. Think of the words you will have to manufacture! Think of the objects and ideas which did not exist two thousand years ago for which you will have to find expressions! For example, is there a Hebrew word for a vehicle propelled by steam?"

"We have two words in Hebrew, one for steam and one for engine. We might combine them and call it a steam engine, just as they do in English, or like the French *machine à vapeur.*

"But you are right, one will have to spend years searching through Hebrew literature and in libraries all over the world for words which once were in the language and disappeared."

"Yes, Eliezer, you will have to be detective, scholar, magician, and midwife all combined."

By the time young Ben Yehuda returned to Paris, so many Jewish publications had reprinted his "appeal" or had commented on it that his scheme for the revival of the language and a return of Jews to the Middle East was the subject of discussion and debate wherever Jewish intellectuals gathered. Most of the reaction, however, was negative.

The opposition had many facets. There were those, like Eliezer's own mother, who wished to sit with folded hands and allow God to have His own unhampered way, without human intervention, which they considered sacrilegious.

Then there were those who thought that an attempt to establish a Jewish state would arouse dormant anti-Semites to new excesses of violence. They argued that better days had finally arrived for most Jews in the Diaspora; that there were now relatively few pogroms; that those willing to give up their identity as Jews and become assimilated would be safe from further persecutions. They even advocated intermarriage and abandonment of religious beliefs. Some went to this extreme because they were personally prospering and wanted no Jewish movement to interfere.

Others contended that the writer who signed himself "Ben Yehuda" had painted too glowing a picture of Palestine; that it was all right to call it a "blessed land" but he had distorted facts when he spoke of "a fertile land upon which nature has bestowed glory and beauty; a land in which only hard-working hands are needed to make it the happiest of all countries."

These critics argued that in the course of two thousand years, through neglect and a stripping of the natural resources, Palestine had become a barren waste which would require generations of back-breaking labor to make productive.

After Eliezer returned to Paris he supported himself by doing translations from French to Russian. He attended classes at the Sorbonne, listened to visiting lecturers, spent hours each day in the Paris libraries, covered hundreds of sheets of paper with amplifications of his ideas, and wrote numerous newspaper articles which he sent to a new outlet, a small newspaper in Jerusalem called *Hahabatzeleth*.

In one article, answering the criticism that he was being blind to reality because the Turks would never allow the Jews any rights in Palestine, he wrote:

"There are times in the history of a nation when it is not the clever ones who are important, but those who have vision to see through the dark curtain of actuality."

While he was in Algiers, Eliezer had been in greatly improved health, but his cough and the attendant pains returned the first week after he returned to Paris.

One night, talking with Tshashnikov, he said:

"I have just about come to a great personal decision. I think I shall leave France and go to Palestine to spend the rest of my life among my own people."

Tshashnikov blinked several times. Finally he said:

"That, indeed, would be a drastic move. What are your reasons?"

"It is a combination of many. A remark I overheard the other day had something to do with it. Some Jewish friends, not knowing that I was listening, said that if I were sincere I would go to the Holy Land myself instead of just urging others to do it. They said my honesty was open to question as long as I remained here myself. This started me thinking.

"After all, there exists over there a nucleus of Jews who, for one reason or another, have already gone back. I must join them and convert them to the use of Hebrew as a spoken language.

"If I am in Jerusalem myself I can send my appeals from there and base them on facts. I can report the true situation. I can speak then with authority. Here in Paris I am an insignificant student. There, perhaps, I can become the leader of a movement.

"Besides—and I hope that this will not offend you, Tshashnikov—but honestly, I am not very happy using Russian and French as my languages. I want to be somewhere where I can speak Hebrew and hear others speak it and perhaps persuade them all to speak it.

"I wish to start work on the language. The time is so short; the work to be done is so great. Palestine—or Israel, as I prefer to call it—is the place. I think I shall go soon. That, I know, is my destiny. I must live and work among my own people."

Tshashnikov had listened patiently to the long speech flow without interruption from the young student's lips. Finally he spoke himself.

"A highly commendable decision, however much I shall miss you. Besides, there are practical reasons why you should go. Perhaps the climate there will be more favorable for you. I care enough for you so that I would rather know there is a living Ben Yehuda thousands of kilometers away than a dead Ben Yehuda here in Paris."

"You have been a good friend, Tshashnikov. You have never once misunderstood me." Eliezer's eyes were blurred as he said it.

Others did not understand him as well. Reports that a young Jewish student named Eliezer Ben Yehuda was leaving the intellectual center of the world for the bare desert sands of the Middle East, where he hoped to create the heart of a movement for the Jewish resettlement of the Holy Land and a revival of Hebrew as a spoken language, only brought forth a fresh wave of criticism.

Some were tolerant enough to call him an idle dreamer. Others labeled him a fool. But there were those who went so far as to say that he should be treated as an enemy of the Jewish people and promptly disowned by them.

But Eliezer's mind was made up and he began packing the battered suitcase which Father Yonas had given him in Glubokiah years before.

9

Determined Chess

ONE EVENING SHLOMOH YONAS CAME INTO HIS wife's room with a letter in his hand. He was extremely agitated.

"Where are the children?" he demanded.

"They are all in bed except Deborah. She is down in the library reading. Why do you ask? Has something gone wrong? What is it, Shlomoh?"

The father sat down and wiped his forehead.

"I had better commence at the start. Here"—and as he spoke he dug into the pocket of his coat—"here is a small article I read in a Hebrew journal several weeks ago. It is only a few lines at the bottom of a column. It says that a young Jewish scholar in Paris known as Ben Yehuda has decided to go to Palestine to start a movement for the speaking of the Hebrew language and bringing Jews back to the Holy Land. When I read it I remembered that Deborah has said our young friend Eliezer had written some articles signed Ben Yehuda. So I obtained his address from Deborah and wrote to him."

"Why did you not tell me about the article, Shlomoh, when you first read it?"

"I did not tell anyone; not even Deborah. I wanted to handle the matter myself."

"I hope you did not write to Eliezer that——"

"Yes, I did! I wrote in a very angry tone, I am afraid. I told him that Deborah has taken seriously the promise he made when he left. I told him she had been waiting for him—waiting for him all these years to complete his education. I told him that she had grown recently into a comely young lady, so fine-looking, so dainty, with culture to the tips of her fingers. I guess I did not restrain myself. I wrote as if I were describing the products of my distillery—as if I were a salesman."

"You told all that to Eliezer in the letter?"

"Yes, and I was very stern about it. I said that we only wished to know what were his intentions. Why had he not given Deborah at least a chance to say no?"

The father was pacing the room. With each sentence he grew more distraught.

"His reply has just arrived. I picked it up myself at the post office a few minutes ago. It is a short note, Rivkah. He writes it all in Hebrew. I can no longer be angry with him. I wish now I had never written the letter to him."

"But what does he say, Shlomoh!"

"He says the article in the paper was true; that he is planning to go to Palestine. In fact, he leaves from Paris next week. We shall just have time to get an answer to him."

"An answer to what?"

"Rivkah, my dear, it seems that the poor boy has consumption. A very bad case of it. He fears that he has only a short time to live. Besides, he is very poor. He says that he has little more than money enough to make the trip to Jerusalem. He apologizes for his treatment of us. He says that he has never forgotten Deborah and has a deep love for her, but that he never dreamed she would be interested in sharing his life, poor and consumptive that he is, and in a land so barren and savage as Palestine. But he writes further that if Deborah would by any chance be willing to accompany him she could join him in Vienna, where he is stopping off to see Peretz Ben Moshe Smolenskin."

"And who would that be?"

"That is the name, Rivkah, of the editor of the paper which published his first article. Remember? He says that if Deborah would meet him in Vienna they could get married there and then continue the journey together."

"But, Shlomoh, you surely are not going to allow Deborah to marry a boy in that condition! And Palestine! It is so far away! We would never see our daughter again!"

"You talk, Rivkah, as if you did not know Deborah. How can anyone stop that girl when she sets her mind to something? You know how she talks all the time of Eliezer and . . ."

It was Deborah's last night at home. For hours the Yonas house had echoed with songs and laughter. Three tables were piled high with wedding presents left by the guests. In the dining room, after the festivities were all over, enough food remained to feed the population of a small village.

Deborah herself had never looked lovelier. At her mother's request she had worn the dress which had been made especially for the wedding in Vienna.

During the evening she had paid considerably more attention to her parents than to the guests. Each time she saw out of the corner of her eye that they were alone, or that they looked as if they were about to burst into tears again, she would dash over to them, put her arms around them, and whisper words designed to make them forget the sorrow which they so ill concealed.

Now the last guest had departed. The other children had gone to their rooms, all except Pola, who had recently celebrated her tenth birthday. Pola had refused to leave the party, even when she no longer could keep her eyes open. Now she was asleep on a couch in the library. Mother Yonas had said good night and had told her husband and eldest daughter not to stay up much longer. But after she had gone upstairs, Deborah turned to her father. With a tone that begged for understanding she said:

"Father, this will be my last night under your roof. Tomorrow I go away on an adventure the end of which none of us can possibly foresee. I know you do not approve, but if it is within my power to make Eliezer happy I shall do it. I shall help him to the best of my ability in his great undertaking. Now, I wish you to do one last favor for me."

Father Yonas looked puzzled.

"I wish," the daughter continued, "that you would play a last game of chess with me before we go to bed."

It was a close fight and lasted almost until dawn. As the father finally admitted defeat Deborah slipped from her chair, put a hand on his shoulder, and said:

"And I am going to win the bigger game I am about to play, too, just you wait and see!"

Because it would have been difficult, perhaps impossible, to obtain for Deborah all the documents needed for her trip, Father Yonas persuaded his own brother to accompany the young woman as far as the Russian frontier and help smuggle her across the border.

Two days later the brother returned. He carried a small paper package with him. The entire Yonas family clustered around him to ask whether Deborah had been shot trying to sneak across the frontier; was she still alive; what dire events had occurred; had there been any "incidents"?

The brother tried to smile. Nothing had happened. She got across all right. They had outwitted the frontier guards. She sent her love.

"But what," asked Father Yonas, "do you carry in the small package?"

The brother opened it. Mother Yonas burst out crying when she saw the small silk cushion she had given Deborah to use on the train when she wanted to sleep.

"As the girl sneaked across the frontier," the uncle explained, "she dropped it. If I had run after her we might both have been caught. So I picked it up and brought it back."

Mother Yonas clutched the pillow to her breast, sobbing with no attempt at self-restraint:

"My Deborah! This is all that I have left of my oldest daughter!"

10

Two Is Company

THE RIDE FROM PARIS TO VIENNA IN THOSE DAYS was a long and tedious one. But the young Jewish scholar had plenty of thoughts to occupy his mind as he traveled across the French countryside and on into Germany.

He would have only several more days to get reconciled to the idea of a partnership, instead of a solitary adventure. In these past few years he had had little feminine companionship. In fact, Deborah was the only girl he had ever really known. Years ago he had occasionally dreamed of the two of them sharing a life together, but since the doctors had warned him about the seriousness of his physical condition, even that thought had grown dim.

Of course he had the natural and normal feelings of any young man contemplating his own impending marriage, but in addition he had to fit Deborah into the plan of his crusade. They would have children, of course, and Deborah would become the first Hebrew mother in nearly two thousand years! She would talk only Hebrew by then, and their children would be the first children in almost two thousand years to know no other language. This would be an example for other Jews. It would be as important in propagating the idea as all the articles and all the books he himself might write. Deborah Ben Yehuda, the first Hebrew mother!

How much had she changed in all these years? Would she be willing to sacrifice for the ideals he believed in? Life would be rugged in Palestine, and the Jews there might not receive them with open arms. They might be suspicious or even hostile. There might be innumerable complications. But the die was now cast. Deborah at this very moment was probably on the way toward their rendezvous in Vienna.

Peretz Ben Moshe Smolenskin, the Viennese editor, greeted Eliezer with an announcement which brought color into the young man's pale face and made his eyes dance with excitement.

They were sitting in the editor's office, after exchanging formal greetings, when Smolenskin smiled and said:

"By the way, I have printed your article entitled 'Letter from Ben Yehuda' and also the third one you sent."

When he saw how pleased Eliezer seemed, he added:

"You will not be so happy, however, when you see that I have printed my own answers to the arguments in your first two articles. I tore them to pieces!"

Eliezer looked crestfallen. Timidly he said:

"Perhaps if I read what you wrote I would be able to reply."

"That is not necessary. Such work has been done by someone else."

The editor paused a moment, apparently enjoying his guest's confusion. Then he continued:

"I did it myself. I have myself written against my own arguments in my own paper.

"I had always thought that Jews could live happily in the countries of their dispersion if they merely announced to the world their intention to be good citizens of the various places where they found themselves.

"But before the ink was dry on my own words, terrible things began to happen in Russia which destroyed all my arguments.

"I have just come back from a long trip through Russia. I have seen myself how wrong I was.

"I saw ugly sights, Ben Yehuda. The pogroms have begun again in certain quarters. Our people are being persecuted, even killed.

I saw how essential it is that we build a sanctuary in Palestine for Jews who wish to escape from the cruelties so often inflicted upon us.

"Of course we shall have opposition among our own people. The battle will be hard. But you are on the right road, young man, and you shall have the full support of *Hashahar,* which now has as its motto, 'The Rebirth of the People of Israel on the Soil of Israel.' "

Elated, Eliezer hurried back to his hotel to see if a telegram had come yet from Deborah. But there was no telegram from her. Perhaps she had changed her mind. Perhaps her parents had argued her out of coming. Perhaps . . .

While he was sitting on the edge of the bed, full of black thoughts, there was a rap at the door. Before he could answer it, the door opened gently. Eliezer looked and blinked several times. Who was this apparition standing there with a half-smile on her face? Not . . .

They shouted each other's names and then greeted each other as lovers should. Several times Eliezer backed away from Deborah and looked her over. Her father had been right.

For an hour they chattered in a mixture of French and Russian, the two languages Deborah had taught him. How was her trip? Why had she not sent him a telegram announcing the time of her arrival?

"But I did, Eliezer. It should have come hours ago. I sent it . . ."

While she was still explaining, the telegram arrived.

That same day they discovered the impossibility of being married in Vienna. Birth certificates and other documents were required, which they neither had nor could easily obtain. They were advised that there would be no such difficulties in Turkey, so they decided to wait until they reached Constantinople.

The two young lovers were together almost constantly during the week they remained in the Austrian capital. They wandered the streets hand in hand, visited museums, and even saw an opera. For some reason which he never explained to Deborah, Eliezer told neither the editor nor several other friends he had in Vienna about his fiancée.

Their last day in Vienna, Eliezer received a letter with French stamps on the envelope. When he finished reading it he turned to Deborah with excitement and said:

"This is wonderful news! Tshashnikov is going with us!"

"And who is Tshashnikov?" Deborah asked rather icily.

"Oh, you'll like him very much, Deborah. He's the best friend I have in the world! He's the Polish journalist I knew in Paris. I wrote to you all about him. Surely you remember!"

Deborah obviously was trying to control her feelings, but her voice was severe as she said:

"What do you mean, he is going with us? Not to Palestine! Not on our honeymoon!"

Eliezer did not seem to understand.

"He writes that he will meet us in Constantinople; that we must wait there for him. It will be wonderful having him. . . ."

"You say he writes that he is going to meet 'us.' Does he know about me?"

Eliezer stammered as he replied:

"As a matter of fact, Deborah, I believe I forgot to tell him about you. But you will like each other very much."

The girl from Glubokiah let the matter drop, but that night she cried herself to sleep.

August of 1881 was a pleasant month. The days were soft and warm, the sky cloudless, the landscape, as the Danube grew wider and wider, extremely picturesque.

The few other passengers on the small river steamer, sensing that the two who spent so much time standing close together on the deck looking out at the scenery were lovers, left them alone.

The first evening Deborah and Eliezer ignored the dinner bell and stood looking into the twilight at the shore line. Suddenly Eliezer turned and said in Hebrew:

"How beautiful it is!"

Deborah, although not sure of the words, sensed what they meant by the way Eliezer said them, so she repeated them back to him:

"Yes, Eliezer, how beautiful it is!"

That was the first conversation they ever held in the language which they were both going to give their lives to propagate.

A few minutes later Eliezer pointed toward the southeast and said, again in Hebrew:

"Off there, Deborah, in the land of our forefathers, on the banks of the River Jordan, you shall someday soon become the first Hebrew mother of our times."

When he translated the words into French, Deborah laughed and said:

"How many times must I remind you, Eliezer, that we are not yet even married!"

In Constantinople there were again difficulties about papers. They were told it would be easier in Cairo.

Deborah wanted to go at once, but Eliezer reminded her that they must wait for his Polish friend. While they waited they explored the Turkish capital, took a boat trip on the Bosporus, wandered through the bazaars, and behaved like two honeymooners, despite the fact that the honeymoon had not yet technically begun.

Finally Tshashnikov arrived. He threw his arms around his frail young friend in greeting. Eliezer watched his face as he presented Deborah, saying:

"I should have told you before. We are going to be married."

Tshashnikov obviously was impressed by her loveliness. His eyes showed that. But as Eliezer said "married," Tshashnikov's face clouded. He recovered himself quickly, however, and took them both by the arm as they headed for their hotel.

Late that evening, after the men had retired to the room they were sharing, Eliezer, with childlike eagerness, asked:

"Tell me quickly, how do you like her?"

"An exceptionally charming girl; very talented, obviously. I like her immensely, except——"

"Except what, Tshashnikov?"

"I do not wish to hurt you, Eliezer, but I think it is a great mistake. I wish you had told me sooner. She is pretty and intelligent, but she is a woman, and you know so little about women! She is frail and delicate. Will she be able to stand the physical hardships? Obviously she has come from a good home, accustomed to a soft life. For her it will be like going from civilization to barbarism."

Eliezer finally managed to say:

"But we are very much in love. Do you understand?"

"That I find difficult to believe. You have not seen her for years. I know a thing or two about love. You could not have been in love with her all these years and ignored her as you have done. This is madness. You should come to your senses before it is too late."

"But, Tshashnikov, she is going to be a very valuable assistant to me in my work. We took an oath on the boat that we would both devote our lives to the ideal."

"That is another point against your marriage, Eliezer. I doubt whether she will be of any help. I myself, who am not a Jew, know more Hebrew than she does. How much will she be willing to sacrifice for your ideal? Now if you had decided to take as a wife one of those Jewish girls we met down in Algiers, it would be different. At least from one of them you could have learned something. I mean something about that pronunciation you like so well. We must talk more about it later, but now I am tired. Let's go to sleep."

Deborah was in a lonely position. She wanted desperately to talk to someone other than Eliezer about his Polish friend. It was years later before she finally was able to confide in members of her own family, but by then the problem was over.

She resented Tshashnikov's presence. He was a discordant note in what had started out as a lovely symphony. Being romantic and having lived so many years for this reunion with the man she loved, she felt that Tshashnikov should have the good grace to leave them alone. But they were seldom alone. Wherever they went it was always a threesome.

Tshashnikov was handsome and intelligent and deeply interested in Eliezer's project, but he made her feel as if she were the outsider.

There was another aspect of the problem which she hardly dared think about. Whenever there was an opportunity, whenever Eliezer was busy, Tshashnikov sought her out and on such occasions was exceedingly charming.

She tried to put the thought from her mind.

Then one day when Eliezer had gone off on a minor shopping trip Tshashnikov said he wanted to have a long talk with her. They walked together along the hill overlooking the Bosporus. For a few minutes they watched the small boats down in the harbor, their movements and the colors of their sails making them look like gaily costumed ballet dancers, Deborah thought.

Then suddenly the Pole turned to her and said:

"How much do you love Eliezer?"

It was a stupid question, but Deborah had decided it was time to speak bluntly.

"I love him with great intensity. You should know that. I also admire him and wish to help him. What more could any man ask from any woman? Now tell me why you try to embarrass me?"

Tshashnikov launched into a long monologue. Doubt after doubt he tried to sow in her mind. But the remark for which she never quite forgave him came at the end.

"I do not presume to advise you, but if you should decide to change your mind and return to your home in Lithuania, I stand ready to volunteer my services. I should be most happy to accompany you. We could have a pleasant trip back north together. Think seriously before you reject all I have said."

Deborah did a great deal of serious thinking in the days that followed. At night as she tossed on her bed, unable to drive away the doubts, she was unaware that in a room a short distance down the hall Eliezer was also tossing; also tormented by doubts planted in his mind by his good friend.

Whenever Deborah saw the two men talking together she suspected that Tshashnikov was making more propaganda against the marriage. All three of them were nervous and irritable. The premature honeymoon no longer had any of the aspects of a honeymoon.

When they arrived in Cairo the tension grew greater.

"The first thing we must do," Eliezer announced, "is to look up a rabbi whose wife I know. There is a reason why I must see him at once."

Tshashnikov gave no sign that he knew what Eliezer meant, but Deborah's feminine instinct told her, so she whispered that she must see Eliezer alone. The conference took place in the hotel lobby. Deborah put her hand lightly on his arm and said:

"Haveevee, let's be honest with each other."

Eliezer smiled.

"You have never called me that before. Haveevee—'my dear one.' How did you learn that Hebrew word?"

Deborah smiled a little sadly.

"First you must answer some questions. Are you sure of me, Eliezer? Are you sure you really want to marry me? We have had our honeymoon, but we have not yet been joined as man and wife. It is still not too late to change our minds."

Eliezer tried to look startled, then said:

"Before I answer, you must tell me whether Tshashnikov has been talking to you, or are these doubts of your own creation?"

Deborah hung her head a moment, debating. Finally she replied:

"I have never had any doubts of my own, Eliezer. Not for years and years. I think I can be a good wife and help in your work. But your friend thinks otherwise. Perhaps he is right. It is really up to you to decide. Only decide quickly, because——"

Eliezer took her right hand tightly in his.

"I shall give you my answer within an hour. And now . . ."

He looked at his watch.

"Now we must hurry, because I have an appointment and we must pick up Tshashnikov on the way."

At the rabbi's house they were greeted warmly by the rabbi's wife, who had known Eliezer in Dünaburg. When the rabbi appeared, Tshashnikov was introduced, and Deborah. Then Eliezer, with a smile to the rabbi, took Deborah's hand and, looking straight into her eyes, said:

"Harei at mekudeshet lee."

There was an exclamation from the rabbi's wife. Deborah also understood the significance of the words. Only Tshashnikov was puzzled.

"This is unfair," he said. "What do the words mean?"

It was the rabbi who explained.

"Translated literally, they mean, 'You are herewith betrothed to me,' and according to Jewish tradition, this alone is sufficient to unite two young people in marriage if spoken in the presence of two witnesses. We have two witnesses, and so . . ."

Then he turned, beaming, to Eliezer.

"And so, congratulations, my son, and now if my good wife will get the wine and sweet cakes we shall have a celebration. How wonderful all this is! I had no idea we would have a wedding party today!"

Deborah, still holding Eliezer's hand, turned to Tshashnikov and said:

"We are both waiting. Are you not going to congratulate us and wish us well?"

11

One Gold Louis

AS THE SHIP BEARING THE BEN YEHUDAS TO JAFFA steamed along the Mediterranean coast it made many stops. At each port tall, brawny young Arabs in colorful costumes came aboard. They fascinated Deborah, but their gaiety depressed Eliezer. Finally he said to his young bride:

"They also are on their way to Palestine, but for them it is 'home.' These Arabs are the citizens; we are the foreigners."

The last night before they reached Jaffa, Eliezer was unable to sleep. He walked the deck for hours. He felt alone on the ship, for there was no other sign of life. Then the stars disappeared and the east began to be tinged with pink and golden shades.

Deborah and Tshashnikov came up on deck in time to see a black streak appear on the eastern horizon, gradually increasing in size until they all knew that this was Jaffa. Small houses cropped up out of nowhere. The decks of the ship began to swarm with passengers.

Eliezer stood at the rail, staring at the shore line. Here was the Holy Land about which he had dreamed so much. Here were the deserts, the hills, the valleys about which he had read so much. How many times, down through the ages, had Jews tried to come back home, only to be driven away again!

Now he, Eliezer Ben Yehuda, Son of Judea, was approaching this place himself, on a mission. Would he, too, someday be driven away, or would his arrival be the forerunner of a great return of his own people?

Deborah came and stood close beside him. There was much she wanted to say, but knowing her husband, she remained silent, merely holding his hand.

The ship anchored half a mile from shore. The passengers were helped into small boats. That half-mile trip was one which neither Deborah nor Eliezer ever forgot. The dark-skinned Arabs who managed the boats seemed as strong as young giants. They were bare to the waist. Their muscles stood out on their arms. They manipulated their small craft with consummate skill through the rocks which dotted the port. As they rowed they raised their voices in a chant, singing prayers from the Koran for a safe landing. The waves were high and angry. Because Deborah was frightened, Eliezer began to talk softly to her.

"This is a place, my dear, famous in our Jewish history. It was originally awarded to the tribe of Dan, but as we shall soon see, it is now an Arab place."

Finally they set foot on "our land," as Eliezer called it. Their dizziness from the buffeting was now heightened by the heat, the smells, the noises around them. Deborah clung to Eliezer's arm. Tshashnikov, the well-traveled man, tried to reassure them.

"This is the edge of the Orient, my friends. A different world! How picturesque! Look at the rounded domes of the mosques!"

"Must picturesque things always be so dirty and evil-smelling?" Deborah asked, wanting an answer.

They stopped at a small hotel to inquire about transportation to Jerusalem. The manager greeted them with several words of Hebrew. When Eliezer replied in Hebrew the man looked as surprised as if he had heard a voice from the dead. He asked Eliezer his name and destination. When he heard the words "Ben Yehuda" his face broke into a broad smile.

"I have read your articles in the Jerusalem paper!"

He told them they should not start before sundown, when the evening dew would begin to temper the heat of the scorching sun.

Meanwhile, he said, he would send a telegram to Editor Frumkin to meet them.

The carriage they finally took, drawn by three emaciated horses, was little better than a large wooden box on wheels. There were no regular seats, only wooden benches without backs. They had to put their luggage under their feet.

"They say that this is luxury traveling," Tshashnikov reported. "I would hate to see what third class is like!"

"When do we get there?" Deborah asked.

"About the time the sun comes up," Eliezer replied as he formed his right shoulder into the semblance of a pillow on which Deborah could rest her head.

Eliezer, while Deborah dozed, had conversation with the coachman, at first in French, which the man said he had learned at the Mikveh Israel school founded by the doctor Eliezer had consulted in Paris. During the night it developed that the coachman also knew a little Hebrew. Before the night was over Eliezer had made his first real friend in Palestine. Hayim Jacob, the coachman, said he must never travel between Jaffa and Jerusalem with anyone else. He would be Mr. Ben Yehuda's "official chauffeur."

(Half a lifetime later, when the Jewish Coachmen's Association held a celebration honoring Hayim Jacob, its oldest member, Eliezer was one of the guests of honor.)

About midnight they reached Bab el Wad (Gate of the Valley). At this point the road began to climb, so the journey was interrupted to change horses for the final, steep twenty-four kilometers.

Most of the other passengers, including Tshashnikov, got out to stretch their legs or have a cup of thick Turkish coffee. This gave Eliezer a chance to spread several coats on one of the vacated benches so Deborah could rest horizontally for a few moments. As she lay there she looked up at her young husband and said:

"Haveevee, I am trying to be kind to the Pole because he is your friend, but ever since we got off the ship he has been looking at me as if to say, 'I told you so!'

"He actually seemed glad that Jaffa was so dirty and smelly. He seems glad that this journey is so long and difficult. He seems so sure I am going to give up and leave you. But I swear, Eliezer, I am not. As long as my body holds out I shall remain at your side."

The young man who arrived at Jerusalem on the twenty-second day of *Tishri,* which is the first month in the Hebrew calendar, in the year called by Christians 1881, was of medium height, blond, with deep-sunk brown eyes, frail, and very aesthetic-looking. He wore European clothes, topped by a blue beret. He was twenty-three years old, but his battle with consumption made him look considerably the senior of his twenty-seven-year-old wife.

She was slightly taller than he was. Although she also had the face of an aesthete, her figure was well rounded, and except for the strains of travel she was a picture of good health.

The carriage left them outside the gates of the city, which was just as well, for from this short distance they could get a view in perspective. The domes and towers of Jerusalem at this moment were painted with the morning's pinks and reds.

"How picturesque!" Deborah exclaimed, to which Tshashnikov maliciously replied:

"But do not forget what goes with picturesqueness!"

Deborah ignored him. Eliezer had not even heard; he was standing with his slim hands clasped behind his back, a strange, almost fanatical expression in his eyes.

"The City of David!" He said the words with religious awe.

Slowly the three approached one of the great gates. It was closed and locked, for the night was not yet officially over; not until the sun actually showed itself above the horizon. The only entrance for humans was by a small gate cut in the large gate and known as the Needle's Eye. In order to enter this small gate it was necessary to stoop very low.

Tshashnikov and Deborah had started to crouch down to go in when Eliezer suddenly shouted:

"No! I shall not enter the Holy City like an animal. I shall not enter with bent back!"

As he finished speaking the large gates suddenly began to creak on their hinges and swing open.

"A miracle!" Eliezer exclaimed, still in somewhat of a trance.

Tshashnikov laughed. "I would call it, instead, merely good

timing. We have arrived, as you will notice, just with the sun; just when the gates are normally opened."

Silently the two men and the girl made their way through the almost deserted streets, but before they had gone far Arab peasants began to clutter the way. The smells were the same as in Jaffa. The filth was just as deep. Deborah put a handkerchief to her nose. Now an occasional *fellah* (Arab peasant) came along, leading a small donkey loaded down with coal, pieces of wood, or sacks of lime. Now an occasional *fellahah* (Arab peasant woman) scuffled by in bare feet on her way to the market place with a basket of vegetables or fruit balanced nonchalantly on her head.

These native peoples looked suspiciously at the European strangers. A few greeted them with the Arabic words for good morning, which meant nothing to Ben Yehuda, who answered in Hebrew, a language which meant nothing to the Arab peasants.

Now the streets commenced to swarm with life. Arabs began pouring in from all sides. The men were dark and mysterious-looking in their long oriental garments. The women, Deborah observed, had a strange, passive dignity. They undulated as they walked. They seemed completely unconscious of the baskets balanced so precariously on their heads.

Tshashnikov said he wished to make a call at the Russian consulate; he would see them later.

Now they were alone. Deborah held tightly to Eliezer's arm. A mutual fear flowed back and forth between them, although they spoke to each other only in monosyllables.

So this was Jerusalem the Golden, with milk and honey blessed? Where were their own people? Red-fezzed Arabs seemed to dominate the place. Where was the spirit of holiness they had expected?

They walked bewildered through the narrow, crooked, ill-paved streets, as if wandering through a nightmare. Was this the city which had seen so many centuries of conflict, siege, plunder, massacre, and misery?

The streets were lined with dingy huts, dilapidated wooden structures or shops which had dirty cloths hung over holes in the wall in place of doors.

"Squalor" and "wretchedness" were the two words that came to

Eliezer's mind. The people all seemed poor and diseased. They were all dressed in rags.

Was this the city which men from all corners of the globe had fought over? What interest could Persians, Egyptians, Greeks, Romans, Assyrians, and Christian crusaders have had in this squalid beehive of depressed humanity?

A cobbler sat in an open doorway stitching a shoe which was so worn out that it looked like a piece of old cheese full of wormholes. Peasant women lined the edges of the roads, haggling over the price of their herbs and vegetables with women shoppers.

Was this the city in which the prophets had preached and from which great religious truths had spread around the world? Was this the city which had been destroyed and reconstructed eighteen times and had suffered two long periods of desolation and had passed from one religion to another six different times?

It was difficult to imagine Abraham here, yet Abraham had walked this very way.

Eliezer saw none of the ancient mysticism and beauty he had expected to find. To him, on this pink-and-red early morning, Jerusalem seemed just another smelly Arab city.

Deborah later admitted that if a thought could have transported her back to where they had come from she would have vanished that morning from Jerusalem and landed quickly in Vienna.

In an especially narrow street they were suddenly accosted by two men who looked unlike the others. In Yiddish they addressed Eliezer, saying:

"Are you Mr. Ben Yehuda? If so, we are to take you to the home of Mr. Israel Dov Frumkin."

Deborah's grip on Eliezer's arm relaxed. "Is he the man you told me about?"

"Yes, my dear, he is the editor of that weekly pamphlet called *Hahabatzeleth*. The name means either a crocus, a lily, a rose, or a lily of the valley. I shall have to do some research someday and find out exactly which flower it is. No one seems to be sure. Anyway, I wrote many articles for the paper from Paris."

As the two strangers led the way, Deborah said in French to her husband:

"Did you notice that they did not even look at me? Why was that?"

Eliezer smiled and patted her hand.

"We shall have to get accustomed to many things, my dear. It is only that they are extremely pious Jews who have a belief that it is wrong for a man to look at a woman in public."

The Ben Yehudas were received politely by the Frumkin family, but as soon as the editor and Eliezer went to his office to talk of serious matters, Mrs. Frumkin, with four children tugging at her skirts, reproved Deborah for not having her head covered by a shawl in the Orthodox manner.

Meanwhile Eliezer and Editor Frumkin, a little annoyed that the young man insisted they converse in Hebrew, were discussing the articles he had written. Finally the editor asked if Eliezer had any money. Where did he propose to live?

"I have," said young Ben Yehuda, "one solitary coin. One gold louis. I am very much in need of employment which will supply us with bed and board."

Frumkin invited them to be his house guests for a few days and said he would propose a more permanent arrangement later.

The few days passed happily. The Ben Yehudas got over their first horror of Jerusalem and began to feel at home in the twisting little streets.

Then the editor made Ben Yehuda a proposition. The young man would become associate editor of the weekly pamphlet. His wife would assist Madame Frumkin in her household duties. For remuneration they would receive their room and meals.

Ben Yehuda quickly accepted, but Deborah that night, after blowing out the light, said:

"Eliezer, I have a suspicion that Editor Frumkin is not at all in agreement with us. We must be very careful to win him over, instead of his winning us over. We must not sell our souls for a few loaves of bread!"

Tshashnikov had found quarters with an old acquaintance, but the day after their arrival he took Eliezer around to the Russian consulate and introduced him to the consul general. After they left the building he said:

"Our paths are going to separate now. You have a long hard road which you have chosen for yourself. Apparently Deborah is going to share it with you.

"Before your marriage I tried to argue you out of it. Deborah is a lovely girl and . . ."

As he hesitated, with the sentence unfinished, Eliezer felt there was something more his friend wanted to say. But Eliezer, afraid to hear it, did not encourage him.

The Polish journalist quickly passed his hand over his face and began a new sentence.

"I shall disappear from your life now and you can forget that I ever existed. I hope you will be very happy and very successful. I shall always follow from a distance your campaign. In case I do not see either of you again, you will say all these things to Deborah, also, for me."

"But, Tshashnikov, you came down here to help me get started on my project. Surely you are not going to leave already!"

"I did not say that I am leaving. On the other hand, I did not say I am staying. My plans are unimportant."

Having said "Shalom," the Hebrew word for "peace," which Jews use instead of "hello" and "good-by," he turned on his heel and walked off. As Eliezer watched his tall form disappear down the crooked street he wondered about many things.

(After that day he never mentioned Tshashnikov by name again, not even in his writings. Years later, in a small book of memoirs, he referred to him only as "our Polish acquaintance.")

It was only a few days before Deborah's phophecy about Frumkin turned out to have been well founded. The editor and Eliezer were in disagreement almost from the start. They were diametrically opposed not only on the ideological plane, but also temperamentally. Their arguments in the newspaper office spread to the house and began to involve Deborah and Mrs. Frumkin. The air was tense, and it soon became clear that the cohabitation scheme would have to be abandoned.

The solution finally arrived at was that Eliezer would continue to hold the job, he and his wife would find quarters of their own, and he would receive a salary of one napoleon per month, about five dollars.

As they packed Deborah said:

"Haveevee, we are like Adam and Eve leaving the Garden of Eden. I am afraid we are going to miss this place very much."

"Yes, and I have not told you the worst. Frumkin insists that he will not pay me my salary in advance. I shall have to wait a whole month for my first compensation!"

"But, Eliezer, how are we going to live? People who rent rooms are not like Frumkin. They believe in 'pay in advance'!"

Eliezer answered by holding out his right hand and displaying the gold louis left over from the trip.

"Let's go now," he said, "and see how much of a living it will buy for us."

That afternoon the two discouraged young Europeans found, finally, a future home. In return for the gold coin an old Sephardic woman rented them two rooms in an abandoned tenement. To reach the building it was necessary to cross through seven dirty courtyards ankle-deep in debris. To reach the rooms it was necessary to climb a rope ladder.

The floors were of bare stone. The walls had been plastered once but now were thick with grime. The ceilings were concave, like those of mosques. There was no furniture in the rooms, not even a chair or a bed.

The two windows looked out onto the Wailing Wall, which for centuries had provoked the lachrymose lamentations of millions of Jews. The sobs and moans seemed to come through the cracks in the walls even when the windows were closed.

Deborah left her husband for a few moments and returned smiling, in each palm a shining gold louis.

She explained that she had gone to a pawnbroker's shop and had sold a jewel which her mother had hung around her neck on a velvet ribbon as she left home.

The next morning Eliezer went to visit a man he had met in a hospital in Paris, Abraham Moses Lunz. He had left school at the age of sixteen in rebellion against an Orthodox education. For the past two years he had been completely blind and yet, although he was only four years Eliezer's senior, he was already well on the road to a career which would bring him fame in the fields of archaeology, history, geography, anthropology, literature, and sociology. He already knew Hebrew, Yiddish, German, French, English, and several other languages and was working on two or three books at the same time.

While Eliezer was gone Deborah called on a neighbor to get some advice about household problems. One of the first questions she asked was where to buy bread.

"Buy bread? Buy bread? One does not *buy* bread, child! One *bakes* bread. Surely you know that much!"

"But I do not know how to bake bread. Could you teach me?"

The old woman agreed, then quickly took back her promise.

"No! I could not help you, and no one else will help you, until you act like a Jewish woman. Good Jewish women never go around with their hair exposed, even in their own homes. Keep your head covered and I shall teach you to bake bread."

Later Eliezer explained that the Orthodox custom of not exposing the hair was based on an ancient theory that the sight of hair has an erotic effect on men and therefore no respectable woman would thus arouse the baser passions of strange men she might encounter on the streets.

At different times, in different countries, among the more or the less Orthodox, the custom had varied. Some shaved the head bare and covered it with a cloth. Others merely hid the hair. Still others, even at this time in Jerusalem, shaved the head and then wore a wig called a *sheitel,* which in turn was covered, as a sign of chastity, by a cloth.

When Eliezer returned from his visit he found his wife's luxuriant crop of reddish-blond hair covered by a scarf, and she was kneading bread.

"Do not be angry, Haveevee. I know how you hate the idea of all those people wailing outside our windows at the wall, and you will like even less some of their other customs. But if we are to win their approval of your ideas we first must win their approval of us as Jews. I must become one of them and so must you!"

Eliezer laughed.

"It is strange, but I was thinking the same thing. It came to me with undeniable potency that we must change many things about our way of life. I was afraid you might not understand, but now that you have led the way, I shall follow."

So they made several more trips to the pawnshop and sold several more articles which Deborah had cherished.

Then one morning Eliezer appeared in the streets of Jerusalem so changed that hardly anyone recognized him. He had become, overnight, an Oriental. His robe was long, olive green in color, and trimmed with the fur of a red fox. A broad girdle encircled his waist. On his head he wore a tarboosh, or red fez. He had started to let his blond beard grow. This was the Sephardic costume of the day. Eliezer preferred it to the dress of the Ashkenazic Jews, just as he preferred the Sephardic pronunciation. It was more flamboyant, less ugly, he thought.

About his beard, Deborah said, cocking her head on one side and looking at him as an artist might at a model:

"What a strange world this is! I must hide my hair and you must grow more hair! Yet as I look at you, Eliezer, I realize how handsome a beard is going to make you look. Already, with such a short growth, you begin to look more than ever like a Man of God! It sets off your eyes, which have a new fire in them these days."

But they went further than that. They kept a kosher household, using food only in the Orthodox manner. They observed *Shabbath,* the weekly holy day. Each Shabbath they went to the synagogue, Eliezer wearing the *tallith,* or prayer shawl, over his shoulders and the tefillin fastened to his arm and head.

These were great concessions for them to make, considering their own personal convictions. Deborah had been brought up by her freethinking father in an atmosphere of books. She had great spirituality, as she was to demonstrate in her life with Eliezer, but she had few conventional religious beliefs. She had studied the philosophies and religions of many lands, and her own ideas were a synthesis of all of them. She hated narrowness and bigotry.

Eliezer had been reared in an Orthodox home and had attended a rabbinical school, but Rabbi Blucker, then Deborah's father, then

Wittinsky, then Tshashnikov, then all the teachers and lecturers under whom he had studied in Paris had made him as un-Orthodox as Deborah herself.

Yet here they were, after a few weeks in Jerusalem, looking and behaving as conventional Jews had looked and behaved for hundreds of years.

It was Eliezer's habit, when he went through the streets on his way to the synagogue with the prayer shawl thrown over his shoulders as if it were a Roman toga, to greet other Jews he encountered with the salutation, "Shalom," but those whom he met looked strangely at him and seldom replied. Small children would gather in crowds and taunt him, following him down the street and shouting at him, in mimicry and not in greeting, the word "shalom."

Inside the synagogue he would follow the service carefully, but while the others prayed he would concentrate on the Hebrew words being uttered. Thus began his philological search for words in the ancient tongue which might be incorporated into a modern, speaking language.

On the first Sabbath, as the service ended, a pious-looking old Ashkenazic Jew wearing long earlocks approached Eliezer and invited him to accompany him home for the light repast which traditionally follows the Sabbath service. Eliezer accepted.

When the old man's wife left the living room to get wine and cakes, the host surreptitiously drew from his pocket a cigarette case, opened it, and indicated that Eliezer should take one. To throw him off his guard, the host took one himself.

Eliezer knew how rigid a rule it was that no one smoke on the Sabbath or on any other holy day. He realized he was being put to a test, so he bowed politely and with a smile said:

"Many thanks, but I do not smoke at all."

The old man's face lighted up as he put the cigarette case back into his pocket. He was satisfied, obviously, that this young man was one who really respected the Law.

Before long Eliezer had new difficulties with Editor Frumkin, whose Orthodox beliefs were outraged by some of the Ben Yehuda articles, yet he apparently did not want to lose the services of his inexpensive young assistant. Finally a compromise was worked out.

Eliezer would start, under Frumkin's supervision, a monthly paper of his own. It would be called *Mebasseret Zion* (The Zion News), would be a supplement to Frumkin's own paper, and Eliezer would be listed as the "responsible editor."

This was just the chance Ben Yehuda wanted. Now he would be able to argue, propagandize, exhort, and proselytize as he pleased, without having to convince anyone but his readers that his ideas were good.

He ran through the seven filthy courtyards to tell Deborah the good news.

12

Like Spinoza

AFTER TITUS LAID WASTE JERUSALEM, THE ROMANS gave him a home-coming celebration which set many new records. One of the "attractions" was that the captured Hebrew commanders were led in chains behind Titus' chariot. Later they were put to death in the Coliseum dungeons.

But some Jews survived this worst of all pogroms and before long they began to drift back to Jerusalem, determined to die in the ruins of their holy city. Jews who remained abroad believed that there were certain long-range benefits to be derived from having prayers said for them on the spot where the Temple had stood, as long as they were not there to pray on the spot themselves, so they sent financial contributions to the handful of rabbis and pious Jews in Jerusalem in return for such prayers.

After two thousand years this system still prevailed.

Down through the ages the Jewish population of Jerusalem had continued to consist principally of a few thousand men and women engaged in what one Jewish historian has called "the business of dying."

No one knew exactly how many Jews there were in Palestine when the Ben Yehudas arrived in the country. Some estimates said twenty-four thousand. Others placed the total as high as thirty thousand. Only about five hundred of them were "on the land." The majority of the rest lived in Jerusalem in varying degrees of poverty.

Most of them spent their days in study and prayer, neither toiling nor spinning. They expected money for their sustenance to come from Jews abroad. Some were sincerely interested in things of the mind and the spirit. Others were merely idle and shiftless. But all were destitute.

Money originally intended for the support of a few learned men and those engaged in religious studies gradually came to be used to support in comparative idleness a growing population of parasitical people.

When sufficient funds from abroad were not forthcoming, "collectors" were sent to Europe, often learned and generally clever men, who received one third of what they raised. Half of what was left went by custom to the rabbis, the pious scholars, and to the religious colleges; the other half (starting in about the thirteenth century) went to the poor. The distribution was made semi-annually. The entire system was called *Halukkah,* the Hebrew word for "distribution."

It was a general practice for a Jewish immigrant not to take out Turkish citizenship but to retain the passport issued to him by the country in which he had been born, in order to have the protection of that country's diplomatic representatives in Jerusalem in case of trouble, and to have certain privileges accorded to foreigners over Turkish subjects.

When the Ben Yehudas arrived in the Holy Land, the Sephardic Jews were the only ones, as a group, who were at all ambitious. Many of them actually saw nothing wrong with working for a living, even on the soil. They were also less pious, or less the victims of superstition, depending on the point of view.

But the Sephardim were greatly outnumbered by the Ashkenazim, whose leaders were vehemently opposed to agriculture, referring to the tilling of the soil as a "vulgarity."

Some of the more ambitious Ashkenazim augmented the charitable doles they received twice a year by carving small religious objects from wood and sending them to individuals abroad with a letter signed by the woman of the household, saying that she was a devout Jew, a widow with seven dying children, and please would the recipient, as a good Jew himself, remit as substantial a sum as his means permitted in return for the "object."

The Ashkenazic and Sephardic Jews had no common language, and there was little social or intellectual intercourse between them.

The Sephardim considered the Ashkenazim their inferiors, while the Ashkenazim looked on the Sephardim as lacking in piety.

But there were even divisions among the Ashkenazim, for they had banded together in this time according to the countries from which they had come. There were bitter rivalries among German Jews, Russian Jews, and Jews from France and England.

Many in these groups spoke, in addition to Yiddish, the languages of the countries of their origin, which made for further disunity.

Out in the Diaspora there were similar rivalries. Jews in various European countries had separate organizations which raised the money that was sent to Jerusalem for distribution exclusively among those who had gone to Palestine from that country.

The administrators of these funds in the Holy Land were often accused of living too well themselves on the money from abroad. The Jews of Jerusalem were, by and large, either antipathetic or openly hostile to these "foreigners." They resisted their efforts to raise the intellectual level and lower the mortality rate, accepting with grace only the alms they received.

A few years before the Ben Yehudas' arrival in Jerusalem three German Jews, visiting the country and seeing Jewish orphans growing up in the streets with no one showing any interest in them, decided to found an orphan asylum. It took them ten years to collect the necessary money, overcome violent opposition, and get the institution opened.

Stories like this depressed Eliezer. The situation obviously was much worse than he had ever dreamed it might be.

Yet knowing all these things made him admire for the rest of his life the courage of a man who paid him a formal call not many weeks after his arrival. The visitor introduced himself as Nissim Behar and said he was in charge of the educational activities of the Alliance Israélite Universelle.

He had been empowered to open a new school for boys and would Mr. Ben Yehuda accept a position on the teaching staff?

"I could do so only on one condition, which I am sure you will not accept. I must be free to teach in Hebrew."

"That is exactly why I have come to you. I wish you to teach Hebrew."

When Eliezer told Deborah about the offer and that he would receive fifty gold francs per month (about eight dollars) for teaching six hours a day, six days a week, she said shyly:

"Fate is being very kind to us, Eliezer. This has happened just at the right time, because . . ."

As she hesitated Eliezer looked into her eyes just as so many sensitive young husbands before him had looked into the eyes of their wives and learned, before any words were spoken, that the miracle of creation was occurring again.

They sat up late that night talking. Eliezer insisted that with the increased income they might now find a better place for the child to be born.

"Deborah, you are going to be the first Hebrew mother in nearly two thousand years," he said, and in his eyes there was a faraway mystical look. "Our child will be the first infant in all these centuries who will come into the world hearing nothing but the beauty of our own ancient language. You must take a solemn pledge right now, Deborah, that you will make this dream of mine come true. Never must the child hear any words but Hebrew!

"Our home must be a Hebrew sanctuary where no one speaks anything else. Whoever crosses our threshold must agree to do so with Hebrew words on his lips. Until our crusade finds popular favor, we must isolate our young one from the contamination of the languages and dialects of the Diaspora. This is even more important than all the writing and teaching I shall be doing, for by this example we may be able to inflame the Jewish world with our idea."

His speech depressed Deborah. This was what she often called his "holy stubbornness." She had been studying Hebrew diligently, but there were few people, even here in Jerusalem, with whom she could speak the language except her own husband, and he was away from home most of the time.

Still, knowing how much it meant to him, she took the oath he demanded of her.

As the Hebrew classes got under way in the Alliance school, the hostility of the Jewish population increased. Eliezer was often stoned on his way to the classroom. From all sides he heard the argument that it was sacrilege for anyone even to dream of using the holy language for everyday speech. They had gotten along all right all these centuries with their various dialects; why change now?

Often, while he tried to conduct classes, groups of teen-age boys would stand outside the windows, either looking in with profound curiosity, or reflecting their parents' hostility by catcalling and jeering.

Sometimes Eliezer would go out and try to make friends with these boys. He succeeded with one of them, Abraham Shalom Yahuda, who developed into an exceptional student. Years later he took his teacher's advice and went to Europe to continue his education, became a celebrated Orientalist and Hebrew scholar, helped with the financing of the Ben Yehuda dictionary, and in 1915 received an appointment to the chair of Semitic languages in a government university in Spain, thus becoming the first Jew since the wholesale expulsion of Jews from Spain in 1492 to receive a government appointment.

It was a long time after Eliezer began teaching in the Alliance school that he heard something which made him admire Nissim Behar even more. The Alliance Israélite in Paris had made no provision in its budget for a Hebrew teacher. Behar had "found" the necessary fifty francs per month to pay Eliezer by cutting twenty-five francs off the salary of each of two instructors in religion.

Yet one of the first articles Ben Yehuda wrote for his own monthly paper was an attack on Alliance Israélite Universelle for opposing the immigration of Russian and Rumanian Jews to Palestine. This was the organization which was paying his salary, yet that did not influence him. For the next forty years he would be rebelling, on ideological grounds, against even those to whom he had to look for financial support.

One of the first friends Eliezer made in Jerusalem was Jehiel

Michael Pines, who represented the Montefiore Memorial Foundation and was therefore the spokesman for British Jewry.

He invited the Ben Yehudas to be his guests over the holidays known as the Feast of the Tabernacles. Pines knew some Hebrew, and Eliezer impressed him so much that he agreed to a pact; at least with their intimate friends and family they would henceforth speak only Hebrew.

The Ben Yehudas were elated over this accomplishment, for they had been told that Pines was one of the most influential Jews in Palestine, but the pact was soon broken. Somehow the gossips of Jerusalem heard about it and subjected Pines to such ridicule that he reverted to the use of Yiddish except when talking to the Ben Yehudas.

It was during these same holidays that Frumkin took Eliezer to pay a call on the Chief Rabbi of Jerusalem.

Despite Eliezer's own un-Orthodox ideas, he was so impressed by the religious leader that he later wrote this glowing description of him:

"He was a beautiful oriental figure. He looked like one of our ancient ancestors, as we like to imagine that they looked. He was tall, erect, and handsome, with noble features and a long beard. He was beautifully dressed in embroidered robes with a silver necklace and a silk hat decorated with a piece of cloth embroidered in silver."

About this time the Ben Yehudas moved from the tenement near the Wailing Wall to a still modest but more comfortable dwelling close to the Mosque of Omar. There Deborah spent every minute of her spare time studying the only language which, by her husband's order, she was going to be allowed to speak to her child.

One day when Deborah and Eliezer were walking down one of Jerusalem's narrow streets, talking in Hebrew, a man stopped them. Tugging at the young journalist's sleeve, he asked in Yiddish:

"Excuse me, sir. That language you two talk. What is it?"

"Hebrew," Eliezer replied.

"Hebrew! But people don't *speak* Hebrew. It's a dead language!"

"You are wrong, my friend," Eliezer replied with fervor. "I am alive. My wife is alive. We speak Hebrew. Therefore, Hebrew is alive."

Thus in many small ways he was beginning to mix the mortar of his dream with the solid stones of reality.

Meanwhile Deborah grew happy as she felt the child she was carrying commence to stir within her. But Eliezer's condition raised doubts in her mind that there would ever be another. His schedule of teaching and writing left him little time for sleep. His face was white most of the time. He coughed incessantly. A doctor whom she had insisted he see flatly ordered him to cut out at least half of his activities.

But Eliezer was stubborn. Deborah knew it, even if the doctor did not. Eliezer argued that his own health was unimportant. He must work at top speed now, partly because the two salaries he received were essential if the "first Hebrew child" were to be brought into the world in decent style.

Also, he could now begin to see his own influence growing. The enrollment in his Hebrew classes increased week by week. Stones were still thrown at him, and the extremists swore they would never give up their fight against his "wild ideas," but he was sure he had one foot planted on the rough road he had chosen.

13

Twice Born

ONE COLD EVENING IN THE LATE WINTER, ABOUT SIX months after the Ben Yehudas had arrived in Jerusalem, Eliezer was sitting at a desk in the bare room which Deborah euphemistically called his "study," working on a new appeal to the Jews of the world. Suddenly his wife burst into the room.

"Eliezer, come quickly. There are many people outside the house. They are shouting your name and calling for you in Hebrew. But I am not sure that you should go. They may mean harm to you!"

Eliezer put down his pen and started for the door.

"If they speak in Hebrew they must be friends."

As Ben Yehuda opened the door there was a cheer from several dozen young men and women who clustered around him. They were a ragged-looking lot. All wore European clothes. Ben Yehuda was perplexed until one, acting as spokesman, began an informal speech.

"Master, we have followed you. We have come from far places to be your disciples. We have journeyed for weeks from southern Russia, Poland, Rumania, Galicia, yes, even from your native Lithuania.

"We are most of us university students. We read your appeal in the Viennese paper *Hashahar,* and it struck a spark in us. We have left everything behind to come and settle in Palestine and be the first to help in the rebirth of the Jewish state.

"So here we are, volunteers in your army. We now await your commands!"

Eliezer clutched at Deborah's arm for support. He closed his eyes for a moment and then opened them slowly to look again and be sure he was not having a hallucination. What were these words he had heard? "Master . . . volunteers . . . your army!"

Their spokesman added:

"We have just walked the forty miles from Jaffa to Jerusalem and —we are very tired. It has taken us weeks to get here. Some have been on the way for more than a month. Could we——"

It was Deborah who finally motioned them to come in.

After Ben Yehuda had regained his composure he asked them questions, and their story came tumbling out.

They were all young idealists whose decisions had been strengthened by a fresh wave of pogroms sweeping eastern and central Europe. Most of them were young, the oldest being the age of Ben Yehuda himself. Many were able to carry on a conversation in Hebrew. Those who did not know the language remained silent as a token of respect.

They had taken a name for themselves. The *Biluyim*. Eliezer asked them to repeat the word. Then, half to himself, he said:

"But that is not Hebrew, unless——"

Their leader laughed.

"It is a word we have created, just as you shall have to create a great many words to make Hebrew a living, useful language. Our full name is 'Sons of Jacob, Come, Let Us Go!' We took the first letter of each of the Hebrew words—*b, i, l, u*—and made *Bilu,* and the plural, of course, is Biluyim."

After half an hour of excited talk Ben Yehuda said to them:

"We keep an Orthodox home here, for reasons which shall be explained to you in due course. This is Passover eve, as all of you know. Tonight, according to ancient Jewish custom, our table is already laid for the feast of *Seder* and also, according to the law, we shall bid welcome to all Jews who have no place else to go."

Then Eliezer smiled.

"Of course we did not expect an army! Yet my good Deborah will find a way to provide enough food and you shall all be our guests. Meanwhile, we have another problem. A few of you can remain the night with us, but our home is not like a hotel. We live modestly and—and there is not much extra room. However, I have a few friends who will be very excited about your arrival. They will help out with the housing problem."

That night one of the most impressive Seder ceremonies that Jerusalem had known in her entire long history took place in that modest house close by the Mosque of Omar. The three girls and several dozen young men who had come from such far places took their seats at the table in the semi-reclining position required by the Seder ritual, while the young schoolteacher-editor led them in the hour-long Passover ceremony which Jews everywhere have observed for so many hundreds of years.

The completion of the service was a signal for a great babble of voices. Each of the guests was eager to tell the story of his own private exodus. Deborah said at one point that they reminded her of some geysers she had once seen which bubbled incessantly, never stopping.

Ben Yehuda listened and was troubled. One fact emerged clearly from their recitals. The older Jews of Europe were going to fight a stubborn battle to prevent their young from migrating. There was not one in the room who had not had a fight to leave. All had had reproaches heaped on their heads. All had had to exert stubborn will power to get away. Only the very strong had been able to break the bonds which tied them to the past; in many cases to the ghettos of the Diaspora. Ben Yehuda knew that they were tenacious bonds and not easily severed. All the arguments which he had heard so often had been used against these young idealists.

Even the new wave of persecutions had not opened the eyes of the older generation. Most of them were determined to die, if fate and the anti-Semites willed it, in surroundings which were familiar. They rationalized their timidity about embarking on bold adventures.

Yet this handful of pilgrims was proof that there were a few who dared. Ben Yehuda looked around at those who had succeeded in breaking away and was encouraged. They had intelligent faces, and the fire of their enthusiasm lighted their eyes.

It was a small army with which to commence a great battle, but they would make good shock troops if he himself only retained the strength to lead them. But every time he coughed, which now was frequently, he wondered how much longer he would be able to carry on.

So they talked and talked. Those who were to stay in the Ben Yehuda home, tired though they were, talked until the gray light of morning began to filter through the windows. It was Deborah who finally forced them to stop, saying:

"We shall have an army of invalids, led by a corpse, if you and my husband do not get some rest."

The next day Ben Yehuda took his followers on a tour of the Holy City. He showed the eager young people all the points of interest, starting with the Wailing Wall, an eternal witness of ancient Hebrew glory; the valley known as Gehenna, or Gehinnom, where children in the dim past were brought as sacrifices to the heathen fire-god called Moloch; the golden gate through which Jews are taught that the Messiah will pass on his triumphal arrival; the well in which the *cohen gadol*, the high priest, drowned himself after throwing the key to the Holy Temple up to heaven during one of the sieges of Jerusalem; the tomb of Absalom, King David's favorite but rebellious son; Jeremiah's cave, the Mount of Olives, and the Temple area.

But the holiday spirit of Passover Week soon ended. Now they had to face cold reality and practical problems. Few of them had any money, and, as Ben Yehuda sadly pointed out to them, idealism does not fill empty stomachs.

A meeting was therefore held, attended not only by the new arrivals but also by some of Ben Yehuda's close friends. The problem of each individual was taken up separately. Some had special talents which could immediately be put to use to enable them to earn a livelihood. For example, one of the young men, David Idelovitch, who had come from Rumania and would become an outstanding Hebrew teacher, was given employment at once in a workshop where knife blades were made. Jacob Shertok was put to work in a carpentry shop.

"I have a friend," Ben Yehuda announced, "who will give a job to one of you as a clerk in his grocery store. However, my friend is a great believer in reviving Hebrew as a spoken language and so there is one stipulation besides honesty. The clerk must agree that he will speak nothing but Hebrew to the customers. It is my friend's way of helping along my campaign."

That job was quickly accepted by one of the Hebrew-speaking youths, Judah Grazovski, who would later become famous under the name of Gur.

The big problem, just as it was to be a problem more than half a century later, was in figuring out what to do with those whose experience had been in commercial fields. They had to be considered without professions, because there was already in Jerusalem a surplus of merchants and shopkeepers. But a solution was found that day; the same one which would be arrived at several generations later. It was Ben Yehuda, then, who suggested the solution.

"Some of you must learn to be farmers, an occupation few Jews in the world have been allowed to practice of late. If we are to make the land blossom again we must return to the soil. There is a group of German agriculturists located near Jaffa who will be glad to teach some of you. The life will be hard, but it will have its satisfactions, for you will be helping to fulfill a great prophecy!"

The meeting was concluded in a spirit of celebration. All of them gathered in a circle and sang the only Hebrew secular song then in existence, so far as any of them knew, the Hebrew poet Gordon's translation of one of Heine's poems set to music by Schubert.

The second wave of mass immigration or *aliyah* (the Hebrew word for "ascent") arrived several months later. But this one was different. Instead of penniless students, these were entire families; husbands, wives, and children of all ages. None was rich, but many came with substantial savings. Some of the men had owned their own businesses in various Russian cities.

They landed at Jaffa and decided to remain there until they could purchase land on which they could learn to become farmers. It was Jaffa which almost defeated them.

They rented quarters in primitive oriental homes (there were few homes of any other kind those days in Jaffa) and tried to adapt themselves to a standard of living difficult for any European to endure.

As Eliezer and Deborah well knew from just one day in the sea-port city, Jaffa was enough to discourage the hardiest soul. Even though some Arabs may have had immaculate homes, they were little interested in the cleanliness of their exterior surroundings. Accordingly the streets of Jaffa were always deep in filth. There were no sewers. The streets were unpaved. Rain water and slops stood stagnant in the thoroughfares, with the heat of the sun making the stench almost unbearable. Flies and mosquitoes thrived in this situation; there were clouds of them everywhere. Stray cats and dogs poked their noses into the refuse which littered the city. Malaria, typhus, and typhoid were as common as the common cold. The mortality rate was so high that only the rabbit-like breeding of the Arabs kept the population from being wiped out. Predatory trachoma caused crossed eyes and blindness. There were few inhabitants at any given time not suffering from mild or serious skin diseases, all of them infectious.

This was the city in which the second wave of immigrants temporarily settled. There were no schools for the children. There was neither rest nor peace for the women.

Each day the men went off on expeditions into the countryside to look for land for the settlement they wished to establish. They would come home each night and report that as yet they had had no success in their search, but when their wives started pleading, they would paint rosy pictures of the paradise they were someday going to create somewhere out there on the brown desert sands. The women grew tired of the promise, but most of them tried to bear their difficulties with courage and patience.

So they stayed, most of them, and some of the children died of disease, and some of the women went almost insane.

Ben Yehuda heard about the group and sent words of encouragement. These people, also, were recruits in his army. His great regret was that he was powerless to help them.

About this time, in the attic of a house on the outskirts of Jerusalem, Eliezer presided over a meeting of a small group of the intellectuals of Jerusalem. The purpose was to discuss ways and means of reviving Hebrew.

That night those present organized themselves into what they called "The Army of the Defenders of the Language" and signed a pact which read:

"The members residing in the Land of Israel will speak to each other in Hebrew, in society, in meeting places, and in the streets and market places, and shall not be ashamed. They will make it a point to teach their sons and daughters and the rest of their household this language.

"The members will watch in the streets and the market places over the Hebrew speech, and when they hear adults speaking Russian, French, Yiddish, English, Spanish, Arabic, or any other language, they will not spare a remark even to the eldest amongst them, saying:

" 'Aren't you ashamed of yourselves!' "

It was almost a lifetime later, however, before it did finally become "shameful" to speak a foreign language in a public place in Israel. That this finally did happen was due principally to the efforts of the group of young intellectuals who met that night in that attic on the edge of Jerusalem in secret conclave.

Soon after that meeting Eliezer had a more personal problem to deal with.

Deborah's time was approaching. He knew she was lonely; that she both needed and wanted her mother. That being impossible, Eliezer tried to be husband and mother too.

One request Deborah made which Eliezer was not able to satisfy was for a spring bed on which her baby might be born. She complained that the rope bed, which was all they had been able to afford, was impossibly uncomfortable. Eliezer tried to borrow a better bed or to get one on credit. Both attempts were unsuccessful.

Then early one morning in the month of *Ab,* in the year 1882, it happened. The child was a boy.

True to her promise, the first word the mother spoke to her infant after it had been placed in her arms was a Hebrew word:

"*Yaldi* [My child]!"

Thus Deborah Yonas Ben Yehuda, daughter of a distiller in

Glubokiah, became, as her husband always expressed it, "the first Hebrew mother in nearly two thousand years"; the first woman in so long a time to address her child in the biblical language.

But the agreement which Deborah had made with her husband raised immediate complications which had not occurred to them in advance.

At the bedside when the child was born was Mrs. Pines, wife of the leader of the British Jewish colony, who would have remained constantly at the young mother's side except that she did not speak Hebrew, and while she and the baby were in the same room Eliezer insisted that she not utter a word. There were many things a bedside companion, such as Mrs. Pines was trying to be, needed to ask and to say at such a time which were difficult to express in sign language.

The situation was saved, however, when the wife of Rabbi Hayim Hirschenson appeared. She did speak Hebrew and so took immediate charge. For weeks after the birth she neglected her own family to run the Ben Yehuda ménage.

The young mother had three other intimate friends: Hannah, a tea vendor; Sheynah Malkah, a strange little woman who spent her entire time looking for some way to accomplish her day's *mitzvah,* or good deed, and a Sephardic Jewess named Simha, a childless widow.

All three came on the run to offer their congratulations, but Ben Yehuda stood at the door and before he would allow any of them to enter put them through a questionnaire about their linguistic abilities.

It turned out that Sheynah Malkah spoke only Yiddish. Ben Yehuda admitted her with the positive understanding that while in the birth chamber she was not to utter a sound.

The other two women contended that they knew "a little" Hebrew. The husband passed them.

When Simha, the childless widow, learned that the baby was a boy she literally went into a dance of joy by the side of Deborah's bed, for Sephardic Jews, along with most oriental peoples, have little respect for female infants.

When her dance was concluded she took the baby from his mother's arms, put him into the bosom of her loose-fitting oriental gown, and finally pulled him out through one of the wide sleeves. As she performed this odd ritual, to the delight of all present except the father and mother, she shouted in Hebrew:

"Now I am not childless anymore! Now I have a son!"

Her actions were based on an old Spanish-Jewish belief that if a childless woman performs this rite with a newborn baby she is automatically childless no longer but shares in the maternity of the actual mother.

The disappearance-into-the-bosom-discovery-in-the-sleeve performance so intrigued the tea vendor, Hannah, that she insisted on doing it also. At the conclusion of her manipulations she kissed the child and affectionately whispered the word "Yaldi," adding in Hebrew, "And now it is partly my child too!"

By frantic signs Sheynah Malkah indicated that she also wanted to share in the maternity. Deborah nodded but put a finger to her lips as a warning that the woman must not give in to a temptation to try to talk to the child, even though by her inability to say the magic words she might be cheated out of synthetic motherhood.

Always after that day Sheynah Malkah was known in the Ben Yehuda household as the "dumb godmother."

Before many hours had passed word spread through Jerusalem that the strange young schoolteacher-editor and his wife had had a baby and that the father had imposed some sort of weird language prohibition. As a result, people came from all parts of the city to verify the report themselves.

One of Ben Yehuda's acquaintances remarked to him:

"If the child is to know nothing but Hebrew, it is to be hoped that he will not grow up speaking stupid things!"

Others made comments which were neither so subtle nor so restrained.

There was excitement all day long in the small house near the Mosque of Omar. By custom Ben Yehuda provided wine for his guests, which had something to do with how loudly they sang and how long they stayed. Oriental Jewish musicians sat on the floor playing primitive guitars and tambourines.

There was excitement enough without the additional news which a messenger brought late in the afternoon. It was a telegram for Ben Yehuda from Jaffa.

His friends who had come in the second small wave of immigration wished him to be one of the first to know that they finally had found a piece of land. It was located one and a half hours by horseback ride to the south of Jaffa.

They already had tents pitched and had moved their families and possessions out of the filth of Jaffa.

This would be the first real agricultural settlement of the New Israel! True, there was the colony of Petach Tikvah (Gate of Hope) which had been founded in 1878 and would someday be known as "the mother of all Jewish colonies," but it was made up of Jewish businessmen from Jerusalem and others who were not *halutzim,* the term used for pioneers who came from far places expressly to settle on the land. There was also Mikveh Israel, which had been founded by the doctor Eliezer had consulted in Paris, but that, also, was not a really pioneering place.

The telegram said they were planning a formal opening and dedication. If Ben Yehuda left Jerusalem at sundown he could get there in time. He *must* come, because (as the telegram expressed it) this was his "baby," his first-born agricultural child. They were his followers and they intended to help him, not only with resettlement of the land, but also with his Hebrew campaign. This would be a Hebrew, not a Yiddish colony. They had suffered greatly in Jaffa. This was the hour of their redemption. Ben Yehuda must come and help them celebrate.

The young father's head was in a whirl. The father of two newborn children the same day! As he pushed his way into his own home he found a violent argument under way. They were discussing the name of his son.

He and Deborah had decided long before this day that if the child were a boy he would be called Ittamar. It was a good Hebrew word meaning "island of palms." They liked its sound.

But the friends and neighbors who had gathered were not in agreement. Ittamar? Unthinkable! Did not Ben Yehuda know the old rule, the old custom? The first-born, if a boy, must always be called Ben Zion, Son of Zion.

Eliezer listened for a few moments to the loud voices and then decided to turn the conversation by reading the telegram. But there was one sentence in the message which caused trouble for Eliezer and Deborah. It said the name of the new colony, chosen by the settlers, was Rishon Le Zion, "First in Zion."

That revived the controversy about a name for the infant which now lay sleeping in its mother's arms.

"Surely," said one of the guests, "you can see now that your son cannot possibly be called by that other name. The colony is to be known as Rishon Le Zion, and your child must naturally be, also, the Son of Zion. If you wish to win favor among our people in Jerusalem, Ben Yehuda, you will not defy custom at a time like this!"

Ben Yehuda's strong feeling of independence was in conflict with his desire to win followers. It might seem to others a petty matter. Yet to him it was a major issue.

The decision was finally made by the young woman lying on the bed, who so passionately hated conflict and yet was to witness and take part in so much conflict before her death.

With a smile that was tinged with both sadness and understanding she took Eliezer's hand and affectionately said:

"Haveevee, I think it is wise that our child be known as Ben Zion Ben Yehuda. I also think it will be well for you to take the evening carriage to Jaffa, to be present at the birth of your other child."

Then she closed her eyes and went to sleep.

14

One Tree

BEN YEHUDA AND SEVERAL MEN WHO ACCOMPANIED him from Jerusalem were met at Jaffa by some of the settlers. Together they covered the last fifteen miles, riding on the backs of horses and small donkeys.

The terrain over which they traveled was nothing to excite a farmer of any nationality. The ground undulated and was bare. The only vegetation was cactus and desert shrubs. It was cause for comment if anyone saw a tree.

Several times they passed Arab villages which did little to relieve the drabness of the landscape.

Suddenly one of the guides reined in his horse, pointed excitedly toward the horizon, and exclaimed:

"Behold! There is our settlement! This is our land, from here on! Welcome to Rishon Le Zion!"

As they approached they saw a line of small tents such as those in which Bedouin tribesmen live. There was nothing else to break the dreary monotony of brown sand except a single tree on a small hill.

Ben Yehuda was hot and tired. It had been a difficult journey for a man in his physical condition. Besides, he had had no sleep last night in the carriage from Jerusalem and little the night before because of the birth of his son. As soon as they had tethered their animals he asked if someone could get him a glass of water.

This request brought a response first of embarrassment and then of laughter.

"You forget, sir, that you are in Rishon Le Zion and not back in Jerusalem! We have only just pitched our tents. We have not yet had time to dig for water. But we can offer you wine. It is better that we have wine, for you must drink a toast with us to our success!"

From one of the tents someone produced a flagon and glasses. During the simple dedication ceremony many toasts were drunk; to Ben Yehuda, to the New Israel, to Rishon Le Zion and its founders, and to the other twin, Ben Zion Ben Yehuda.

Ben Yehuda was perplexed that the only immigrants he saw were men. But it developed that he had misunderstood the telegram. The women and children were still in Jaffa and would remain there until several cisterns had been dug, until the men had gathered a mountain of dead cactus branches for firewood, and until they had built ovens of stone and tin for communal baking.

As proof to Ben Yehuda that they meant to keep the promise they had made to him, practically all the conversation that day was carried on in Hebrew, except when someone stumbled for a word which did not exist in the ancient language and had to use its Yiddish or Russian equivalent.

Each time they raised their glasses they used the Hebrew expression *"Lehayim!"* meaning "Here's to life!" the traditional Hebrew toast.

Just before the men from Jerusalem left on their long homeward journey Ben Yehuda said:

"Your names will all be written in history; in the new history of an old people.

I know you will have your heartaches and your troubles. Weak men among you will wish to give up. Even the strong will get discouraged. It is not an easy fight any of us is facing. We have many enemies, but nature is not among them. Always remember that nature is not to be defeated or conquered. She is only to be understood and tamed and put to use. This sandy soil, if you treat it in a right manner, will blossom for you as it once did for our ancestors.

"And the hills of Judea before long will be echoing with the deep, rich sounds of the Hebrew tongue again.

"And the hills of Judea will begin to welcome back more and more returning sons.

"And someday there will be peace throughout the Promised Land and a good life for all of our people who hunger and thirst for shalom.

"And so I leave you with my blessing and great good wishes.

"To the first settlers, to the people of Rishon Le Zion, lehayim!"

One day Eliezer Ben Yehuda presented himself at the Russian consulate in Jerusalem and announced to the doorman that he wished to see one of the officials on an important matter.

The doorman ushered him into an office at the end of a long corridor. Behind a large desk sat a man with a finely chiseled face and with a beard much bushier and more handsome than the one his visitor wore.

"And what may I do for you, sir?" he inquired pleasantly in well-polished, precise Russian.

"I have come to renounce my Russian citizenship and turn in a passport for which I no longer have any use," Eliezer announced in a determined tone as he placed the passport bearing the Czar's coat of arms on the desk.

"This is a rather unusual procedure, Mr.—Mr.——"

"The name is Ben Yehuda. Eliezer Ben Yehuda."

"You say your name is Ben Yehuda? That is not the name in this passport. This belongs to a Mr. Elyanof." The official looked up suspiciously at his visitor. "This is all rather mysterious."

"Not at all," Eliezer replied. "Elyanof was my name before I left Russia. I have changed it now. That is one reason I wish to get rid of this passport. When I get one here it will be in the name Ben Yehuda."

The official looked startled. Then Eliezer continued:

"From now on I shall consider myself a citizen of the Land of Israel."

"Palestine, you mean."

"I said the Land of Israel."

"I think you speak of a country which does not exist. You will have difficulty getting a passport issued by a state called Israel!"

"That is beside the point. I no longer consider myself a Russian subject and am announcing it to you officially at this time."

At that point Eliezer turned on his heel and started from the room, but before he reached the door the man behind the desk stopped him, saying:

"You might be interested to know that we have been holding a letter here for you."

As he spoke the official walked forward with a long white envelope in his outstretched hand.

Eliezer took it, glanced at the address, and then handed it back.

"This letter is addressed to Eliezer Elyanof. As that is no longer my name, I could not possibly accept a letter that does not belong to me."

A smile spread across the official's face.

"I assume, then, that you wish me to have the letter returned to the expediter, who, in case you did not notice, is a man named Leib Perlman, who lives in the country of the Czar at a place called Luzhky. Do you know who this Leib Perlman is?"

"I think he is my youngest brother."

The official took no trouble to hide his astonishment.

"You think? What do you mean, you think? Is your family so large that you do not even know the names of all your brothers?"

"Yes, my family is very large," Eliezer said gravely. "My family is now the whole of the people of Israel, and all of its sons are my brothers."

"That is a very fine speech, Mr. Elyanof—pardon—Mr. Ben Yehuda. But if it does not annoy you, may I ask if by any chance you know my sister? I had a sister once who lived many years ago in this same village from which you apparently came."

Eliezer unbent a little and replied:

"I lived there only as a boy. I am afraid I would not know your sister."

"That is too bad, because you are the first one I have ever met who came from Luzhky. I have often wondered about my sister;

whether she is still alive; whether she has ever married. She had a lovely name. They called her Feygaleh."

In the split second it took the official to say the name, eight years suddenly dropped away for Eliezer. His mind now was back in Luzhky the last time he had seen his mother, when he was on his way to high school in Dünaburg.

Eliezer held onto the desk for support. "Feygaleh is my mother. She had a brother. I even remember his name. It was Leib Beer. She often told us about him. When he was only seven he was kidnaped by the Cossacks and taken away for the army. She never heard from him again. Would that—— What is your name, sir?"

Without replying the older man suddenly threw his arms around his slim young visitor and embraced him as a father might a son he had not seen in years. There were tears in his eyes when he finally backed away and looked Eliezer over from head to foot.

"So! So you are my nephew then. You are dear Feygaleh's boy and I am your uncle. How strange a world in which we live! And to think that we meet in this far-off place, Jerusalem!"

For the next quarter hour they sat on opposite sides of a table while the uncle gave the nephew a brief résumé of his life. It was true that at the age of seven, as Feygaleh had told her children and anyone else who would listen, he had been kidnaped. His captors took him to Siberia and when he was old enough to carry a rifle put him in the Czar's army. His teachers converted him to Christianity, and he took the name of Davidson, having forgotten what his own family name was, but remembering that his father's first name had been David.

Before the session was over the uncle picked up the envelope again. With a smile he slit it and pulled out a sheet of paper and a smaller envelope.

The sheet of paper was addressed to Eliezer. It had been dictated by his mother, who still did not know how to read or write, to her youngest son, Leib. In it, besides several personal messages to Eliezer, she said:

"I am enclosing an envelope addressed to Leib Beer. You may remember, Eliezer, that I often spoke about him. He was my favorite brother who was kidnaped by the Cossacks when he was only seven.

But just recently I have been talking with a woman who passed through Luzhky, and she said she had reason to believe that your uncle is still alive and is employed by the Russian consulate in Jerusalem, where you now are. Would you try to find him and give him the enclosed letter?"

15

Miracle of the Rain

ELIEZER AND EDITOR FRUMKIN FINALLY CAME TO the point of dissociation. It had been inevitable to Deborah from the start. The younger man was far too radical for the older. On Eliezer's side, he desperately wanted independence. His dream was to edit a sizable daily paper of his own, "as attractive in appearance as *Le Figaro,* the Paris daily."

He took his first step in this direction by resigning as the "responsible editor" of the monthly supplement. His next problem was to get a license from the Turkish government to start a paper of his own. But he found that it took knowing the right people in government circles, knowing which ones to bribe, and then much waiting. Ben Yehuda was not a patient waiter.

A solution was suggested by Rabbi Hayim Hirschenson, whose daughter a generation later would become well known as the wife of Dr. David de Sola Pool, Chief Rabbi of the Spanish and Portuguese congregation of America. Rabbi Hirschenson possessed such a license as Eliezer needed. It permitted the bearer to put out a weekly paper called *Hatzebi* (The Deer). If Eliezer wished, the rabbi would be glad to rent him the permit.

That night Eliezer discussed it excitedly with Deborah.

"Just think, my dear, in a few weeks I may be a free and independent editor, able to express what I please, how I please, and when I please!"

"But, Haveevee, how do you feel about the name, the *Deer?* It seems rather an odd name for a paper of *yours!*"

"In a way it is a ridiculous name, except that in the Book of Daniel there is a reference to *Eretz Hatzebi,* which has been translated figuratively to mean 'Israel, Glorious Land.' But *Hatzebi* does not explain in any way what the paper will stand for. There is nothing about a deer which is even symbolic of what my paper will be!"

"That is not quite correct, Haveevee. A deer *is* beautiful and your paper will be beautiful, I know. Remember what you have always said about wanting a paper that looks like *Le Figaro?*"

"Well, we might as well get reconciled to it, because the *Deer* it is going to be. Anyway, I now have a more pressing problem. I need money, desperately this time."

"I wish, Haveevee, I could find something else to take to the pawnbroker, but I do not have a single piece of jewelry left, and most of the clothes I brought with me have found their way to the same place. Do you have any ideas where——"

"Yes, I am going to talk tomorrow to Hayim Calmi, the French teacher at the Alliance school."

The next day Mr. Calmi seemed as startled as if someone had asked him for a million sovereigns when Eliezer said quietly to him:

"I am trying to start a newspaper, Calmi, and I need one gold piece to finance it. Could you possibly loan me a single gold piece for a short time?"

"Start a newspaper on such a sum as that? Are you mad, man? You know a great deal, I am sure, from bitter experience, about making money stretch a long way. Anyone who teaches school for a living knows that. But how can you start a newspaper with such small capital?"

Ben Yehuda did not convince Calmi that day that it could be done, but he got the gold coin, half a napoleon, worth in American money about $2.50.

He also got this parting word from the teacher:

"There is, as you may know, an old Jewish superstition which says that if you dress a child in borrowed clothes when it is very young, the child will thus be protected from the evil eye. And so, good luck to your third child, the *Deer!*"

Rabbi Hirschenson came to the rescue a second time by introducing Eliezer to the owner of a small print shop located in the cellar of his home in the old quarter of the city.

There were no typesetting machines in Jerusalem at that time; it was necessary to add one letter of type to the next, painfully, slowly, by hand. The printers were not Hebrew scholars. They made so many mistakes that finally Eliezer, in addition to writing all the articles, actually set them into type himself. It was a tedious job for one so inexperienced. The cellar was lit by a single kerosene lamp. The young editor's eyes burned with the strain on them. Because of his ambition to make the *Deer* attractive to look at, as much like *Le Figaro* as possible, Eliezer also arranged the type in the steel forms; "made up the paper," as the printers put it. In addition he helped with the proofreading, anxious that there should be no errors. Meanwhile he tried to teach the printers a few essentials of Hebrew so that eventually he would not have to do so much of the work himself.

The *Deer* was to be dated Friday, in order that the readers would be able to enjoy it over the Saturday holiday. There was only one mail a day out of Jerusalem. It left early in the morning. If the papers missed that mail they would lie over in the post office until after the week end.

The first issue, just a few hundred copies, finished rolling off the press at midnight Thursday. As soon as the ink had sufficiently dried Eliezer took the bundle under his arm and ran the mile and a half from the shop through the dark streets to his home, lighting his way with a lantern containing a candle. There Deborah was waiting for him.

"How does it look, Haveevee? I can hardly wait to see!"

"You *must* wait, my dear. We shall look at it later. First help me quickly to fold them, get them ready for the mail, put on the stamps. We do not have a minute to lose if we are going to catch the morning post."

So all night long they folded, wrote addresses, and licked stamps. When they came to the last operation Eliezer announced:

"Because you are the careful member of the family, my dear, starting tonight you are responsible for this part of the work. It is most important because I am told that under Turkish law there is a fine of half a Turkish pound for each piece of mail which is posted without a stamp. And you know what a fine like that would do to us!"

The first issue of the *Deer* came out on the fifth day of the month of *Heshvan* in 1884. It consisted of a single piece of paper folded to make four pages, five by nine inches, smaller than the ordinary business letterhead. Although the editors of *Le Figaro,* had they seen it, might not have noticed much resemblance to their own paper, when Eliezer came home from the post office and sank exhausted on a couch, Deborah said:

"You have a right to be very proud, Haveevee. I have been reading every word of it several times. Just wait until the letters start pouring in!"

Eliezer's answer was to cough deeply several times and rub his hands over his burning eyes.

The reaction of the Jews of Palestine to this first real European-type Hebrew newspaper was at least not apathetic. Everyone admitted there was a great deal of news packed into its four pages. But they objected to the way this Ben Yehuda wrote. Instead of the pompous style of the scholars, who often copied whole sentences out of the Talmud, this man wrote simply, in conversational style. Many complained that he did not write "the language of the angels and the prophets."

They were also violently antagonized by what he said. Who was this young upstart who defied all conventions? He was worse than a *goy* (a non-Jew), for he had been brought up in the faith and should know better. What did he mean by arguing for the use of Hebrew? Hebrew was to pray in. God would be greatly displeased by this heretic who claimed that his own son, although almost two years old, had yet to hear a single word of any other language.

But at least the *Deer* was talked about, and as a result before long it had three hundred paid-up subscribers, which meant that each Thursday night as Eliezer trudged through the dark streets his load was heavier than the Thursday before. Sometimes the wind almost blew him off his feet. Sometimes the rain soaked him to the skin and almost ruined the bundle he carried so affectionately close to him, as if it were Ben Zion, his own child. Sometimes his cough would be so bad that he would have to set down his small lantern while he went through one of his "spells." Several times he fell flat on the unpaved street because he had failed to step over a hole.

Deborah called this weekly trip "Haveevee's Night Watch." She tried to persuade him to "put his paper to bed" a few hours earlier so there would not be such a mad Thursday-night rush. He refused because, he said, he must get into the paper news that happened right up to the last minute. Deborah knew him better than to argue. This, she told herself, was his Via Dolorosa along which he felt he had to go in order to achieve his goal. So she tried to help him with love, with patience, with understanding.

Before long Eliezer's friends had nicknamed him the "Deer," and Deborah became known as the "Deer's Wife."

One week, annoyed with the compulsory use of this meaningless word, Eliezer put the paper out under the name *Haor* (The Light). But the next day the Turkish government ordered him to revert at once to the name which he and Rabbi Hirschenson had been licensed to use.

In these days there often was not enough money in the Ben Yehuda purse to buy flour for bread. Any money which came in went first to pay the expenses of the paper. Sometimes there was not even enough money to purchase the newsprint for the next edition. At such times Eliezer would borrow the small sum needed from a stationery dealer with whom he had become friendly, a pious character and a lover of the Hebrew language who looked on the young man with the short beard almost as if he were a living prophet. Often Eliezer would say to Deborah:

"We have enough now to buy food *or* pay back my friend. I think we had better let the food wait. I must not allow anything to happen to my friend's faith in me!"

No one, not even Eliezer, was aware in these days of what Deborah was going through. First she had a child to take care of and always had to be on her guard lest a "foreign" word be spoken in the infant's presence. On this point Eliezer was now more fanatical than he had been at the time the child was born. Then there was the problem of running the household with so little money that Deborah sometimes wondered herself how she did it.

Yet not a day went by but that Eliezer had at least one glass of milk and one slice of meat for his evening meal. Deborah would put the food before him and start to walk away. Eliezer would then quickly say:

"But, my child, I do not like to eat alone. You know that!"

And then Deborah would reply:

"You should know by now, Eliezer, that I have a baby to care for and I cannot wait until you get home for *my* food. You sometimes come home, Haveevee, so late!"

Then Eliezer would apologize and go back to the book or paper he had started to read.

Deborah never told him the truth. She never told him that she ate alone so he would not see that all she ever had for *her* evening meal was a slice of bread and radishes.

Such sacrifices did not bother the young wife. This was the sort of life she had always expected to have with Eliezer. What did bother her was her inability to make Eliezer take some regard for his own health.

Before long the schoolteacher-editor was being called by some by a new name, *Ha-Apikoros,* a word derived from the Greek for "the heretic."

The *Deer* had begun to print criticism of the institutions in Jerusalem supported by funds raised abroad. One article said it was ridiculous for all this money to be used to house Jewish students in ramshackle buildings in Jerusalem. Why was not the money used to buy land on which the students could live and work while they did their studying? In this way they could help bring Israel back to fruitfulness, and when they died they would leave something constructively accomplished behind them.

This radical suggestion horrified even those who agreed. It horrified them because of their fear that Jews abroad would be offended and would stop sending charitable contributions to Palestine.

But the *Deer* grew in size and in strength as the months went by. It grew to six and then to eight pages. It brought its readers news of the outside world, news of inventions and discoveries, news of general interest. It brought light into places of darkness, and sunshine into the lives of some who up to now had been almost afraid of sunshine.

Slowly Ben Yehuda introduced new Hebrew words to his readers which were needed if one were to use Hebrew for other than religious purposes.

Eliezer Ben Yehuda might have been called a fanatic, and indeed he was by many. During this period he worked as if the entire future of the Jews of the world rested on his own weak shoulders. He was being constantly warned by Deborah, by his doctor, and by friends that he would soon burn himself out if he did not slow down. They gave him all the arguments of caution which wives, doctors, and friends have given men with a touch of fanaticism down through history: he must husband his strength; he must realize that if he worked himself into an early grave his whole campaign would collapse and his small accomplishments would quickly be wiped out by his enemies.

But Deborah, the doctor, and the friends quickly learned that such advice was wasted on a man like Ben Yehuda. If such men were able to slow down, the advice would never be needed.

Over and over again Eliezer would press his right hand to his tired forehead and say to Deborah:

"The day, my dear, is so short, the work to be done so great."

He taught school seven hours a day. He wrote and edited all the articles for his paper, set them in type, proofread them, carried the papers home, folded and addressed them, then delivered them to the post office.

Because there was a great need for textbooks in Hebrew, he worked with teachers and instructors, helping them to compose such textbooks in their individual fields.

Then he got the idea that if there could be plays in Hebrew which children could perform it would help popularize the language, so he enlisted the help of Hayim Calmi in writing such plays. He began working himself on a play with David Yellin, a young instructor whose grandfather had settled in Palestine and whose father had been active in the development of the country. Yellin had been brought back to Palestine from London by Nissim Behar and had married the daughter of Jehiel Michael Pines. He and his father so antagonized the reactionaries of the day that both, about this time, were excommunicated, but Yellin went on to found an association of Hebrew teachers, translated many books, including the *Arabian Nights,* into Hebrew, and was one of Ben Yehuda's most ardent Hebrew-revival colleagues.

Eliezer never stopped his intellectual labors before midnight, and every morning he was up in time to greet the dawn. When Deborah would argue that he should have more sleep, he would reply:

"I get the strength I need to carry me through the day by watching the miracle of the sunrise each morning. Please do not deny me that! Next to your help and advice, Deborah, it is the greatest inspiration I have!"

There were thus nineteen hours in each of Eliezer's days, and he had undertaken already enough work to fill every one of those hours. But now he had a new idea.

"Our crying need is for an up-to-date dictionary. Just think! Here we are trying to teach people to speak a language and there is no dictionary of that language. There is not even a Hebrew word that signifies 'dictionary.' We must invent a word for dictionary and then we must make the dictionary itself."

"But, Haveevee, that is not a task for a single man, is it? Surely it would take a great many scholars a whole lifetime to make a dictionary, would it not?"

"I shall not deny, Deborah, that it would be a colossal job, but there is no group of scholars likely to undertake it. I must do it myself. Somehow, I must find the time!"

So Eliezer Ben Yehuda added the creation of a dictionary to his list of activities, not realizing that he had set for himself a half-century task which would become his great lifework and would someday completely consume him, as the candle destroys the moth.

As the size of Ben Yehuda's newspaper grew, so also did the size of his family. A second son was born. This time Eliezer chose the name he wished for the child and made it clear that there would be no changing it. The boy was to be known as Avi Hayil (Leader of the Army). It was an odd name for a scholar to pick for a son, but even in those days Eliezer Ben Yehuda was dreaming of the time when Israel might become a nation and, like other nations, have an army of its own. He had the wild hope that this second son might become the founder of such an army, or at least its commander.

The birth of Avi Hayil was not the great event that the birth of the first child had been. There was no ceremony or celebration, principally because the Ben Yehuda family was now in the very nadir of its poverty. There was not money enough to buy a single bottle of wine with which to toast the arrival of the child. There was not even money to buy bread.

Deborah had worried during her pregnancy about the economics of the situation, but Eliezer's mind had been too occupied with intellectual matters even to think of such considerations. It was only when Deborah took to her bed that Eliezer was forced to give some concern to what practical men would call "practical problems."

The Leader of the Army had been born, but there was no bread, so Eliezer, knowing of no other way to raise money, took his own gold watch, which had been Deborah's wedding gift to him and which he had faithfully promised he would never sell, and offered it to Dr. Wilhelm Herzberg, who had been sent to Jerusalem by the Jews of Germany to administer the funds raised by them for Palestinian charities. He asked for a loan of half a napoleon, with the watch as security.

It was an embarrassing step for Eliezer to take, because these leaders of nationality groups had been and still were violent in their opposition to him. Each group wished to preserve its own language and resented Eliezer's attempt to get Jews from Germany, Poland, Great Britain, Russia, and the Spanish-speaking countries to come together on a common linguistic basis.

Dr. Herzberg smiled and said:

"If you are in financial trouble you must have the money. Pay me back whenever you can, but please do not insult me by offering me security."

The half a napoleon bought bread, but it was not enough to pay the back rent which Eliezer owed. At this time the Ben Yehudas were living in very modest quarters in an Ashkenazic section outside the Old City. The landlord was a Jew named Shalom Blesher. He had been very tolerant about the rent bill until one day when there appeared in the *Deer* an article entitled "The Cruel Landlords." It was typical of the sort of editorials Eliezer was writing these days. It had nothing to do with the Hebrew language or the establishment of a Jewish state.

The editorial pointed out that a number of Jerusalem landlords who owned large cisterns were profiteering in water and were hoping that the drought would continue so they could keep raising the price they charged for each bucketful of the precious liquid. It so happened—and Eliezer must have known it—that Shalom Blesher owned one of the largest cisterns in Jerusalem and was making a neat profit on water. What the young editor did was therefore little different from a modern newspaper exposing one of its advertisers for fraud.

Shalom Blesher was indignant.

"He can't pay his bills and he prays for rain and preaches morals to us!"

So one arid day Eliezer, Deborah, and their two children, the youngest a baby in arms, were dispossessed. Their meager belongings were literally put into the street.

Shalom Blesher personally engineered the eviction.

"You want rain, do you? Well, you troublemaker, now you can stand in the street and pray for rain!"

A crowd gathered. Even those who had been critical of the Heretic were moved to sympathy. Deborah sat on a suitcase with Avi Hayil in her arms, trying to hold back the tears. Eliezer, who was incapable of any violent emotions, stood beside her, trying to comfort her.

Suddenly the sky grew dark. The crowd scattered. Shalom Blesher also disappeared, frightened by what he apparently decided was an omen from heaven.

Within a few minutes the rains came. For a full hour the deluge continued. This was the rain which the *Deer* had said would put an end to the profiteering of the "cruel landlords." All Jerusalem welcomed it, even the young man and woman who sat on their baggage trying to shield their two offspring from the downpour.

As soon as the storm had passed, men, women, and children poured out of their homes and gathered around the Ben Yehudas. Some even got down on their knees in the mud to offer the young man with the beard their thanks and congratulations. They gave him and God full credit for what had happened.

For a brief moment Eliezer Ben Yehuda was a local hero.

To the crowd the villain in the piece was, of course, Shalom Blesher, so they flocked to his house and shouted his name, threatening him with all manner of punishment unless he allowed the Ben Yehudas to return to their quarters. Blesher did not dare appear, but he sent out word that the evicted tenants could have back their rooms.

There are two old sayings which Eliezer thought of several weeks later:

"Glory dies quickly; misery has a long life."

"Poverty always follows the poor."

When news of the Ben Yehudas' difficulties with the landlord spread through the quarter, shopkeepers to whom Eliezer also owed money decided to close in on him. Almost every day there was a parade of creditors banging at the door with bills in their hands.

To make matters worse, about this time Eliezer had to give up his schoolteaching. His cough had grown so much worse that the Alliance directors decided it would be better for all concerned if he had a vacation—without pay.

It was Deborah who suggested, as a solution, that he take a trip to Moscow, where her own family, the Yonases, now lived.

"If you can borrow money for the trip, Haveevee, it will be a good investment. I know that my family will help if you just explain the situation to them. Besides, you yourself have said that you have worked up a good following among the Jews of Russia. Surely, in this emergency, they will come forward with some financial support for both the paper and the dictionary you wish to write, if you can only meet them and explain everything."

"But it will take weeks to make such a trip," Eliezer pointed out. "How can I leave you with two small children for such a time?"

Deborah forced him to forget this consideration. Then Eliezer brought up another problem.

"I know you think I go too far in not wanting our children even to hear any other language except Hebrew. But I wonder if you, by yourself, are strong enough to prevent it?"

Suddenly Deborah burst into tears.

"I have had much trouble already which I have kept from you. Your friend, Mr. Pines, the last time I saw him, tried to fill my mind with many doubts. He begged me to have pity on our children before it is too late. He said I owe it to them not to try to teach them Hebrew, in order to prevent them from becoming idiots!"

Eliezer waved his hand to stop her. Then in his calm, soft voice he said:

"Deborah, my child, do you remember when Ben Zion was two years old? On his second birthday he had still not said a word. Do you remember how Pines and all the others told us that this was proof it could not be done? They tried to tell us that Ben Zion was going to grow up to be an idiot. They try to frighten us with this word.

"But you also remember that it was only a short time later that the boy began to talk. And now! Now he is five and speaks beautiful Hebrew! And nothing except Hebrew! Not a word of any other language has ever passed his lips.

"Deborah, this is our great experiment. Nothing in the world is going to stop me from trying to make it succeed.

"However, I promise that if we find it impossible to bring up our children speaking only Hebrew, then I will admit publicly that I have failed. I shall publish it in my newspaper and say to the world that I was wrong; that it is impossible to revive a dead language.

"Meanwhile, we must not weaken. What Pines talks is nonsense! You and I must show him how wrong he is!"

So in the summer of 1887 Eliezer Ben Yehuda took leave of Jerusalem and headed for Moscow. Before going he entrusted his newspaper to the only man willing to take on the responsibility, Jehiel Michael Pines, representative of the British Jews in Palestine, the same Mr. Pines who was so sure the Ben Yehudas were raising a family of idiots.

16

Time for Deborah

SOON AFTER ELIEZER LEFT FOR MOSCOW, DEBORAH moved from Shalom Blesher's house to a less expensive place in a large courtyard where only Sephardic Jews lived, hoping that they would be more tolerant of her than the Ashkenazic Jews had been. The Sephardic women, she had discovered, never tried to force her to adopt their other religious customs and superstitions so long as she conformed in the single matter of covering her head with a kerchief and wore a piece of black velvet on her forehead.

Eliezer had left her with money enough to last little more than a week. There was an immediate necessity of earning more. Her good Sephardic neighbors came to the rescue. They taught her how to do embroidery work and to knit. She learned quickly and spent innumerable hours at it every day, her fingers flying. Then the neighbors helped her market her handiwork.

They also taught her many tricks of living on a minimum of money. Her main food, all the time Eliezer was gone, was dark bread dipped in olive oil, which she purchased a liter at a time from men who went by the door with clay pots and bottles strapped to the backs of their small donkeys.

Once in the middle of her knitting Deborah jumped up, ran to a mirror, and studied her face. She was now thirty-three, yet she appeared a worn-out, middle-aged woman. She remembered how Eliezer used to tell her how lovely she looked. It had been years since he had made such a comment. So that day Deborah swore that before he returned she would do something to try to regain what she had lost.

She remembered that the book of ancient Jewish law said that women as well as men must beautify themselves; that "women become ugly unless they use cosmetics."

So the next day Deborah spoke to one of her Sephardic neighbors who had learned from the Arabs about roots whose juice kept the hair from turning gray; about a liquid which, when dropped into the eyes, made the pupils bright and exciting; about painting the fingernails; about how to accentuate the eyes with antimony, ancestor of modern eye cosmetics.

By the discreet use of these ancient tricks Deborah hoped she would be able to improve her appearance so much that when Eliezer returned he would find her almost as fresh and charming as when they had met in Vienna six years ago.

Also while her husband was in Moscow, Deborah devoted hours each day to reading his books, studying geography, brushing up her knowledge of the sciences, and digging deeply into the history of the Jews and of other peoples. She even decided, as a surprise, to prepare herself to teach Hebrew the same way Eliezer did. He called it "teaching Hebrew in Hebrew." It was a method which generations later would be used by one of the most successful language schools in the world. In Eliezer's classrooms no word was ever spoken of any language except the language being studied, Hebrew.

All this time the young wife kept writing encouraging letters to Eliezer in Moscow. She was happy and comfortably situated. Neither of his sons had yet heard a single word of any foreign language. They played happily by themselves. They would all rejoice when he returned, but he must stay there until his mission had been fully accomplished.

Pola, the baby of the Yonas family, was about eighteen years younger than Deborah and nearly fourteen years younger than

Eliezer. Yet the first love of her life was the frightened boy her father had found in the synagogue of Glubokiah and had brought home for breakfast one cold morning in 1872. She had cried when he cut off his curls, and years later, before she was even ten years old, she had wrangled with her older sister, whenever his name was mentioned, over whose sweetheart he was.

Now, in the summer of 1887, Eliezer was her brother-in-law and she was no longer a child. Yet as she stood in the family reception line to greet him on his visit to Moscow she realized that her childhood feelings for him were still little changed. He was almost twice her age, yet to her, despite the worry lines on his face and the emaciation caused by his repeated illnesses, he was still a romantic creature. He had come from that far-off place where he and Deborah lived and where they had been fighting a battle the purpose of which she did not yet really understand.

Father Yonas still considered Eliezer his own protégé, as well as his son-in-law, and greeted him with both love and admiration. As the young man sank exhausted into the cushions of a sofa in the library, where his education had really started, he told them of his long trip, commencing with the difficulties he had had obtaining a Russian visa because he had given up his Russian passport.

"And what nationality of man am I now entertaining?"

"I am a Turk."

"And why did you ever become a Turk, of all things?"

"Because I feel it is a person's duty to take the citizenship of the country in which he makes his home and to share in the obligations as well as the advantages of that place. I have no other reason for becoming a Turk except that the Turks now rule our Holy Land, and as long as they do, I must be a Turk. Also, by changing my nationality I was able to change my name!"

From the moment Eliezer entered the house the conversation was all in Hebrew, for Deborah had warned her father about her husband's fanaticism. The result was that the children understood little of what was said, which especially irritated Pola, who had to be content with just staring discreetly from under her long eyelashes at the man she had "always loved."

Mother Yonas understood a word here and there. She understood what Eliezer meant when, in Hebrew, he asked her if it would be possible to have his food prepared in the Orthodox manner while he remained with them. She understood the words but was perplexed by the idea.

"You know we do not follow Orthodox rules, Eliezer, and you never did either!"

"You are correct, but when Deborah and I settled in Jerusalem we decided to abide by all the customs of the majority so we would be accepted. We try to live as they live."

"But," interjected Father Yonas, "you are not in Palestine now, so why keep up the subterfuge?"

"I would feel myself a hypocrite if I did things differently behind their backs, and so I hope it is possible for me to observe the dietary laws and dress in the Palestinian fashion while I am living with you."

When he later appeared in his long coat trimmed with red-fox fur and his oriental fez there was amusement on the part of the Yonas children. All except Pola. She whispered to one of her sisters:

"Doesn't he look romantic! Just like an ancient holy man, with his beard and those strange clothes! Just like in a picture book."

The next morning Eliezer had a frank talk with his father-in-law about the Ben Yehuda financial problem. The older man at first was indignant.

"Why did my daughter not tell me you were suffering from lack of money?

"I know you do not want charity. What you need and deserve is support from Jews here and elsewhere. Let us commence at once to make a list of people you should see."

Several days later a delegation called at the Yonas home to see the man from Palestine. Among them were many destined to play leading roles in Palestine and in latter-day Jewish history, but now they were all young university students. One was Menahem Ben Mosche Ussishkin, engineering student, who eventually was to become one of Ben Yehuda's greatest enemies. Two others introduced themselves as Jehiel Tschlenow, medical student, and Reuben Brainin, a young Hebrew writer.

The student group arranged a number of meetings at which Ben Yehuda made appeals for subscriptions to his paper and to the dictionary on which he told them he was working.

In his speeches Ben Yehuda stressed the necessity for quick action in Palestine, warning that this small piece of land was a prize on which many nations had their eyes.

Most of those who flocked to the meetings were young. Many vowed they would soon be at Ben Yehuda's side on the fighting line in Palestine. Their contributions were small but numerous.

Before going home Eliezer made a quick side trip to Paris. Many important French Jews received him with respect. Six years ago they had called him a dreamy idealist, a wild-eyed visionary. Now, although many did not agree with him, they listened.

When he brought up the matter of financial support, the Jewish leaders of France promised to consider helping him if he did nothing to raise the older generation against him in Palestine.

"Be content to work on your dictionary and encourage people to emigrate to Palestine," they told him. "Above all, do not stir up our French representatives in Jerusalem against you. Follow this advice and you probably shall receive our help."

Eliezer Ben Yehuda returned to Jerusalem, after an absence of several months, full of energy and hope.

Deborah's double transformation heightened his happiness. In between sentences of his report on all he had seen and done, he complimented her on her appearance.

"It is just as if we were back in Vienna again!"

Nothing he could have said would have flattered her more.

It took a few days for him to discover her mental transformation. When he did he was even more pleased.

Several days after his return Deborah said to him:

"While you were gone someone passing through Jerusalem told me that your old friend Tshashnikov has settled in one of the Scandinavian countries; that he has never married; that he has been following your activities with great interest. I wonder, Eliezer, why he has never written to you."

Her husband shrugged his shoulders and changed the subject.

The happiness reflected in Eliezer's face quickly disappeared, however, when he discovered what Mr. Pines had done in his absence. The acting editor had thrown the full support of the paper behind the forthcoming observance of Shemittah, an ancient Orthodox custom under which land is given a rest one year out of every seven. For twelve months no field is plowed, no planting is done, no crops are harvested, trees are neither sprayed nor pruned, nature is allowed to run rampant.

Eliezer knew that behind the old custom, as with all Orthodox practices, there was a sound, practical consideration. He knew enough about farming to be aware that the earth occasionally needs a rest; that originally Shemittah was in the nature of a crop-rotation scheme.

But he also knew, as with so many Orthodox practices, that Shemittah was taken too literally; that it was used as an excuse for laziness; that young trees would die of neglect, and that years of hard work in trying to bring patches of the desert back to fertility would be undone.

So he summarily dismissed Mr. Pines and then wrote a series of diatribes against the observance of the sabbatical year. Never before or afterward did he write with such an acid pen.

The next issue of the *Deer* caused a sensation. Groups of men gathered on street corners and talked excitedly about the articles. Families were divided. Neighbors took sides against each other. Jerusalem was in an uproar.

The elders of the Holy City felt they finally had a chance to put a noose around the neck of the young heretic. They appealed to the rabbis to declare a ban on the *Deer*. They were joined by the Halukkah leaders who managed the charitable funds and saw an opportunity to get even with Ben Yehuda for his articles calling them "parasites."

The ban was imposed, with all the old Orthodox formalities. Black candles were burned in the synagogues. A "town crier" went through the streets blowing the wind instrument made from a ram's horn and called a *shofar*.

"The *Deer* is banned! The *Deer* is banned! It is officially forbidden for any good Jew to buy, possess, or read this paper!"

On Sabbath eve great posters appeared on the walls of Jerusalem, not only repeating the wording of the ban, but also denouncing the paper and its editor in scathing language. One section, in the form of an open letter to Ben Yehuda, said:

"You thought you could deceive Jerusalem by appearing before us in your long robe and your fez. You are mistaken. We are not deceived. We declare you a heretic, an unbeliever, and in addition you are a hypocrite. We shall know in the future how to guard ourselves from your lies and shall not fall into your trap."

Rushing home from reading one of the posters, Eliezer burst into Deborah's room. He forgot that she was expecting the birth of their third child. He forgot his customary restraint. He forgot everything but that he had been held up to public scorn.

"It is impossible to meet these people halfway! It is impossible to fight their misguided leaders in a subtle fashion. Perhaps your father, after all, was right. I should have listened to him! But now I shall really start to fight! I hope they remember that they began this!"

Deborah looked up and in a frightened little voice asked:

"Haveevee, what are you doing?"

Eliezer had taken off his long coat trimmed with the red fur of the fox and was trampling it under his feet. Now he threw his oriental red fez to the floor.

"Haveevee, this is so sad. You liked that coat so much! Surely you remember once saying you would like to see such coats worn by all Jews as a national costume instead of as a religious requirement."

"I did, Deborah, but not any more. I shall never wear it again. Also, I am going to remove one more sign of my attempt at conformity. I am going to shave off my beard!"

Deborah let out a small cry of pain.

"No! Not that, Haveevee! I shall never recognize you without it. You look so well with a beard, Eliezer!"

"All right, I shall compromise with you," he promised after a short argument. "I shall trim it down so that I look like a Frenchman with a short Vandyke. It will still indicate that I am no longer following the Orthodox custom of letting the beard grow."

When Editor Eliezer Ben Yehuda next appeared in the streets more people stared at him than ever before. He looked, except for the lines on his face, just as he had the day he arrived, nearly seven years ago, dressed like a gentleman from Paris.

The next issue of the *Deer* came out with its front page in a wide black frame as a symbol of mourning. In that issue appeared an article which was due to become one of the most celebrated pieces of writing to come from the Ben Yehuda pen. It was entitled:

THE
CRIME

Instead of going on the defensive, the young editor did what any good military leader does when the enemy strikes hard at him. He made a counterattack.

The article lit into the Halukkah. It accused the leaders of "social crimes." It blamed them for holding back the progress of Israel. It called them "reactionaries" in the worst sense, men with their eyes on the road behind, afraid to look forward toward the bright future.

The answer of his opponents was another ban, announced with all the excoriation of the first. The building in which the *Deer* was printed and the Ben Yehuda home were now placed under a boycott. No religious Jew must enter either place, under pain of severe punishment.

In the midst of all this tension Deborah's third child was born, a girl whom they called Yemeemah, an old biblical name.

Deborah needed friends now, yet many who had been intimate deserted her, afraid to defy the elders of Jerusalem.

Nissim Behar, the Alliance-school director, publicly came to Ben Yehuda's defense. He also told him he would try to get from the "Great Benefactor," as Baron Rothschild was called, the financial support which the French Jews had promised.

As reactions to the Halukkah fight came in from around Palestine it was evident that the rest of the country did not reflect Jerusalem's attitude.

There was by now a large Jewish population in Jaffa, and it was almost wholeheartedly behind the *Deer's* stand. A number of new settlements had been established. The pioneers working on the land were unanimously on Ben Yehuda's side.

The big gun he fired in the next issue was a demand that the directors of the Halukkah publish an exact accounting of the moneys they had received in the past year from abroad and an explanation of how they had spent all of it.

He demanded that they give the name of each recipient. He implied that the officials would refuse because they would never reveal how large their own salaries were, nor allow the public to discover that after the payment of organizational expenses there was so little left for the poor.

He also demanded that the religious schools draw up and announce a tangible, orderly, scientific program which would lead to improvement in the curriculum and a degree of efficiency.

This new double-barreled attack increased the intensity of feeling on both sides.

As soon as Deborah was well enough she obtained a position teaching Hebrew in the Evelina de Rothschild school for girls, which had been established by English Jews, with Behar's sister as principal. This permitted Eliezer to spend all his time on his paper and his new project, the dictionary, although he did sandwich in the writing and publishing of a modern Palestinian geography book.

His enemies were unable to silence him.

17

Thrice Death

DEBORAH BEN YEHUDA DIED ON THE TWENTY-SECond day of *Elul,* in the late summer of 1891. She died of the disease which she had contracted from her husband.

It was irony that doctors had been telling Eliezer since his youth that he had only a few years to live and that he had hesitated about marrying Deborah because she might so soon become a widow. Yet it was Deborah who died of tuberculosis.

She was thirty-seven. Eliezer was thirty-three.

It was also ironical that Deborah, after fighting with so little complaint at her husband's side through the grimmest part of his life, should be taken away just when, finally, there was a chance for a modicum of comfort and security, a taste of success.

The Ben Yehudas had moved into a larger house surrounded by a garden. Deborah had a Sephardic woman as a maid. Two more children had arrived, both girls. One had been named Attarah, from the Hebrew word for "tiara," and the other Shlomit, derived from the Hebrew word for "peace."

Ben Zion now was nine years old, and Avi Hayil was six. Both, thanks to Deborah's consideration of her husband's fanaticism, spoke beautiful Hebrew and not a word of any other tongue. The first daughter, Yemeemah, was now three and already had begun to talk her father's language. The two babies had thus far been sheltered from the "contaminating languages."

The Ben Yehuda house and garden echoed all day with the laughter of the children and the babble of Hebrew words, many of which the father had dug out of old books or had actually created. Hebrew was the language of their games. It was the language in which they studied, for now in Nissim Behar's school it was possible for pupils to learn geography, history, and even mathematics in Hebrew.

When Yemeemah had begun to talk Eliezer had had a new excitement, that of hearing his favorite language spoken in the mellifluent, euphonious tones of a small girl.

The Ben Yehuda home by now was furnished in European style, which was a novelty in this part of the world. In the dining room there was a round European-type table, six chairs, and a mirror in a large ornamental gilded frame.

Life had begun to take on a more pleasant hue, and Deborah had started to enjoy her role as "the first Hebrew mother in nearly two thousand years."

But then she commenced to cough. She had a terror from the start that it was the White Plague. She refused for a long time to allow Eliezer to send for a doctor, fearing to be told what she knew she would be told.

But a doctor finally came and confirmed her fear.

Eliezer wrote to the Yônas family, and in return Deborah received an immediate invitation to come to Moscow, alone or, if she wished, with all five children. But by the time the invitation arrived her condition had deteriorated so much that the doctor said such a trip was out of the question.

Eliezer then wrote to his own mother, with whom he had had little correspondence in all these years. She agreed to come at once, but then a difficulty arose. The Turkish government had begun to get suspicious of the nationalistic activities of Palestinian Jews and had issued a ban against any more Jewish immigation, just as another nation was to do half a century later, with more tragic results.

Eliezer suffered mentally as well as physically in these days. He knew that his disease was going to take Deborah. Every day she grew weaker and there was less of a sparkle in her eyes. Yet she wanted so desperately to live!

Eliezer had many problems. First, the children. It was not easy to prepare five small boys and girls for the imminent death of their mother. It was not easy for a man as impractical in a household way as he was to edit a newspaper, work on a dictionary, run a home, play nurse to a dying wife, and take care of five children, the youngest a baby in arms.

In desperation Eliezer went to the Turkish pasha of Jerusalem and appealed to him to make an exception in the case of Mrs. Perlman of Luzhky, his mother. He explained that she was almost seventy; that she was harmless to the Turks or to anyone else, for she was too old to bear arms, or children either. Besides, Eliezer pointed out, she would be here for just a short time; just until the death of his wife.

The pasha's answer was a cold, stern "No."

So Eliezer arranged to have his seventy-year-old mother smuggled into the port of Jaffa disguised as a sack of potatoes!

Thus Feygaleh came to the shores of the Promised Land, in a burlap sack loaded in a small boat with other pieces of cargo. She arrived, finally, at the Ben Yehuda home more dead than alive.

She arrived to find Deborah melting away like a rapidly burning candle. There was fever in her eyes and the terror of approaching death.

Mother Perlman knew the Hebrew words of the Bible, but she had never really understood what the words meant. Spoken Hebrew was a complete mystery to her.

So Eliezer made his first concession. He permitted his own mother to speak to Deborah and the older children in Russian, on the understanding that she would never converse before them in Yiddish.

Mrs. Perlman was a perfect nurse. She and the invalid quickly acquired a mutual love for each other. But Deborah wanted her own mother at her side during what time was left. So she dictated a letter, which Eliezer wrote for her, imploring her mother to come at once.

Mother Yonas was also smuggled in. By the time she arrived Deborah had been taken to a hospital.

One month later she died in her sleep. She was too weak in those last days even to say good-by.

She died with her mother, her mother-in-law, her husband, and her children clustered around her.

The first Hebrew mother in nearly two thousand years had gone to her ancestors, leaving behind five small hostages to fortune.

Deborah's death provided the enemies of Eliezer Ben Yehuda with a new opportunity for revenge. They thought that this time, because he was so weighed down with grief, they could break him completely.

The Ashkenazic undertakers who had charge of the body said they were sorry but they had just been officially informed that Mrs. Ben Yehuda, being the wife of a man against whom a religious ban had been issued, had been declared *terefah,* or unclean, an ugly little word in any language; an especially ugly word to be used about so sweet a character so soon after her death.

Instead of being crushed by the announcement, Eliezer reacted like an infuriated wild animal.

"And what does this all mean?" he demanded.

"It means," the undertakers replied, "that we are digging a grave for your wife outside the walls of the cemetery. It is not allowed that an unclean body be placed anywhere near the others, for fear of their contamination."

Eliezer shouted his defiance.

"This is an insult I shall not tolerate! You need not dig any grave at all. I shall make other arrangements."

Whereupon he went to the leaders of the Sephardic congregation and asked them if they would take charge of the burial. They agreed, and Sephardic undertakers went to get the body from the Ashkenazic undertakers.

This caused the Ashkenazic leaders to hold a quick consultation. Perhaps they had gone too far. It would not do to let Ben Yehuda outwit them this way.

Eliezer eventually won the battle. He argued with them until they agreed that Deborah would be buried within the walls of the Ashkenazic cemetery in the place of highest honor, on the summit of the Mount of Olives.

Readers of the *Deer* waited impatiently for the next issue. But they were disappointed. After the conventional seven days of mourning called *Shivah* the paper appeared with no reference to the death or the controversy, except a short quotation from the Book of Jeremiah, surrounded by a thin black border:

> I remember thee, the kindness of thy youth, the love of thine espousals, when thou wentest after me in the wilderness, in a land that was not sown.

After several weeks Mother Yonas returned to Moscow, leaving Eliezer's mother to manage the household.

One bright spot was the reunion of Mrs. Perlman with her brother who had been kidnaped as a child by the Cossacks. But this minor joy was quickly overshadowed by fresh tragedy. Within two months after Deborah's death, Avi Hayil, who in Eliezer's dream was to become leader of an Israeli army, became ill and died. In the same month death also took the two younger Ben Yehuda daughters. All three children were buried on the top of the Mount of Olives beside the body of their mother.

It was a sad household after they left: Eliezer, his first-born son, one daughter, and the aged grandmother who, although she rarely said it aloud, saw in all this tragedy the hand of God meting out punishment to her son for his un-Orthodox behavior.

Mrs. Perlman's continued ignorance of Hebrew and Eliezer's continued insistence that she not talk Yiddish to the children made life difficult in the Ben Yehuda home, especially when little Yemeemah would burst into tears and demand to know when her mother, her two sisters, and Avi Hayil were coming back.

The grandmother finally solved the problem by learning the Hebrew word for "someday," which she not only used to answer the question the child kept asking, but even made into a song which she sang to put Yemeemah to sleep.

Eliezer's grief was both increased and ameliorated by another tragedy which occurred at this time. The young wife of Nissim

Behar died just after Deborah, leaving the director of the Alliance school with two small children.

Friends already, the two men now became brothers in misfortune. Each morning for months Behar would call at the Ben Yehuda home for Eliezer, and together they would take a long walk into the outskirts of Jerusalem. This exercise and the invigorating air of the Judean hills did much to help them regain the courage and strength they needed to carry on.

18

Intrigue and Bribery

ALTHOUGH THE BARREN SANDS OF PALESTINE WERE gradually being populated by Jews, with nearly a dozen agricultural colonies already established, the Turkish government went to great lengths to enforce the law against Jewish immigation. But the Jews, just as they were to do half a century later when the British would try to close the doors of Palestine, organized an underground and smuggled in a considerable number of immigrants.

The more conservative Jews not only tacitly approved the restrictions imposed by the Turkish government but imposed some of their own.

Settlements which had ignored the pronouncement of a sabbatical year by working their fields were placed under the stigma of a religious curse. Schools were banned if they encouraged the study of Hebrew. Hebrew teachers were castigated. Pupils who insisted on studying Hebrew were placed on a black list which was even enlarged to include their relatives.

Eliezer Ben Yehuda was the archangel of evil. But his enemies were sure God would take care of him; that he would quickly follow his wife and children to the grave. There were even those who were happy if they received a report that his cough was worse.

In their fanaticism they persecuted even those who had never been very enthusiastic supporters of the Ben Yehuda program.

One of their victims was the same Mr. Pines who had managed the *Deer* while Ben Yehuda was in Moscow. Pines was placed under a ban and even made the butt of cheap jokes. One day a paper listing all the complaints against him was tied to the tail of a mangy dog, which was chased through the streets until it had advertised the Pines case in every corner of Jerusalem.

Pines, unable to stand such attacks, moved to Jaffa, where he established a "Society for the Support of Farmers and Artisans."

About this time Ben Yehuda and Behar concocted a piece of political intrigue.

Although the Jews were second-class citizens here, the Ottoman Empire gave them a small voice through an officially recognized representative, called *Hacham Bashi,* to the Turkish government. The man who was the Chief Rabbi of the Sephardic community was automatically Hacham Bashi. It was a position of great power, yet in the past it had generally been held by an extremely antiquated Jew with few progressive leanings.

"Why," asked Ben Yehuda, "should we not try to find some young, well-educated, cultured, and forceful person, pleasing in appearance, who can win the respect of governments and fight for us in the diplomatic field, and at the same time raise the status of the Sephardim in the eyes of the world?"

Behar and Ben Yehuda chose as their candidate a young rabbi named Jacob Meir, who had many but not all the qualifications. His greatest asset was that he did not have what Ben Yehuda always called "the ghetto mentality." However, he knew not a word of French, the language most widely used in social and government circles in the Middle East.

Behar and Ben Yehuda had many talks with Rabbi Meir, who was just two years older than Eliezer himself. Rabbi Meir was a little overawed at the idea of aspiring for such high office, but they finally convinced him that there was a chance of success if he would agree to work diligently preparing himself. Then when the time for action came Ben Yehuda would throw the support of the *Deer* behind his candidacy, and Behar would use his influence with the

Chief Rabbi of France and with Baron Rothschild if necessary.

They told him he must learn to speak fluent French as quickly as possible. But he must do his studying in secret, for if the conservatives even suspected, they would organize violent opposition.

Accordingly, for hours each day, Rabbi Meir studied in a locked room. His servants had orders to admit no one but Ben Yehuda or Behar.

But in spite of such precautions the secret leaked out and an uproar ensued. The flames of the controversy spread to Jaffa and the settlements. Again, as in each other dispute which Ben Yehuda had generated, neighbors fought with neighbors; parents argued with their children.

Finally, as a compromise, Ben Yehuda and Behar agreed that they would not try to force the young rabbi's appointment. Instead they offered to throw their support behind the selection of the elderly and conservative head of the Elyashar family, in return for which their young protégé would be made his assistant and upon his death might succeed him.

Controversies like this one kept the Jews of Palestine in a state of high tension and also had an effect abroad. Many saw in them proof that Jews could never live together in peace, even if they had their own state and their own language.

But Ben Yehuda was not discouraged by such talk. He answered such critics by saying:

"This is life. Wine must ferment. Bread must rise. Brothers must quarrel. Thus it is written."

Those who came to Palestine on a visit were favorably impressed by the progress that had been made on the land. There were Jewish agricultural settlements now in all parts of the country. Hebrew was being taught in many schools, by many teachers, in the Ben Yehuda manner, without recourse to the use of any other language. Young mothers were even singing Hebrew lullabies to their children.

Ben Yehuda had also succeeded in having Hebrew introduced into the curriculum of several of the old theological schools, although such schools were citadels of reaction. Only Ben Yehuda's most intimate friends knew how it had been accomplished. It was simple bribery. Each week he paid each teacher who gave lessons in spoken Hebrew a secret and unofficial "salary." Also, each week each pupil who submitted to Hebrew instruction was likewise paid a bribe for his willingness to defy convention. The fact that teachers and pupils were always on the verge of poverty made them very amenable to such an arrangement. (A book of accounts in Ben Yehuda's own handwriting listing such payments is still preserved.)

Ben Yehuda's major activity was still the *Deer,* although he spent hours each day doing research for his dictionary. The paper continued to grow in size and circulation. Even his enemies were forced to subscribe so they could attack the ideas he advanced.

He often worked all night translating British, French, and German literature into Hebrew for serialization in the *Deer.*

Because the Turkish government was violently opposed to foreign culture and prohibited the publication of any foreign literature, Ben Yehuda was compelled to withhold the names of foreign authors and even change titles.

He published Victor Hugo's *Notre Dame de Paris* under the title, *The Stolen One,* author anonymous.

When he printed Molière's *Le Tartuffe* and his *L'Avare* his critics wrote that he was giving circulation to anti-Semitic writings. Palestine's wealthiest Jew was sure that he personally was being lampooned.

When the *Deer* carried articles about new inventions and scientific discoveries the opposition said such items undermined religion.

When Ben Yehuda tried to encourage the start of an endemic Palestinian literature they argued that Jews should keep their minds on the study of biblical law. But Ben Yehuda, undisturbed by their clamor, continued to help every young poet, novelist, or journalist who came to him.

There was hardly a field in which the young editor did not try to raise the cultural and artistic level. But most important, each issue of the *Deer* contained at least one new Hebrew word which had been discovered or created by Ben Yehuda. Thus each week Hebrew was becoming more and more a language in which women could do their marketing, children could play games and call each other names, and men could discuss scientific and political developments.

On the first day of each month, which in Hebrew is called *Rosh Hodesh,* Eliezer Ben Yehuda would put on his best suit, pack a grip with books and papers, and go to Jaffa. These monthly trips were partly business, partly pleasure. After Deborah's death Eliezer looked forward to them with relish.

From early morning until late at night a Jewish money-changer named Baruchin sat in a stall close by the Jaffa Gate. Often Eliezer would not have the necessary capital for the trip, in which case Baruchin the Money-Changer would advance him however much he needed, knowing that forty-eight hours later, when Eliezer returned, he would have money enough from selling subscriptions to the *Deer* to repay the loan.

Baruchin also grew accustomed to another piece of routine. Twice each year Eliezer would come to him with a worried frown and say:

"Baruchin, my friend, I have just received word that Baron Rothschild's representative will be in Jaffa next week. As you know, I receive a small subsidy from the baron, and so it is necessary for me to make a good impression on his administrator. For that reason . . ."

So each six months Baruchin would advance the money for a new suit, which Eliezer always found some way to pay back. Baruchin, out of his regard for Ben Yehuda, never charged him interest.

What Eliezer liked best about Jaffa was that here one could get away, temporarily at least, from the bickerings and petty squabbles of Jerusalem. Here a fresh breeze blew in from the sea, and the moral atmosphere was invigorating too. Jaffa was a modern, thriving city. There was conviviality here, and intellectual awareness. This was part of a new world.

Each visit, for Eliezer Ben Yehuda, had its financial rewards. He not only collected new subscriptions to the *Deer* but also sold Hebrew textbooks which had been written and published in Jerusalem.

He sat in on conferences at which the establishment of new colonies and the purchase of additional land were discussed.

The most productive of his meetings was one which resulted in the establishment of the first school anywhere in the world, in nearly two thousand years, in which no other language but Hebrew would be spoken. The founder was Israel Belkind, who started the school without a bit of financial support from anyone, although Ben Yehuda gave him generous assistance in less material ways.

The conferences in Jaffa sometimes ended in arguments and disagreements. In the matter of acquiring new land Ben Yehuda took the minority position that two considerations should always be kept in mind; whether the tract to be purchased was defensible in case of Arab attack, and whether the tract had any historical significance for Jews. The majority always argued in favor of buying land merely on the basis of its fertility.

On one trip Eliezer took exciting news to his Jaffa friends. He had just received a letter from Deborah's youngest sister, Pola. In Moscow, she wrote, she had met a fine-looking, cultured Russian Jew named Halperin who, although only twenty-six years old, had built up a small fortune in Smolensk. For nearly a year he had been trying to convince his wife that they should take their money, their three small children, and all their worldly possessions and emigrate to Palestine. His wife had heard so many discouraging tales about the barrenness of the land and the prevalence of serious diseases that she refused even to listen.

According to Pola's letter, the husband in exasperation had divided his fortune into two equal parts. One part he turned over to his wife and children; with the other half he had started for Palestine.

The next time Eliezer went to Jaffa he learned that Halperin had arrived and had spent most of his money buying a large tract of land in Judea, which he presented to a group of settlers who were establishing a community called Nes Ziona. The philanthropist Halperin would become a common laborer on the land with the rest of them.

About this same time a group of Jewish immigrants from Warsaw acquired a large tract not far from Jaffa and established a colony named Rehovoth (Expansion). Although the Rehovoth pioneers were men of great faith and ambition, they could hardly have dreamed that within fifty years their settlement would grow into one of the greatest beauty spots in the new Israel, its hills covered with orange groves, eucalyptus forests, and vineyards, its streets lined with some of the most sumptuous homes in the country, and that tourists would someday come from distant places between Purim and Passover to see the display of almond blossoms covering the ground like deep snow.

These were not the only new settlements. An entire network of Jewish villages had now been formed, each a spot of green against a dull brown background.

It was still dangerous, however, for Jews to travel on roads at night between villages. Arab highwaymen would waylay them, take their money, strip them of their clothes, and even force them to remove and hand over the shoes they wore. If the victims protested too loudly they often were murdered.

Arabs made surprise raids on Jewish shepherds at sunset and stole their flocks. At night, as the harvest season approached, they would raid Jewish fields. When the patience of the Jewish settlers finally wore thin, they appealed to the Turkish government for protection, but the Turkish government was extremely uninterested in their problem.

Then young Jewish men procured rifles and organized guard units. One of the leaders of this defense movement was a youth named Branitzky, who was to go down in history as a fabled character. He was from Rishon Le Zion, a towering, robust settler who owned one of the finest horses in all Palestine. Ben Yehuda heard many stories illustrating his fearlessness. Eventually, while Branitzky was traveling alone down a deserted road, he was waylaid and killed. His memory, however, still lives in legend.

Another founder of the Jewish guards was Israel Feinberg, who was nicknamed by the Arabs *Shaitan Lulu* (Devil Lulu). He spoke perfect Arabic, and something about him struck terror into the heart of every brigand. If the silhouette of the Devil Lulu on horseback appeared on the horizon, all Arabs in sight fled.

Feinberg did more than all his followers together to bring some degree of security to the Jewish settlements. He died, not at the hands of Arabs, but in his own bed, on his own small piece of land.

Eliezer heard many stories about the Jewish guards. But what pleased him most was the discovery that Jews really were beginning to take to the soil. Many of them were living more happily under their fig trees now in the Promised Land, despite all their troubles and difficulties, than they had ever lived out in the Diaspora.

They were beginning to learn how to get along agriculturally. Now when they bought goats from the Arabs they did not make the error of accepting male goats and trying to milk them.

No longer did they sow wheat on worthless soil.

No longer did they plant orange groves and expect them to bear fruit at once without irrigation.

No longer did they clean out their stables, throw away the refuse, and then have to buy manure from the Arabs to fertilize their fields.

Slowly progress was being made.

David Idelovitch, who had come to Jerusalem in the first small wave of immigration, was now a recognized teacher of Hebrew. Judah Grazovski, for whom Ben Yehuda had obtained a job in a grocery store, was now the author of several Hebrew schoolbooks. He was later to take the name of Gur.

Saplings which had been planted ten years ago were already growing into healthy trees.

19

Industrial Childbirth

ELIEZER BEN YEHUDA KNEW THAT NO NATION CAN rise without a thriving industry of its own and so, although economic matters were far out of his field, he took a keen interest in any sign he saw of the industrialization of Palestine.

Those who had settled on the land had had their greatest success growing grapes. That led Baron Rothschild to send a Russian who had once been an orchestra conductor in Kiev to Bordeaux, France, to learn all he could about wine making, and then to Palestine to take charge of the new industry. The Palestinian wine was praised by everyone who drank it. Soon it was being marketed abroad and received prizes at exhibitions and fairs.

The baron was so pleased that he embarked on a second experiment. The profit of the winegrowers was slight because of the necessity of importing shiploads of bottles. Palestine also needed chimneys for kerosene lamps and other glass products. So the baron paid the expenses of Meier Dizengoff (who later became the mayor of Tel Aviv) to go to Belgium and learn the glassblower's art. In less than a year Dizengoff returned and helped establish a factory at Tantura.

Not long after the factory was opened Dizengoff arrived excitedly one day in Jerusalem and called on Ben Yehuda. His hands trembled as he unwrapped a package and spread the contents on the editor's desk.

"Look! Made in Israel! The first products of our first real factory!"

The gifts he had brought were glass and porcelain jars, bearing on their sides the Hebrew words:

"From the Land of Milk and Honey."

Then he explained.

"We do not have milk, but we do have jam and honey. The more our orange groves and vineyards flourish, the more bees and the more honey. Our factory will turn out thousands of jars like these which will be shipped all over the world to advertise the land of the Jews!"

Ben Yehuda complimented him but added:

"I hear that the real need is for wine bottles. I was told today that the wine vats at Rishon Le Zion are already overflowing. Being religious people, they take the Bible literally and are ignorant about the aging of wine, thinking it should be bottled and consumed when it is new. Have you started making wine bottles yet?"

Dizengoff assured Ben Yehuda that the factory would soon be turning out wine bottles as good as any made in Europe.

But the day after an initial shipment of wine bottles was made to Rishon Le Zion, a report came back of an industrial tragedy.

Hundreds of the bottles had been filled and corked. But within an hour every bottle had broken at the neck. The floor of the winery ran ankle-deep in wine.

A second tragedy quickly followed the first. An epidemic of yellow fever and malaria swept through the factory. Dizengoff and his wife were among the victims. Many of the workers and their families died. Those who did not fled from the seacoast town, cursing the place. The factory windows were boarded up.

Experts came and examined the sand on Tantura's beach and reported it highly unsuitable for the making of glass.

That ended Industrial Experiment No. 2.

Baron Rothschild at this time was young, still in his forties, and he was adventuresome as well as wealthy. He refused to be discouraged. Far from Tantura, at Rosh Pinah in Upper Galilee, he established a third industry, a silk factory, knowing that for hundreds of years in two neighboring countries, Syria and Lebanon, a thriving silk business had been carried on.

Mulberry trees were planted and huts were built in which the children of Rosh Pinah and nearby Safed were to care for the silkworms. But the experiment was abandoned when it was discovered that there was no one who knew anything about silk weaving.

Project No. 4 was perfume. The baron sent chemists from France to manage the distilling of perfume from flowers at Yessod Ha'maala. Farmers in the neighborhood began growing geraniums and roses on every spare foot of land. But the perfume was not good. When it was shipped abroad it found no favor.

Despite the failure of many of the baron's experiments, there was a degree of prosperity in the colonies which he had helped establish. Jewish families which had known nothing but persecution and privation in the ghettos were enjoying, here in Palestine, a relatively secure and peaceful existence. Through the philanthropy of the international banker they had been enabled to buy land, build houses, educate their children, have decent medical care, and produce a "pay crop" of oranges and grapes each year.

But now a nationwide grumble of discontent began to be heard. Many of the Jewish settlers resented the paternalism of the plan. They complained that they were little better than slaves. They figured out that they would never be able to repay Baron Rothschild for the purchase of land and the construction of homes.

Most of all, they resented the attitude of the administrators sent to Palestine by the baron to manage his affairs. They complained that these men often acted like slave owners.

Jealousies and antagonisms deepened. What little social intercourse there had been between administrators and their families and farmers and their families gradually disappeared.

Finally the farmers appointed representatives to go to Paris and present their complaints verbally. The men came back with a black report. The baron had listened but then had practically thrown them out of his office, saying that although there might be some slight justification for their complaints, if the Palestinian Jews were not appreciative of his help, and if they continued to grumble about petty matters, he would immediately cut off all further financial aid to them.

When this report reached Ben Yehuda he was worried. Baron Rothschild had no consuming interest in a rebirth of a Jewish state. If the Jews of Palestine angered him he would almost certainly deviate funds being sent here to other areas where Jews were in need. That would cause hardship and suffering among the very people who were now complaining.

For these reasons Ben Yehuda threw his paper into the fight on the baron's side. In one article he called on the farmers to stop their "nonsense." He likened them to soldiers in an army who must obey the orders of a superior, even when thinking such orders foolish. He never argued that the administrators were without blame; he merely implored the farmers to forget their small grievances.

But the colonists were in no mood to listen to reason. Many who had admired Ben Yehuda now turned against him, accusing him of being a traitor to everything he had previously believed. They charged that he was now on the side of slavery instead of freedom; that he was trying to "sell them out" to the Paris banker.

But the accusation which really hurt was that Ben Yehuda was receiving financial support from the baron for his newspaper and his dictionary project (which was true) and that he was merely trying to protect his own financial position.

Mass meetings were held at which paper and editor were denounced. Ben Yehuda's closest friends advised him that it would not be wise for him to travel into any of the colonies because of the intensity of feeling against him.

This upsurge of anti-Ben Yehuda sentiment was not merely a financial blow. For years his greatest support had been from a small intellectual group in Jerusalem and from the inhabitants of the new colonies. Frequently he had made tours of the country, getting not only new subscribers but also an emotional uplift from seeing the development that was taking place. Now such contacts were denied him. Also, the Jerusalem intellectual circle was split on the issue.

A few devoted friends such as David Idelovitch, Judah Grazovski, and Israel Belkind remained his allies, but all were young and had not yet the prestige that they later would acquire.

20

Love by Mail

WHEN POLA YONAS WAS SIXTEEN YEARS OLD SHE had a formal photograph taken in a Russian embroidered dress, with her hair hanging in long dark braids over her shoulders.

When Mother Yonas went to Palestine to be with her eldest daughter during her dying days she took a copy of that photograph with her.

After seeing it, Deborah one day from her hospital bed wrote to her younger sister:

"Today Mother showed me your picture. You are as beautiful as Aphrodite. I had a dream about you the other night, Pola. I saw you standing before me and I said to you:

" 'Sister, if you wish to become a princess . . .' "

The letter ended there. Apparently Deborah had not had the strength to finish it.

When Mother Yonas returned to Moscow one of the first questions Pola asked her was:

"What did Deborah mean that I should do if I wanted to become a princess?"

The mother hesitated, and from her hesitation Pola guessed the answer.

Love by Mail

Pola was only nineteen when Deborah died. She was a student at the women's branch of the University of Moscow, specializing in the natural sciences. But she was not happy because there were few opportunities for a girl in Russia in those days to go far along scientific or intellectual roads.

Frustrated in her dream of a scientific career, Pola began to have another vision. The thin, aesthetic face of Eliezer kept coming before her eyes. She remembered her parents telling her how, when she was only an infant, she had cried because the young guest in their home in Glubokiah had cut off his curls; how he had carried her around the house in his arms; how she had hero-worshiped him even then.

She had seen him again when she was six and he was almost twenty. A dashing young man, she thought him then. She had even had fights with her sister Deborah over whose suitor he really was, because once, to make her stop crying, he had laughingly said something about taking her off to Paris with him.

But she best remembered the visit he had made to their home in Moscow five years ago. She considered herself a "grown-up young lady" then, although she was only fifteen. By then Eliezer was a member of the Yonas family by marriage, for Deborah was his wife.

Eliezer and Pola had spent a great deal of time together that summer in Moscow, and they had had some violent arguments. Eliezer had told her she was "too Russian," with no real feeling for anything Jewish.

But despite such scoldings, Eliezer Ben Yehuda had always remained a romantic figure in Pola's young eyes. She had envied the experience her older sister had had, going off to an exciting country like Palestine to share an adventurous life with a man who defied convention and had the courage of his own deep convictions.

So Pola one day wrote a letter to Eliezer. She told him that she was considering changing her first name from Pola to something more Hebraic and would Eliezer please send her some suggestions.

Back from Jerusalem came a quick reply. Eliezer was delighted to hear from her and was happy over her interest in Hebrew. He was enclosing a list of twenty names, with a translation of each one. Pola should pick the one she most fancied.

Pola wrote back that she had chosen "Hemda." She had not yet informed her family, but from now on Eliezer could address her as Hemda. What she did not write was that it was not the Hebrew letters of the name that appealed to her, nor even the sound of the word, but the meaning of it. Eliezer had written that Hemda meant "My Cherished One."

When Eliezer finally wrote and proposed that Hemda also change her last name and become Mrs. Ben Yehuda, Pola wasted no time in debate with herself. She knew that this was the career she wanted most and had always wanted.

When she broke the news to her father, he simply shrugged his shoulders and said:

"I suppose you two will be happy, because, after all, you are both a little crazy!"

Mother Yonas did not take the announcement so well. She was terrified, she said, that Pola would meet the same fate that Deborah had.

But the greatest opposition came from the brothers, sisters, and other relatives. They bluntly pointed out the difference in ages. They argued that Pola ought to finish her university studies first. They warned her how different it was in Jerusalem than in Moscow; that she was going to have to renounce civilization when she went off to that barbaric part of the world.

But nothing anyone said had the slightest effect on the headstrong young woman. She had already quietly begun to sever the ties which bound her to family, to friends, and to Moscow.

Fellow students gave a farewell party for her. The Yonas family decided that it would not do to allow so young a girl to go off on so long a trip alone. She would be accompanied not only by her father and mother, but also by her youngest brother and youngest sister.

All preparations for the journey had been made, when the letter arrived.

Eliezer Ben Yehuda's neighbors began to get suspicious when he had his house painted inside and out. They became more suspicious when he had a gardener trim the rosebushes and prune the vines. They began whispering to each other when they saw him planting with his own hands two young eucalyptus saplings at the entrance to the house.

But what made them certain that the rumor being circulated around Jerusalem must be true was the sparkle in the young editor's eyes. Also, his friends and neighbors noticed that his shoulders suddenly were no longer as stooped as they had been since Deborah's death. They pointed out that he even greeted the mailman who brought the "not wanted" newspapers back to him with something less than bitterness.

No one was ever certain exactly who it was who confirmed the rumors. It might have been Ben Yehuda's own mother, for she was overjoyed when her son told her that Deborah's young sister had agreed to become the second Mrs. Ben Yehuda.

When the story of Ben Yehuda's impending marriage to Pola Yonas was definitely confirmed, the tongues began to wag in earnest. Even Eliezer's best friends were against him on this issue. Some used the difference in ages as their talking point. Others, infected by his own fanatical interest in the language, argued that this was the second time he had chosen a girl who knew no Hebrew.

When the news reached Dr. Schwartz, chief of the Rothschild Hospital, he sent for Nissim Behar.

"Is it true our friend is about to take another wife; a child nearly fourteen years younger than he is?"

The Alliance-school director said the rumor was correct.

"He has no right to marry this—this girl!" said the doctor, looking the schoolmaster in the eye. "You know he has tuberculosis. You know Deborah contracted her fatal illness from him. Ben Yehuda himself has little longer to remain in this world. It is a crime for him to kill another life, especially one so young!"

Nissim Behar nodded sadly and said:

"You should know, Doctor, for he is your patient and you attended his first wife. But what is there to do?"

"One of us must talk coldly to him, and you are the one to do it because you are his best friend."

Ben Yehuda and Behar were accustomed to go on long walks each morning. The next day, climbing the Mount of Olives, Behar said:

"There is something I must tell you, Ben Yehuda, that I know will be painful to you. I do it only with the understanding that you realize what I am about to say comes from a devoted friend."

Ben Yehuda looked at the schoolmaster with an expression of anguish on his face.

"I have taken all the blows I can bear. What new catastrophe does fate have for me now?"

Behar then repeated exactly what Dr. Schwartz had told him, even including the remark about how little time Ben Yehuda had left to live. He concluded with a demand that the marriage contract be broken.

For a moment Ben Yehuda said nothing. Then he clasped his hands behind his back and started walking in the direction from which they had come. As Behar caught up with him he tried to talk to his friend, saying:

"Be strong, Ben Yehuda! Remember those words? You said them to me one day after my own wife had died. 'Be strong,' you said. Now I say your own words back to you."

Ben Yehuda did not reply. As they approached the house Ben Zion and Yemeemah came running to meet their father. He dismissed them, sending them into the garden to play, while he went to his study, asking Behar to accompany him. There he sat down and wrote a short note to Pola Yonas, whom he addressed as Hemda.

He told her what Dr. Schwartz had reported. He told her that the marriage was now out of the question. He concluded:

"You are free, therefore, and please do not worry about the two children. You have no right to sacrifice your life for them and for me. They will grow up like all other orphans. Besides, their grandmother is here to look after them."

When he reached the end and signed his name he put the letter in an unsealed envelope and handed it to his friend.

"I beg you to give this to Dr. Schwartz. Ask him to read it and then mail it himself so he will be certain it is on its way. Now I should like to excuse myself. I wish to be alone."

The next day Behar and Ben Yehuda took their customary walk and talked, as usual, of the affairs of the day. No mention was made of the letter or the broken engagement. Day after day they walked and talked, and not once did the editor reveal what was going on in his heart and his mind.

Ben Zion, the elder child, was puzzled. There was no longer the excitement around the house that there had been. His father did not even answer when he asked questions about when his new mother would arrive.

For two weeks it went on that way. Then one day a cable came.

BE CALM. LETTER FOLLOWS. HEMDA.

Ben Yehuda showed it to Nissim Behar.

"What do you suppose it means?"

The schoolmaster smiled.

"I would guess that she is not taking your advice!"

Two weeks later the letter arrived. It was full of affectionate phrases and profuse reassurances. One paragraph said:

"Please express my thanks to Dr. Schwartz for his special interest in my fate. Tell him it has touched me deeply. Also tell him that I am coming to you, whether for many years, or for a month, or only for a day. Whatever it is, you and I shall spend together the time left for the two of us."

Ben Yehuda handed the letter to Behar, saying:

"I am grateful to Dr. Schwartz. Now if anything happens to my second wife we all have clear consciences. But I am also grateful to him that as a result of this correspondence the tie between Hemda and me is stronger than ever. Tell Dr. Schwartz that!"

Ben Yehuda's mother and the two children did not need to read the letter to know that things were again as they had been. Once more the house hummed with excitement.

One day Ben Zion was called to his father's study and given some instructions.

"My son, I am going away in a few days to meet your new mother. While I am gone you must be head of the household. When I return to Palestine I shall send you a cable to meet us. You shall hire a carriage and be the head of the reception committee. Be sure, now, that you and your sister create a good impression!"

21

To Become a Princess . . .

THE RUSSIAN STEAMER WHICH HAD TAKEN THEM from Odessa to Constantinople began nosing its way toward shore. Suddenly Mother Yonas was beside Pola, saying excitedly:

"Look, my dear! Look! There is Eliezer!"

Pola held tightly to the rail and looked.

He was not at all like the picture she had been carrying in her mind. His long blond beard was short-trimmed and pointed. Instead of being dressed in the manner of an Orthodox Jew, as he had been in Moscow, he now wore elegant European clothes. His trousers were checkered and his jacket was of black velvet. He was more frail than he had been, which gave him a more youthful appearance. He was vibrant with energy. It showed even in the way he walked. He did not look at all like a man who had been weighed down for years with troubles. There was even a bit of dash and swagger about him.

Pola stood rigid, trying not to display any reaction, but to herself she said:

"Doesn't he look just like an English artist! He is more romantic in real life than he ever was in my dreams!"

There was only one touch which annoyed her. On his head he wore a red fez.

She was a little disappointed when he greeted her so formally.

From the ship they went directly to the hotel rooms Eliezer had engaged for them. Pola's room was banked deep with flowers.

In addressing her at dinner he used her self-selected name.

Father Yonas wheeled on his daughter.

"What is this name he calls you?"

Pola laughed and explained.

Father Yonas held his hands out in a helpless gesture.

"Not only do I lose two daughters to this man, but he tries to rob me even further by taking away the names I gave you."

Conversation that first evening was difficult. Eliezer insisted on talking Hebrew. He reverted to French only when addressing Pola, who was therefore out of the conversation most of the time.

The two children, Oniah and Peninnah, who were five and seven, were put to bed early, and Mother Yonas left with them. Father Yonas finally gave up late in the evening. At last Eliezer and Pola were alone for the first time.

Taking her hand, the young editor said:

"Hemda, I can hardly believe you are here!"

Then he made his first love speech to her, in the course of which he said it was difficult for him to express such intimate thoughts in French. She must promise to learn Hebrew quickly.

As they sat close beside each other he said softly:

"Hemda, when your sister was in the hospital she told me one morning when I went to see her that she had had a dream the night before. You appeared before her, looking just as charming as you now look to me. As you stood there, she suddenly said to you:

" 'Pola, if you wish to become a princess, marry Eliezer.'

"Of course I pretended to get angry. I said she and I would live together for many years, and the subject was dropped. But a few days later, as her strength began to fail, she whispered to me that she was going to die and hoped that you would take her place after she was gone.

"I would never have told you this unless you had already agreed to marry me. It would have been using an unfair weapon. But I hope it will make you happy to know you are carrying out your sister's last wish."

Pola tightened the pressure of her hand on Eliezer's and silently debated whether she should tell him of the letter she had received from Deborah. Instead, she changed the subject.

It was the wedding day of Eliezer Perlman, now called Ben Yehuda, and Pola Yonas, now called Hemda.

While Mr. and Mrs. Yonas were out making the necessary arrangements, the principals went for a walk. As they started Hemda turned to Eliezer, fixed her eyes on his red fez, and said:

"I hope you do not think me rude, but is it not possible to buy a—a regular hat down here somewhere?"

Eliezer blushed and replied:

"Of course!"

A few minutes later they passed a men's shop and he disappeared inside. When he came out he had a smart-looking European hat on his head. It was only then that he explained that all subjects of the Ottoman Empire were morally obligated to wear the fez as a symbol of respect for their rulers. Then he added:

"As long as we are being so frank, I do not much care for that foolish little student's hat you wear!"

So they stopped in a women's shop and bought not only a new hat but a chic umbrella, gloves, and a French handbag.

Although Hemda had lived in busy Moscow, she was impressed by the shops of the Galata section, the horse-drawn vehicles, the oriental excitement and confusion, and most of all by the Street of the Dogs.

Eliezer explained that for Moslems in Constantinople the dog was a sacred animal, not to be killed or even injured under pain of civil and ecclesiastical punishment. For some reason the dogs had taken over this one particular street. They seemed to know that here they would receive especial attention.

When they arrived back at the hotel, the Yonases were in a state of indignation. They had been searching the city for the two young people. The assistant Hacham Bashi had already arrived to perform the ceremony.

As the service began Eliezer interrupted with a demand that the assistant Hacham Bashi speak exclusively Hebrew.

Just as the ceremony ended a messenger arrived with word that their ship was about to sail without them. There would not even be time for a wedding feast.

With feminine foresight Mother Yonas had procured a roasted chicken and several bottles of wine, which she carried herself aboard the Russian steamer *Zesarevitz*. As they reached the dock the boat whistle was being blown for the third and last time.

Father Yonas, although an aristocrat in his inclinations, had insisted they travel in the most humble manner possible (as deck passengers) because he said he wanted to enter Israel in austerity, to share the experience of those pioneers who were forced by economics to travel in this manner.

They were only a few hours out of Constantinople when Hemda received her first Hebrew lesson. She had given Eliezer the keys to her baggage. Now, in Russian, she said:

"Please give me the key to my suitcase. I want to get something."

As he handed her the key Eliezer said: *"Zeh mafteach."*

When Hemda asked him what that meant he said it was Hebrew for: "This is a key."

Slowly the girl repeated the words until she had memorized them. In later years she would always say that "mafteach" to her was the most important word in Hebrew, because it was the "key" which Eliezer gave her on her wedding day to the language for which she eventually was to develop his own deep love.

After stops at Smyrna, Alexandria, and Port Said they finally came within sight of Jaffa. Standing at the rail peering toward the shore, Hemda said:

"It is just like a giant bird, isn't it? Just like an eagle with its wings outspread!"

Eliezer was vibrant with excitement. This, now, was "his" country. This was the place where he had suffered so much, yet it was the place which meant more to him than any other. In excited Russian words he tried to explain it to Hemda.

"This is *our* land, Hemda! This is where we all once lived and where we really belong! I hope you feel it and understand!"

But Hemda did not understand. To her it was just another shore line, not nearly so attractive as Constantinople or Smyrna. But she knew that if she admitted this to Eliezer he would be unhappy, so she made no answer.

Small boats in the harbor were dancing wildly on the waves, waiting like birds of prey for the signal which would permit them to encircle the steamer.

Government officials boarded the *Zesarevitz*. There was an inspection of passports, a medical examination, then questioning by police. Now a flag was hoisted as a sign that the medical men had found no contagious diseases aboard. Instantly the small boats swarmed in. Hemda clapped her hands excitedly and pointed to one in which there were four men.

"Look, Eliezer! What do all those beautiful flags on that little boat mean?"

Eliezer smiled.

"One is the flag of the Ottoman Empire. Another is the banner of the Cook's travel bureau. Then there's a flag advertising a hotel. But wait—those four men are all friends of mine! Four of my young Hebrew teachers! Where did they ever get those banners? They're coming for us! Our reception committee!"

Soon the four men were clambering up the rope ladder. They pressed around Eliezer after giving him a military-type salute. They talked rapidly in Hebrew. Hemda understood nothing they said. Finally Eliezer turned to his bride.

"My friends offer their congratulations to both of us."

Hemda in Russian asked Eliezer to thank them.

By now the steamer was vibrant with the noise of haggling porters, shouting boatmen, annoyed officials, and almost hysterical passengers. Hemda was dizzy, but she remembered for years how impressed she was by the young Arab boatmen, so sunburned and iron-muscled, filling the ship with the noise of their lusty speech and filling the air with the gesticulations of their hands. They literally tossed the baggage from man to man and finally down into the boats. They literally dragged the passengers after them down the rope ladders which were flapping loosely in the wind. Those were the lucky passengers; the ones who had been cleared by the officials. The others waited with panic written on their faces for someone to "fix" a permit for them.

When Eliezer said they must now descend into the small boat, Hemda replied:

"And my family?"

"They must stay on the ship because they have no entrance permits. But as soon as we get into town we will do everything possible to have them released."

It took a great deal of arguing to persuade Hemda to pull herself away from her parents.

Hemda's reaction to Jaffa was not at all what her sister's had been. She found the city gay and exciting. She liked the mixture of Arabs, Turks, and oriental Jews swarming through the streets, talking, singing, and crying their wares.

They had lunch at a table Eliezer had reserved in a small hotel. It was set with flowers and there were bottles of red wine. Friends came by and shook the young editor by the hand and stared at his young wife. Hemda was annoyed that they all talked only Hebrew. There was always the "comedy" of translation. She sensed that all these people could speak some language she understood if Eliezer would only permit them to. She thought of it as a conspiracy to try to convince her that no one here spoke, or even knew how to speak, anything but the ancient language.

When the luncheon was nearly over Hemda's family suddenly appeared. Father Yonas' face was pale with suppressed anger. He had revolted bitterly against his reception in this, the land of his own ancestors. He had hoped that here, at least and at last, he would feel safe ground under his feet; that no one would tell him "this is allowed and that is forbidden."

Eliezer had hired two carriages, drawn by three horses each, for the trip to Jerusalem. While the baggage was being loaded he took his bride into what she admitted was the most beautiful garden she had ever seen. It was just across the street from where they had had luncheon.

Although the two carriages were now ready, several of Ben Yehuda's friends said that the night before Arab bandits had attacked a party of Jews on their way to Jerusalem and had robbed them of all their belongings. Some of the victims had been wounded. It would be foolish to travel during the night just to avoid the heat.

Better to start early in the morning, rest during the midday at the halfway spot, Bab el Wad, and make the ascent of the Judean hills in the relative cool of the late afternoon.

Ben Yehuda agreed and sent a telegram to his son, Ben Zion.

The sunrise the following morning was so radiant and the air so refreshing that Hemda grasped Eliezer's arm and said:

"It makes me feel as if the world has just been created; as if I myself have just been born; as if all life lies ahead of me!"

"It does," her husband replied, smiling.

Leaving Jaffa, the road at first ran between groves of orange and lemon trees. This being the month of *Nisan,* the air was heavy with the fragrance of fruit blossoms, heady and almost as intoxicating as strong wine. Then they drove through fields of growing wheat and barley. Then vegetable plots. Hemda, looking for a lake, a river, or a small pond and seeing none, asked:

"How do all these things grow if there is no water?"

"The groves are irrigated with water from wells," her husband replied. "The fields are watered all summer by night dew from heaven. In the winter there is much rain."

Gradually the cool of the morning was conquered by midday heat.

Often the two carriages had to pull to the side of the road to allow vehicles coming from Jerusalem to pass. Each time there would be a volley of greetings from those going in the opposite direction.

"You act as if you were all members of one large family," Hemda remarked, to which Eliezer replied:

"Because we are!"

Finally the carriages came to a stop at Bab el Wad. The coachmen put their horses in the stables. The elder Yonases and the two children went into the inn to rest. Ben Yehuda and his bride went for a walk, then sat under an olive tree.

Stretched out on her back, looking up at the sky, Hemda said that in spite of her imagination and her desire to picture Jerusalem as it might be, the closer she approached the city, the more distant and blurred it became in her mind's eye.

"Nevertheless," Eliezer said, "you will be sleeping tonight in the Golden City!"

22

"Shalom Doddah!"

TEN-YEAR-OLD BEN ZION BEN YEHUDA FELT HIMself a real man with "responsibilities" while his father was gone. He was not content just to collect articles from contributors and deliver papers. He spent much time learning the art of typesetting. He also began his own writing career, which would someday make him a well-known literary figure. One of the many articles he composed and persuaded the temporary editor to publish in the *Deer* was entitled: "We Shall Not Give Up Nissim Behar!" It was based on rumors that the head of the Alliance school was to be deposed.

Then came the telegram:

"We have arrived. Come and meet us at Bab el Wad. Daddy."

Ben Zion was as excited as his father had been weeks before over the receipt of the cable from Moscow. He took his four-year-old sister by the hand and ran to the house of the coachman, who lived in another section of Jerusalem, and insisted that they start out immediately.

It was an "occasion" for the small boy. It was his first trip out of Jerusalem. Then there was the excitement of meeting Hemda, although he was afraid he was not going to have one tenth the affection for her that he had had for his own mother.

They reached Bab el Wad without incident and found the Ben Yehuda-Yonas party lined up waiting for their carriages to be brought to them. Ben Zion's first impression was that they all looked like foreigners, even his own father.

When Eliezer took his son in his arms to greet him, Ben Zion noticed that he appeared younger than he ever had before.

Then the introductions began.

"You remember your grandmother, Ben Zion, even if maybe Yemeemah doesn't.

"And here, Ben Zion and Yemeemah, is Hemda Ben Yehuda, your new mother!"

The little girl looked at the ground and shyly said:

"Shalom."

Ben Zion stared at Hemda. She wore a large fancy hat, unlike any he had ever seen on a woman in Jerusalem. She carried a bright-colored parasol. There was a pleasant smile in her eyes. With a childlike spontaneity of decision Ben Zion made up his mind he liked her, so he reached up, put his arms around her neck, kissed her affectionately, and said:

"Shalom, *Doddah!*"

Yemeemah, taking the cue, then did likewise.

For Hemda the happiness of that moment was marred by the necessity of responding to the children through a translator. Turning to Eliezer, with a choked-up voice she said:

"Tell them quickly that they must not use that word 'doddah.' I know that it is Hebrew for 'aunt.' Tell them I *was* their aunt but now I am something more. I can't be their real mother, but I shall try to take her place. They call you *abba,* which means 'daddy,' not father. They called Deborah 'mother.' But why should they not call me *imma,* which means 'mamma'?"

The children agreed. They would never use the word for "mother" to Hemda, but they would call her "imma."

It was three o'clock when they began the ascent of the Judean hills. At first the horses seemed to enjoy the climb, but soon they were sweating. Often the passengers had to get out of the carriages to lighten the load.

It was nine o'clock when they saw the first lights of Jerusalem.

One hour later they drove into the city. The streets were unlighted, which meant that Hemda saw nothing but the shadowy outline of buildings. Few human beings were in sight. Finally the carriages pulled to a halt and Eliezer said softly:

"This is your house!"

As he led her across the threshold, her heart sank. It was a house, all right, but not a home. The entrance hall was also partly a dining room. Overhead there was an enormous vaultlike dome, similar to the cupola of a Christian church. Off the circular hall were the bedrooms.

The reception committee consisted of Ben Yehuda's mother, who had put on her Sabbath dress for the occasion, and her brother, the official from the Russian consulate, with his wife, who was even younger than the new Mrs. Ben Yehuda.

Hemda was tired. She went to bed almost immediately. As she tossed herself to sleep she wondered what her first impressions of Jerusalem would be when she saw it in the morning. Whether Jerusalem appealed to her or not, she had made her decision. Despite what she might think of the place, it was now her city as well as her husband's.

When Hemda awoke the next morning the first thing she noticed was a bouquet of roses on a chair beside her bed. Drops of morning dew were still on the petals. She had almost forgotten, but this was Eliezer's way of saying that he had remembered. This was her twentieth birthday. As she bent over to smell the flowers Eliezer came in. She smiled her thanks to him.

"Good morning, my husband. And why are you up so early?"

"You will soon learn, Bitti, that I never miss the sunrise."

"Bitti? What does that mean?"

"Bitti means 'my child.' It is an affectionate little word which just seems to fit you."

"I like its sound. I hope you will call me that often!"

At breakfast Hemda realized how sizable a family she had. There were her own father and mother, Eliezer's mother, her two stepchildren, her brother and sister, and Eliezer's niece, a woman about thirty-five years old whose parents had sent her to Jerusalem at the time of Deborah's illness, hoping that perhaps she might become the second Mrs. Ben Yehuda. There were ten at the table, a big responsibility for a girl of twenty.

After breakfast Eliezer took her for a walk in the garden. It was not as magnificent as the one in Jaffa, but there were olive and fig trees, grapevines and almonds. It was Passover eve and spring was in all its beauty.

Eliezer showed her the two eucalyptus trees he had planted for her.

"This one," he said, pointing to the more delicate of the two, "I have named Hemda."

"So we shall call the other Eliezer, yes?"

As they returned to the house and entered her husband's study, a large room with a domed ceiling, Hemda's first reaction was displeasure that the windows were covered with an iron grillwork that made them look like windows of a prison. The walls were a full three feet thick. A wide stone divan ran along one entire wall. It was covered with cushions in the oriental manner. In the center of the room was a round table littered with papers, and against a wall was Eliezer's desk, deep with notes in his own delicate handwriting.

Eliezer sat down beside his wife on the divan, produced a Bible, opened it at the first page, and asked her to read.

"But, my dear husband, I hardly know the Hebrew alphabet!"

Ignoring her remark, he pointed to the first word in the first verse of the first chapter of Genesis and said:

"That is *bereshith.* It means 'at first,' or 'in the beginning.' Now look at it again and repeat the sound."

The second word she learned that morning was "created," and the third "God." The lesson went on for half an hour. Hemda's head was swimming.

Finally Eliezer put the Bible away and asked:

"Would you like to go for a walk?"

They wandered first through the streets of the city. Hemda, in her childlike imagination, had thought of Jerusalem as like Rome or Athens, which she knew about from pictures and paintings. But Jerusalem was unlike either of them. It had no great crumbling forum. Its streets were narrow and ugly. They were full of refuse.

Animals and even children played in the garbage. Hemda was depressed by it.

Later they climbed the rough path that ascends the Mount of Olives. Then they threaded their way through rows of tombstones until they came to Deborah's grave. At her feet were the even fresher graves of her three children.

They stood in silence for many minutes, without sharing their thoughts.

Finally Hemda lifted her head, looked at Eliezer, then put her arms around him. From that moment on she realized that her life was not her own.

23

Like a Beautiful Flame

HEMDA TURNED OVER THE MANAGEMENT OF THE household to her mother-in-law so she could devote all her energy to her two stepchildren who had been so neglected by their invalid mother and later by their bereaved father.

Mrs. Perlman had dressed ten-year-old Ben Zion like an Ashkenazic boy, in a frock coat, long trousers, and a large-brimmed hat which, in the Orthodox manner, he always kept on in the house. He even had earlocks like those Eliezer wore when he arrived so many years ago in the village of Glubokiah.

Yemeemah, although four, had never had her hair trimmed. Her clothes were hand-me-downs from Moscow, much too large for her.

"She looks like a dwarf from the land of Lilliput," Hemda complained.

The two children were pale, emaciated, and walked as slowly as if already on their way to the grave. They spoke with timidity, had no playmates, and knew no child games.

First Hemda took scissors to their hair, to the dismay of the paternal grandmother. As she did so she smiled, remembering her parents' story of how she had cried when Eliezer cut off his earlocks.

Then she cut the legs off Ben Zion's long trousers, making him look like a boy rather than a dwarfed man. She made little dresses for Yemeemah which actually fit.

She bought two large hats in a German shop in Jerusalem so the children would have protection from the sun and their skin would not turn the shade of an Arab's.

Now the offspring of Ben Yehuda the Rebel began to attract more attention on the streets of Jerusalem than ever before. In addition to being the only Hebrew-speaking children in the city, they now also looked different from any others because of their European dress. But that did not bother Hemda.

Next she dug out of one of her suitcases a large doll she had brought for Yemeemah. At first the child was terrified because it was so lifelike, but eventually she overcame her fear of even touching it.

Then Hemda bought a rubber ball and taught the children how to throw and catch it. But they were so self-conscious that they were reluctant to play, even with a ball.

There was great danger now of the Ben Yehuda home losing entirely its Hebrew character. Mrs. Perlman spoke Yiddish. Hemda spoke Russian and French. Ben Yehuda was being subjected to violent criticism by his colleagues. Why did he not do something to prevent this? Why had he not taken a Hebrew-speaking wife?

His enemies rejoiced. The structure had begun to crumble. Obviously he was having to abandon his own teachings himself. How could he now expect others to follow?

Eliezer met this situation by doing a decisive thing. He had the printing press moved into his home. That added four or five printers to the population of the house. All were men who had been given their jobs with the understanding that they would never speak anything but Hebrew. As they worked putting Ben Yehuda's articles into type, they sang. Hemda said they sang more than they worked. They sang nothing but Hebrew songs: "The Sun of the Spring," "The Rose of Jacob," and "Jerusalem."

Father Yonas, tired of the same three songs over and over again, morning, noon, and night, composed a fourth for them. He called it "Hebrew Is Our Language" and taught the children as well as the printers to sing it.

Then there was Chaim ha Halabi, a Syrian servant who ran errands for Ben Yehuda and helped in minor ways on the paper. Now he was given a new assignment. He was to be with the children from the time they arrived home from school until they had their dinner and went to bed; a male governess. He was to speak nothing but Hebrew to them. Also, he was to correct the Hebrew pronunciation of everyone in the house, so that eventually all the words might be said in the same melodious oriental way.

Nevertheless, Hemda realized that in the long run it was up to her to decide whether this would remain a Hebrew household or not. So she began to spend all her spare time over her books.

Day after day she would sit in one of the deep window sills, curled up on a pillow with a Hebrew grammar in her lap, looking occasionally out at what she had nicknamed "our Garden of Eden." Often tears would well up in her eyes because of her fear that she would never be able to learn the language.

Although she had previously mastered several other languages, she found Hebrew grammar next to impossible.

"Never," she once told her father, "will the Semitic spirit be able to vanquish the Slav in me."

But she kept all these doubts from Ben Yehuda. Day after day she took lessons from him. He taught her first to read the entire Book of Genesis, but each day he gave her a sprinkling of purely household words to learn.

Although he corrected her patiently, she persisted for weeks in saying the Hebrew word for "he" when she meant "she," and mixed up her present, past, and future tenses.

But finally, after three months of study, she made a little speech to her husband, all in Hebrew:

"Eliezer, I did not think that this day would ever come, but I have now a big announcement to make to you. Beginning right now, I wish you to speak nothing but Hebrew to me. If you talk slowly I think I will understand. I do not yet promise that I shall always reply in Hebrew, but someday that also may even be possible."

Eliezer smiled, kissed her, and called her "Bitti" with an extra degree of warmth.

In all this period Hemda asked her husband not to invite guests to the house. She did not want to meet people until she could talk to them in his language. The only exceptions were Nissim Behar and Hayim Calmi, close friends, with whom she spoke French.

Six months to the day after Hemda arrived in Palestine, on the Feast of Sukkoth, she walked into Ben Yehuda's study and made a second announcement. In almost perfect Hebrew she said:

"I know you have waited patiently for what I now say, so I hope you will be pleased. From this moment on I shall speak exclusively Hebrew, not only with you but with everyone we meet.

"I do not yet have as large a vocabulary as I would like, but I feel able to conduct a two-way conversation on most subjects. If you wish to start planning trips for us, I promise never to embarrass you by speaking a 'foreign language' again."

"Bitti," he replied with a trace of tears in his eyes, "you make me very happy. You are like a beautiful flame, giving both light and warmth. I shall thank you repeatedly for what you have brought into my life!"

Hemda's reward for her accomplishment was a trip to the Jewish settlements. When Eliezer asked her if this would please her, she clapped her hands and kissed him on the forehead.

As they made plans for the trip Eliezer smiled and said:

"It will be a real honeymoon, Bitti. Call it our second if you wish, but really it is our first; the first trip alone. To make it more exciting, we shall do part of it by railway."

"Railway? Railway to where?"

"I thought I had told you. The new railway between Jerusalem and Jaffa has started running. Maybe you will laugh at it, but to many of our people who have never seen a train it is like a miracle."

The train consisted of a small engine and three miniature cars. As the Ben Yehudas took their places she said:

"It is really like a plaything, Eliezer, isn't it?"

The conductor apologized for the lateness in starting. This railway, he said, had more problems than any other in the world.

Jews who lived anywhere within a mile or two of the right of way congregated twice a day to watch with infinite excitement the slow passage of the train.

But the Arabs reacted differently. To them this was an instrument of the devil. The more religious the Arab, the more he felt it his holy duty to destroy the monster that screamed up and down the Palestinian hills belching fire and smoke. In superstitious fear the Arabs at night placed large rocks between the rails.

"The trouble is," the conductor explained, "our timetable allows no time for the removal of these Arab barriers. How late we are depends entirely on how many Arabs went without their sleep to place how many rocks on the tracks during the night."

But when the Arabs discovered that the rocks, no matter how high they piled them, did not defeat the devil on wheels, they adopted another technique. They gathered in droves on the right of way and defied the engineer to run them down. This called for more strategy than strength on the part of the train crew.

There was also a certain not entirely unlaudable nonchalance about the way the train was run. If some prominent Palestinian or distinguished visitor from abroad sent word that he would be late making the train, the train would wait for him. Or if some woman passenger dropped her umbrella out the window, the engineer would stop and the conductor would wander back looking for the lost article.

In Jaffa, Ben Yehuda insisted on taking Hemda to the homes of many friends before going on to the settlements. He did not admit it, but he wanted to show off her ability to speak Hebrew, and his wife, knowing it, tried to put on a good performance. Never once did she allow a Russian, French, or Yiddish word to slip its way into her conversation.

Jehiel Michael Pines, Israel Belkind, and many of Ben Yehuda's other friends expressed their astonishment. Some refused to believe that six months ago Hemda had known no Hebrew. Several accused Ben Yehuda of playing a joke on them.

The story spread quickly through Jaffa and soon, wherever the Ben Yehudas went, a crowd gathered and there was a hushed silence, as if an opera singer were about to begin her great aria, and when Hemda finished speaking there would be a babble of comment.

This was one of Eliezer's moments of glory. Here, in the person of his second wife, was living, talking proof that it could be done. Just half a year after setting foot on Jewish soil Mrs. Ben Yehuda was talking Hebrew, if not like a scholar, at least like a normal intelligent person; talking of the weather, of their railway journey, of Jerusalem, of common everyday matters. If Hemda could do it, so could others.

Eliezer did not say all these things with his lips. His whole attitude said them. He was an often defeated man reveling now in this hour of small triumph. His eyes sparkled. His shoulders, Hemda noticed, were thrown back at a defiant angle. He had not coughed once all day!

But that first night Hemda in her exhaustion said to her husband:

"Eliezer, I know how happy you have been today, but now we must go on to the settlements. I cannot possibly go through my 'performance' again tomorrow. I felt all day like a dancing bear in a circus!"

The next day, Friday, they started out in an "omnibus" drawn by three very old and lazy horses.

What Hemda saw as the carriage laboriously made its way down deep-rutted roads through clusters of Arab huts frightened her. She kept a handkerchief to her face to ward off the stench which, Eliezer explained, came from fires over which Arab women were baking bread.

"But why should smoke have such a vile smell, Eliezer?"

"Because, Bitti, the only fuel these people have is dried manure; dried human and animal dung."

Hemda could see that the same windowless huts served as shelter for both man and beast. At the entrance to several she noticed old women, obviously blind, sitting grinding corn just as their ancestors had done for hundreds, perhaps thousands, of years. Hemda shuddered and held the handkerchief closer to her nose.

"Cheer up," Eliezer said, "we shall soon be approaching Rishon Le Zion."

But what if the Jewish settlements were even a little like these

Arab places? How much could the Jewish immigrants have done in a mere ten years to change this ancient and filthy way of life?

So Hemda was afraid to look when her husband suddenly shouted out enthusiastically:

"Look, Bitti! Off on the horizon, just to the left, you can see the roof of the synagogue of Rishon Le Zion!"

24

Printer's Ink

THE BEN YEHUDAS AND THE SABBATH ARRIVED IN Rishon Le Zion simultaneously. The sun was just going over the horizon as their carriage approached the settlement, which meant that all work must cease immediately for those following Orthodox custom.

Years later Hemda wrote in a book:

"Never in all my life had I seen such a beautiful village!"

As soon as the red roof of the synagogue came in sight the landscape suddenly changed. Now the road was lined with orange trees and mulberries. There were fields of grapes and beds of flowers. The predominating color became green instead of brown; green of many shades, sprinkled with dots of brighter hues.

Ben Yehuda became rhapsodic as he grasped Hemda's hand.

"This, Bitti, is *our* earth! Here Jews have changed the desert into a Garden of Eden. Look! Here we have triumphed, just as someday we shall triumph over all the hills and deserts of the Holy Land!"

As they drove into the settlement they saw men, women, and children streaming from a low wide building. They all seemed cleanly dressed and happy. Each had a small parcel under the arm. They were on their way from the public baths.

Some of the houses were painted white, others pink, yellow, blue, and red, which prompted Hemda to remark:

"They look like flowers in neat little rows in a garden, don't they, Eliezer? But what is that long low building with so many windows? It looks like a museum. Does someone live there?"

Eliezer laughed.

"That is the stable, Bitti. Just horses live there."

Hemda thought of the Arab villages, where no one was housed as well as animals were here.

In one street there were some small children at play. They politely said "Shalom" to the two strangers and then went back to their game. Hemda asked Eliezer why just hearing this commonplace Hebrew greeting had put such a bright light on his face.

"No, Bitti, it was not their 'shalom.' It was something else. Perhaps you missed it, but I heard the words they were saying to each other even before they looked up and saw us. A few years ago I would not have believed it possible. But, Bitti, they were talking *Hebrew* to each other! Children, speaking Hebrew of their own volition! Imagine that!"

They headed immediately for the home of David Idelovitch, the young man who had arrived in the first wave of immigration and for whom Ben Yehuda had found a job making knife blades in a German workshop. Now he was one of the best Hebrew teachers in Palestine.

After the evening meal the house filled up with young people who sang Hebrew songs and told stories of their adventures in helping to conquer the desert.

The next day the Ben Yehudas celebrated the Sabbath by making a house-to-house tour.

The only man in Rishon Le Zion who did not speak Hebrew was Baron Rothschild's administrator, but few of the women could even understand the questions Hemda asked them in Hebrew. They excused themselves on the ground that "sickness and all the difficulties and demands" of their pioneering life had left no time for mastering a new language.

Hemda, determined to keep her promise, insisted on conversing through an interpreter with the women of Rishon Le Zion, many of whom had been in Palestine for years and some of whom had been born there.

"How do you like life in Rishon Le Zion?" Hemda would ask in Hebrew.

Then Idelovitch or someone else would repeat the question to the woman of the house in French or Yiddish.

"I have been happier these last few years than ever before in my life, even though I do work harder," the woman would reply in Yiddish or French.

Then the interpreter would translate the answer into Hebrew for Hemda.

It was a little comedy, for Hemda could easily have carried on the entire conversation herself in the woman's language. It was even more amusing when Hemda realized that six months ago the situation had been just reversed.

In every house the men's conversation, from the first "shalom" of greeting to the final "shalom" of good-by, was filled with politics, which meant the issue of Baron Rothschild and his administrators versus the settlers. And each conversation eventually turned to a discussion of the *Deer*. The men of Rishon Le Zion were almost brutal in the frankness of their criticism.

The *Deer* gave too much news of Jerusalem and not enough about the colonies.

Ben Yehuda defended the Rothschild administrators too much and too seldom took the side of the settlers.

They did not like the paper on which the *Deer* was printed. They even went so far as to complain about typographical errors.

They said too much of the paper was written by Ben Yehuda himself. Why didn't he print articles by others, with a different style and different point of view?

Then they discussed the new Hebrew words which Ben Yehuda sprinkled through each issue. What was the origin of these words? Was it true that he invented many of them himself? If so, what right did he have to originate words? Shouldn't everyone have a voice in deciding such a vital matter as enlarging the language?

It pained Hemda to see him subjected to such an ordeal, almost as if he were on trial for a crime. She tried unobtrusively to lend him her moral support. Several times, when he began to cough or seemed worn out, she found a subtle way to bring the visit to a close.

Nearly everyone wanted to know how the Hebrew dictionary was progressing and how soon it would be ready. The first time such a question was asked, Ben Yehuda answered by pointing to his wife and saying:

"It all depends on her."

Hemda tried not to show her astonishment.

"On her?" someone asked. "Surely she is not going to make the dictionary!"

"I mean," Ben Yehuda replied, "it depends on her help. The more help she can give me in my other work, the more time I shall have for my dictionary."

On the way home Eliezer announced that he was taking back with him more new subscriptions to the *Deer* than he had ever obtained before on such a trip.

As they discussed the future of the weekly Hemda asked:

"Why wouldn't it be a good idea for me to write letters to many of the people whom we have met, suggesting that they send us news from the settlements?"

"It would be," Eliezer replied, "except that many of them would expect to be paid, and others will presume that because they correspond for the paper they have a right to influence its policies. I'm willing to sacrifice a great deal, but not my principles. You have seen yourself the opposition even among my friends. A man must be strong to face it, but with your help now, I think it will be much easier."

That gave Hemda an opening to ask what he had meant about the additional help he expected from her.

"For one thing," he replied, "I want you to start writing articles for the *Deer.*"

"But, Eliezer, I am not a writer, I am a chemist. I have no desire to be a writer. Besides, I don't know the language well enough."

Ben Yehuda made a gesture as if to sweep aside all her arguments.

"Remember, I have proof of your writing ability. Have you forgotten all the letters you wrote me from Moscow?"

"But, Eliezer, it's one thing to write a letter; quite another to write articles for a paper!"

"Your letters were beautifully written, Bitti. They were even more beautiful than the famous letters of Madame de Sévigné. As for the language, I shall correct what you write before it is set into print."

When Hemda persisted in her refusal, he took a new line of attack.

"This is not just a matter of filling up columns or satisfying a few hundred subscribers who cry for fresh material, or even of giving me more time to work on the dictionary. You must understand what a vital contribution you can make to the creation of a living, breathing, vibrant new Hebrew language.

"The hour demands that women enter the field of Hebrew literature. The language needs a feminine touch. You can help give it the softness it lacks, the flexibility, the delicacy, the subtle nuances."

As Hemda thought back later on this conversation she realized that it was the final speech which won her.

Her first contributions to the *Deer* were entitled "Letters from Jerusalem." She patterned them after the letters of Jean Joseph Charles Louis Blanc, in which the celebrated French journalist discussed affairs of the day as if he were writing to a friend. In her letters Hemda wrote about life in the Holy City in an intimate, feminine style.

More and more Hemda began to share her husband's professional problems. Gradually she eased the demands on his time. Gradually the fanatic look in his eyes came into hers too.

Their chief worry, always, was financial: where to obtain the funds for rolls of paper, stamps, the wages of printers, and still have enough left for bread.

Then there was Ben Yehuda's desire for foreign literary contributions for which he would not have to pay. Together he and Hemda made a list of half a dozen young Hebrew writers scattered around Europe, and she wrote a pleading letter to each of them explaining how hungry Jews in Palestine were for European ideas. The percentage of affirmative replies was good. Now the size of the paper was increased. The back page was devoted to advertisements. One day, looking over the latest issue, the editor said to his wife:

"If we could only get a few more advertisements, I could afford to add a two-page literary supplement."

Hemda made no comment, but the next day she started out as an advertising solicitor. She discovered that the businessmen of Jerusalem had a queer attitude toward advertising. They considered it an indication of a firm's approaching bankruptcy.

One of the city's most successful merchants told her that even if she offered to insert an advertisement without charge he would still refuse to allow his firm's name in the paper.

In a shop specializing in women's wear she found some embroidered dresses on a rack in an obscure corner and talked so vociferously to the owner about advertising them that he finally sighed and gave in. Within a few days he had sold all the dresses and became a regular advertiser.

Hemda received no congratulations for that success because the profit all went to pay for a subsequent piece of folly. She was in another dress shop and was telling the owner of the success his rival had had. In the second shop she had seen some old-fashioned women's suits which the merchant had imported from Vienna, so she asked:

"Why don't you advertise these?"

"If I did, would it influence you to buy one yourself?"

Hemda could think of nothing to say but "Yes."

The deal which was finally consummated provided that Hemda would buy one of the Viennese suits, paying half in cash, half with an ad.

The advertisement bore no fruit and was the last one the merchant ever took. But Hemda, having paid a goodly sum for "half a suit," had to wear it. It was many sizes too large and looked like an ancient hand-me-down from a prosperous relative with very bad taste.

Up to this time no one had ever bothered about setting up a bookkeeping system for the paper, so Hemda undertook that additional chore.

Then she began to assist Ben Yehuda with work on the dictionary itself. She wrote letters to important personages in Europe, soliciting their support, copied philological material, and even helped search through musty volumes for traces of Hebrew words.

During the second six months of their marriage the bonds which held them together grew strong, and a beautiful companionship developed, despite the great difference in ages.

Eliezer Ben Yehuda, who appeared to the world as a fanatic, had a warm side to his nature too. But Hemda knew better than anyone else his singleness of purpose, how often his mind was occupied solely with academic matters, how primarily the scholar he was.

Hemda never forgot Deborah's story of the time she and her young husband were walking together in the woods. They sat on a log to rest. It was cool and pleasant in the shade of the trees. Deborah felt in a romantic mood, but suddenly she saw a scorpion and, jumping up, shouted in Hebrew:

"Help, Eliezer! A scorpion!"

Ben Yehuda did not come immediately to her rescue. Instead, very reproachfully, as a teacher to an errant pupil, he said:

"Deborah, how many times have I told you that the Hebrew word for 'scorpion' is *akrab* and not *akreb!*"

25

Saul Killed Thousands

ALTHOUGH HEMDA WAS ALMOST FOURTEEN YEARS younger than her husband, it took her a very short time to establish herself as the ruler of the household and the final authority when any important domestic decision was to be made.

Eventually she found a new house for them on the upper Jaffa road, opposite the government hospital and next door to the police station, which the brothers Kukiah agreed to lease to her for ten years. The garden was lined with great acacias and was surrounded by a high wall, giving the privacy Hemda wanted so much.

About this time she began writing a fashion column, much to the disgust of Orthodox Jerusalemites, who contended that this was the extreme in the sacrilegious use of the holy language.

With Eliezer's help she even created a new Hebrew word for what British and American women called "fashion" and the French called *mode*. The word was *ofnah,* derived from the ancient Hebrew word *offen,* meaning style or manner. For many years the women of Jerusalem fought against this word, preferring to say *modah,* because it was more like the word Paris used.

In the Ben Yehuda camp there was one real rebel who, although he had affection for his "mother," was determined not to acquiesce as his father had done. Ben Zion later in life wrote:

"I insisted on showing my new mother that I had ideas of my own and therefore refused to surrender to her will and whims, for I considered myself heir presumptive and determined that my place should not be usurped by anyone else."

Ben Zion was a little older when he became involved in what he called "My First Scandal." He told about it in this manner:

"One day the news reached me that the Great Donor, which was the nickname we had for Baron Rothschild, was planning a second visit to our land. This was enough of a spark to revive in me an idea which had been in my heart and mind for some time, the idea of a Hebrew army.

"I was still then only eleven or twelve years old, but this is what I did:

"I called my young sister Yemeemah, my child-uncle Oniah and my child-aunt Peninnah, who were both younger than I was, and two or three other little friends to a meeting in the full of the moon. This was to be a secret meeting at which I would expose my idea for an army for our people. I realized that for such a project a great deal of money would be needed.

"Oniah, who called himself my uncle, got cold feet and refused to participate. The other children, while in favor of my idea, refused to have their names mentioned, being afraid of their parents. So they appointed me to launch the project by myself in the form of a letter to Baron Edmond de Rothschild, which I agreed to do.

"After much serious deliberation with myself I wrote what I called 'A Letter of Freedom for an Israeli Army' and I read it to the others. A majority of the group agreed to it and the letter was sent off."

Ben Zion addressed the communication like this:

Great Sire, Baron Edmond de Rothschild.
Paris Palace,
Next to the Palace of the President,
Paris, France.

When the boy was asked later where he got such an address he explained that the principal of the school he attended once told the class that Baron Rothschild "lived in a palace in Paris more beautiful than the home of the President of France."

The letter, which the boy wrote in French, read as follows:

> Do not be surprised to receive this communication from your faithful servant.
>
> The current events in some of the colonies of Your Excellency, at which a few farmers have been killed by their own so-called Arab guards, have caused great disturbance and excitement among the Jews of the country.
>
> It is because of this that I, the undersigned, on behalf of my many friends, boys and girls (already a few hundreds), appeal to Your Excellency with this proposition, daring, perhaps, at first sight.
>
> I am ready to undertake the responsibility for the formation of a Hebrew army which will defend the colonies of Your Excellency.
>
> This army, like the French army, will be made of Jews and Arabs, the latter to be named *Légion Etrangère.*
>
> As it is clear to me that such an army requires great funds, I propose to start small. One hundred men will be sufficient for the beginning, eighty Jews and twenty Arabs.
>
> According to my estimate, it will be necessary to have one hundred pounds per month, in addition to the money required for uniforms and armament.
>
> In order that Your Excellency will not suspect us of desiring the whole sum immediately, we shall appreciate it if we receive by the return of the mail the first one hundred napoleons for the purchase of uniforms for the officers.
>
> We have already also started maneuvers. We also have already a flag which is herewith enclosed, along with my picture when I was four years old. The flag was drawn for us by David Idelovitch from Rishon Le Zion, whom I call my uncle. This banner, as Your Excellency sees, is white, like the color of Israel in its white conscience.

Your Excellency will be pleased to hear that I have translated into Hebrew, for the purpose of a marching song, the first verse of the French "Marseillaise," in abbreviation.

In olden times we had Samsons, Maccabees, Bar-kochbas. Why should we not today have "Rothschilds"?

Yes, Rothschilds, for this will be the name of our soldiers. Rothschilds with rifles and many napoleons, for, according to the Hebrew saying, "Money is the answer for everything."

Please, Your Excellency, answer with money and your name will be written in the history of Israel not only as our "Great Donor" but also as "Leader of the Army of Israel."

Saul has killed thousands.

Your Excellency will kill tens of thousands!

I sign, with complete humbleness,

Ben Zion Ben Yehuda,
Colonel of the Hebrew Army.

"Days, weeks, months passed without a reply from Paris. Then one day my father's friend, David Idelovitch, whom I called uncle, arrived from Rishon Le Zion, together with the secretary of Baron Rothschild, to see my parents, and said that the baron was shocked at the receipt of the letter, saying that this was the biggest scandal in the history of our land and that he therefore decided not to carry through his visit to Palestine as he had planned.

"The baron said that if the son of Ben Yehuda, his great and devoted friend, could write such 'stupid things' in order to get funds, he felt obliged to withdraw his interest in various undertakings in our country, and of course withdraw his support of my father's newspaper.

"Needless to say, both my parents were shocked and dumfounded. An investigation was made and the perpetrator was found to be myself. I was brought before my parent and I acknowledged my guilt, but then I quickly added:

" 'But I do not retract!'

"There was then a big uproar which was quieted down by the intervention of my 'uncle' from Rishon Le Zion. He influenced the secretary to the baron and persuaded him to forget it and consider it a dead thing, which the latter promised to do."

Despite the necessity of regulating the impetuosity of young Ben Zion, this period of Eliezer Ben Yehuda's life was probably the least troublous he had ever known.

Hemda faithfully kept her promise to follow in her sister's footsteps. There was just one exception. If there were a shortage of food, which there often was, she divided what they had in exactly equal portions. She refused to "starve" herself, as Deborah had so often done.

Despite Ben Zion's prank, the Ben Yehudas continued to receive a subsidy of ten napoleons per month from Baron Rothschild. The newspaper brought in a profit of one or two napoleons a week. In addition there were occasional "windfalls," like the one thousand rubles Eliezer received from a Russian publisher for a small dictionary, the sums paid for articles from the *Deer* reprinted in other publications, and the fee received for Ben Yehuda's translation into Hebrew of Jules Verne's *Around the World in Eighty Days.*

One minor problem which developed in these days was a family conflict over Hemda's insistence on regular baths for the children. There was no bathroom, no bathtub, no hot water, all of which made bathing a rather complicated procedure. The naked child would stand in a large copper basin in the middle of the room, would soap himself, and then would be given a cold shower by Hemda from a pitcher. Ben Zion led in the rejoicing when Arabs one night stole the copper basin. But Hemda somehow managed to save money for another.

In this period Eliezer was spending much time searching through Spanish, Italian, and Egytian literature for "lost" Hebrew words and would often come from his study with a book in his hand and read the family a passage he considered especially beautiful. Hemda required the children to memorize many of these selections.

But the tranquillity of the home was shattered by what Ben Zion later called his "Second Scandal." As he told it:

"I came back from a visit in the colonies one day full of excitement at what I had seen, and a new idea was born in my mind:

a newspaper for the children of Jerusalem and the settlements.

"One day as I was walking through the Old City I stopped as usual at the stationery store of Mr. Hagis, who was holding in his hand a stenciled copy of a poem, and thereafter he showed me the little machine on which he could produce many more copies. He said it cost only one medjidie [a Turkish coin worth less than an American dollar].

"At this point my dream came back to me, a Hebrew children's paper with me as the editor. But here I was stuck. I did not have the great sum of one medjidie to buy the machine, and of course the whole thing had to be done in secret because I wished it to be a bombshell to the public.

"Now I approached the oldest of my intimate acquaintances, Baruch Homah, who was known in our school for his beautiful handwriting, in Hebrew, French, and Arabic. He said that for the remuneration of one quarter of a medjidie he was willing to write up the whole paper in special ink for the stencil. But I still had no money.

"Thereupon I went to see the writer Yavetz, whose eldest son agreed to write literary articles for the children. The rest of the editing I took upon myself.

"The contents for the paper were soon ready for the first issue. The following were the contents:

"a. To the Young Readers.

"b. The Duty of Hebrew Children in Our Land.

"c. Hebrew Only, or French and Turkish Also?

"d. The Boundaries of Our Land Before Our Fathers Abraham and Moses.

"e. Through the Land of Israel in Eight Days.

"f. Children's Plays.

"g. The Children's Press in France.

"h. Jokes for Children and Charades.

"Having everything ready, I went to our great friend, Nissim Behar, who was about to leave the country, and to Mr. Calmi, also a dear friend of the family, and told them my proposition. Mr. Nissim Behar gave me immediately five French francs, and Mr. Calmi one half a medjidie.

"Happy with my success, I ran to Baruch Homah, the boy with the beautiful script, and gave him the half medjidie, and then to the stationery shop and bought from Mr. Hagis the hectograph or duplicating machine, to which he added five hundred sheets of paper.

"A week later our paper appeared on the market. We sold fifty-seven copies and sent twenty to my uncle David in Rishon Le Zion, five to Rehovoth, and a few to Jaffa to Mr. Krugliakov, who refused to accept them.

"The bombshell was enormous and the copies were handed from one to another.

"When I told Mr. Hagis, the stationer, of our success he said:

" 'You will be a great man one day, son!'

"When I got home, however, full of the glory, my father met me with scorn, not because of the whole enterprise but because of the article, 'The Boundaries of Our Land Before Our Fathers Abraham and Moses.' He reminded me that after the first scandal I promised that I would never mention a Hebrew army or anything connected with it again, and yet in this article I declared that we must fight for the ancient boundaries.

"Well, there was a feeling of panic in our circles. Yavetz reprimanded his son. Baruch Homah's father made his son stop his participation.

"Luckily a sensational event took place in Jerusalem at this time which drowned the importance of my paper and the article. A Russian Jewish merchant by the name of Goldberg, seventy years old, and his wife, fifty-five, were shot dead by a Turkish policeman.

"This aroused great excitement all around and caused complications in the Russian and Turkish diplomatic corps.

"I took advantage of this turmoil and threw away the duplicating machine in the only pool in Jerusalem."

26

Behind Bars

IN THE DYING YEARS OF THE NINETEENTH CENTURY Palestine was populated by only a few tens of thousands of Jews spread thinly across the land. Yet there was little unity among them.

The relationship between Ben Yehuda and Jehiel Michael Pines was typical of the times.

The lexicographer-editor was actually a great admirer of the man who represented the Jews who had emigrated from Great Britain. It was Pines who, when Ben Yehuda first came to Palestine, helped him form the Hebrew-Speaking Group. Yet it was Pines who had terrified Deborah, telling her that her first-born child would grow up to be an idiot because the father insisted it speak only Hebrew.

It had been a strange relationship. Now Pines was involved in a new controversy.

There was a Russian-Jewish group called *Bney Mosheh,* which sponsored some of the Hebrew schools in Palestine. Its leader was a Russian intellectual who had changed his name from Ginzberg to Ahad Haam, meaning "One of the People." Ahad Haam was a Ben Yehuda ally in that he proselytized for spoken Hebrew, but he was an enemy in that he was against the colonization of Palestine, contending that Jews were inadequately equipped, intellectually and spiritually, for a pioneer life. He favored concentrating exclusively on improving the culture of Jews here and abroad. Pines and Ahad Haam had had a feud, and Pines had been read out of the group by its leader. The controversy came to a climax at a meeting in Jaffa which Ben Yehuda attended.

Many vitriolic speeches were made, leading to an outburst by Pines himself in which he vowed that he would "fight to the last breath" against the Bney Mosheh.

Ben Yehuda warned Pines that by his stand he was endangering all that both of them had been working for; that if he persisted he would destroy the entire Hebrew movement.

"Then let it be destroyed!" Pines shouted.

This remark so angered Ben Yehuda that he retorted:

"Then I shall destroy you first!"

When Ben Yehuda reached home after the meeting he went immediately to bed with bloody coughing spells. For days he was in a serious physical and emotional condition. He already deeply regretted his outburst of temper against a man for whom he had such deep personal affection. Talking about it to Hemda, he said:

"Maybe I was wrong, Bitti, yet this is a war we are fighting, and I suppose in a war a good soldier must fire at his adversary, even if that adversary be his own brother!"

Hemda tried to nurse him back to health, but she had her own problems at this time.

She and Ben Yehuda had been married for more than a year, and already the gossips of Jerusalem were raising their eyebrows and questioning the fact that the child bride had not yet conceived.

She and Eliezer had talked about it months ago. She had subtly mentioned the fate of Deborah's three children and her husband's lung disease. She had told him of her horror at the infant and maternity mortality rate in Jerusalem and the prevalence of malaria, dysentery, and "that terrible eye disease."

Eliezer each time expressed his understanding of her hesitation. Yet she felt that he hoped she would bear him a child.

So when Hemda finally felt new life stirring within her, she quickly confided the secret to her husband, who took her hand and softly said:

"Bitti, I am very glad!"

But that same evening she extracted a promise from him. It must remain a secret. She would hide it from everyone, even from her mother and his, for as long as possible. This would be her small way of annoying the gossips of Jerusalem.

So Hemda continued to preside at her Friday-evening soirees, to write for the *Deer,* to attend receptions, and to travel to the colonies, cloaking her secret by an ingenious use of the dressmaker's art.

The second Mrs. Ben Yehuda was almost twenty-two years old when she bore her first child, which was the sixth child of Eliezer, who was thirty-five.

Mrs. Yonas announced the birth in these words to the father:

"A perfect little girl! Five fingers on each small hand and five toes to each small foot. Bright open eyes and a sweet, tiny mouth. You should be happy and proud, Eliezer!"

To perpetuate the memory of the first Mrs. Ben Yehuda, the child was named after her, and the following announcement appeared in the next issue of the *Deer:*

"A daughter has been born to Eliezer and Hemda Ben Yehuda, and her name is Deborah."

Congratulations poured in from Jaffa and the settlements, but with them came some loud complaints. The announcement in the paper said a name had already been given. What did the Ben Yehudas mean by such defiance of religious convention? Were they not good enough Jews to know that a name is given only after prayers have been said in the synagogue?

Eliezer Ben Yehuda was so excited over the birth of Deborah II and so eager to remain in constant attendance upon mother and child that he persuaded Father Yonas to take over temporarily the management of the newspaper.

Father Yonas, the rebellious freethinker, had undergone something of a conversion during the brief time he had been in Palestine. Gradually he became less and less the rebel he had been most of his life. He warned the Ben Yehudas that they were making a great mistake in not bringing up the children in the strict ways of religious orthodoxy.

The elderly distiller from Glubokiah took pride in the issue of the *Deer* which he had the privilege of editing. It was a special issue for *Hanukkah,* the eight-day candlelight festival which commemorates the victory of the Maccabees and the rededication of the Temple and is celebrated by putting one candle in the window the first night and adding one more each subsequent evening, through the eighth.

Father Yonas was especially proud of the leading article he wrote entitled "Good Deeds Require a Purpose," which praised the courage of the Maccabees and exhorted present-day Jews to follow in the footsteps of their illustrious ancestors. Like the Maccabees, the article said, "we must collect our forces and move forward."

Palestinian editors in those days had to be very careful of what they wrote. Under Sultan Abdul Hamid II, the Ottoman officials were severe in their censorship. Jewish editors could comment on Jewish affairs and their own internal politics, but that was about all. They were not allowed to discuss, let alone criticize, the Ottoman Empire. If Ben Yehuda ever wished to publish even news items about world affairs, he had to be sure they were carefully phrased, with the import half concealed.

Yet as Eliezer read over the special issue of the *Deer* he could see nothing wrong with anything his father-in-law had written. That was why what happened surprised and shocked him.

On Friday afternoon, the fourth day after the birth of Deborah, and only a few hours after the Hanukkah issue of the *Deer* appeared, the walls of buildings along Jerusalem's Jaffa Street were suddenly plastered with placards signed by officers of the Central Administration of the Halukkah, by the Hacham Bashi of Jerusalem, and by the chief Ashkenazic rabbi.

The placards denounced Ben Yehuda for using his paper to try to stir up armed revolt against the Turks, a scheme with which the signers hereby completely dissociated themselves.

As proof of the accusation, the placards quoted the single phrase from the Yonas article, "Let us collect our forces and move forward." This, of course, meant military forces, they said.

All day Saturday, Jerusalem, which thrived on controversy, buzzed with excitement. Some said:

"Obviously Ben Yehuda is proving too much of an annoyance for the old generation. They finally realize that he represents a new element which has entered the country and will not be put in its place and is changing the very foundations of Jewish life here. Therefore, they are out to get him!"

The opposition, however, charged that Ben Yehuda had been "poking his nose into everything"; that every week his paper made some new attack on Jews; that he had tried to interfere in the election of the Hacham Bashi; that he had printed exposés about the distribution of charitable contributions from abroad; that he had criticized the way Jewish religious institutions were run; that he had made public a list of rabbis and scholars who had been receiving free medical service from charitable funds.

Jerusalem, they argued, must be freed of this man's evil influence by any means possible. The placards were right!

Ben Yehuda himself dismissed the entire affair with one word, "Ridiculous!" and went on about his business.

But on Sunday morning a policemen in Turkish uniform appeared at the Ben Yehuda home and said Eliezer must accompany him.

After getting his hat and coat, the editor stopped at his wife's bedroom and called to her:

"I shall be back soon. I am just going to the censor's office!"

After he was gone Hemda's instincts told her that something was wrong. It was the first time since their marriage he had ever left the house without kissing her good-by.

Hours went by. Still Eliezer did not return. Late in the day Hemda became anxious and sent someone to bring Nissim Behar to her. The messenger returned saying Mr. Behar was with Mr. Ben Yehuda.

Finally, early in the evening, Mr. Behar appeared.

The process of interrogation had been long and protracted, and it had not yet been concluded.

"However, do not worry. Your husband will surely be home in the morning."

Hemda, finally realizing that Eliezer had been imprisoned, burst into tears.

At midnight a man wearing long earlocks and a dark coat arrived with what he said was a message from Mr. Ben Yehuda. He must deliver it to no one but the wife.

Speaking in a whisper, he identified himself as Alter Kossover. He ran a store at the prison where the watchmen bought their groceries. Therefore, he had certain privileges. When he had heard that Ben Yehuda, whom he greatly respected, had been imprisoned, he persuaded a guard to let him visit the prisoner. When he asked Ben Yehuda if there was anything he could do for him, the editor had said:

"Yes, go at once to my home and tell my wife it would be wise if she cleaned up the house because she might be having some unexpected guests soon."

As the man talked Hemda studied his face and finally decided he was a trustworthy character. Yet she had a fear that this might be some sort of trap. What did Eliezer mean about cleaning up the house? And guests? He knew she was bedridden, and so . . .

But then she suddenly realized what he was trying to tell her, so she quickly replied to the messenger:

"Say to Ben Yehuda that I understand and shall clean up the house at once!"

As soon as the prison shopkeeper had gone she went to the study and collected all the documents and letters which might in any way compromise her husband with Turkish authorities. She made a package of these papers and had them delivered to a neighbor.

The morning after the imprisonment another messenger arrived with a note from Ben Yehuda. It read:

"I am in prison, but many friends are working to get me out. Do not worry. Take care of yourself."

Hemda, however, had no faith in Ottoman bureaucracy. She considered the Turkish officials more unpredictable, more evil than even those of the czarist regime. In her wild imagination she decided that even now Eliezer might be on his way to an execution chamber in Constantinople. So she announced she was going to the prison in person and began dressing.

David Yellin, the young Hebrew instructor, accompanied her. As they walked through the Old City businessmen stood in their doorways to stare at her, and a crowd gathered. As they walked Hemda said to Yellin:

"It is all so quiet. It is almost as if the angels of death were hovering around us already!"

When they arrived at the prison gates the watchman said they were too late; it was after sunset; the prison was closed; they could not possibly be admitted until midnight, when the director would arrive for his nightly inspection.

"Have some pity on this poor woman!" Yellin pleaded, at the same time surreptitiously handing the guard some coins.

The guard said, "Wait a minute!" and disappeared. When he returned Ben Yehuda was with him. The husband and wife talked from opposite sides of the iron gate. Hemda thought Eliezer looked very pale and terrified. They had exchanged only a few words when the watchman said he would now have to take Ben Yehuda away; this was strictly against the rules.

Nissim Behar was waiting for Hemda when she returned home. Her first request was that he send a report at once to Baron Rothschild in Paris. Maybe he would help.

By this time it had become clear that the arrest had been made after the Orthodox leaders had taken a translation of the Yonas article to the Turkish officials, along with their own statement disavowing responsibility for the "diabolical" suggestion advanced by the paper. The arrest itself had been ordered by Sultan Abdul Hamid II, who had previously issued the decrees forbidding Jewish immigration into Palestine.

Nissim Behar was the leader of the fight for Ben Yehuda's liberation. He worked day and night without rest, hardly taking time for meals. He went to the Turkish governor of Jerusalem and tried to explain that the accusation was merely a vengeful act of old enemies. But the governor, obviously afraid of his own superiors in Constantinople, replied:

"You had better have nothing to do with this man or his affairs, else you might find yourself in a cell with him."

"I am ready to go whenever you decide to send me!" Behar replied, and stalked off.

It was Nissim Behar who sent a long cable to Zadok Kahn, Chief Rabbi of France, imploring him to take the case up with Baron Rothschild. Behar knew that the baron's representative in Rishon Le Zion had already cabled Paris that the Rothschild standing in Palestine would suffer greatly if the baron intervened in the case.

It was Nissim Behar who appealed to Ben Yehuda's friends throughout Palestine to contribute what they could to a fund. He explained that it would cost one thousand gold francs per day to bribe the prison officials, from the director down to the doorkeeper, in order to obtain permission for Ben Yehuda's acquaintances to visit him, which was essential so they could hold consultations about what he was to say at his own trial.

The money was raised quickly. Behar's own daughter, Henrietta, pawned the jewelry left to her by her mother and gave the proceeds to the fund.

Hundreds of people came daily to the prison. A Jewish businessman and his Arab partner opened a special café outside the gates so Ben Yehuda's visitors could get coffee and other refreshment.

Telegrams by the hundreds came from all parts of Europe.

Numerous progressive Arabs, among them many high officials, risked the ire of the Turkish government by openly lining up on Ben Yehuda's side.

Many offers of help came from Christians, some of them diplomats, some Catholic priests. One group of Freemasons sent a resolution of protest against the "crime" of the imprisonment.

The most encouraging repercussion was that Ben Yehuda's arrest finally brought about some degree of solidarity among those Jews who were not actually in the camp of the opposition.

Even Pines, with whom Ben Yehuda had so recently had such a violent feud, came to Hemda with an offer to do anything he could. He was in such a state of indignation over the arrest that at times he actually wept with anger.

It was well known that Father Yonas was the author of the article which had started all the trouble. But he was still a Russian subject, whereas Ben Yehuda had become a Turkish citizen and also was listed on the masthead of the paper as the "responsible editor." Furthermore, it was Ben Yehuda they were after.

For eight days the emaciated, consumptive editor was kept behind bars. At first he was put in a cell already occupied by fifteen assassins, a cell so small and crowded that he had to remain standing all night, his face thrust against the small opening at the top of the door in order to get air to breathe.

The next day the prison doctor, influenced by a sizable bribe paid to him by Nissim Behar, decided that Ben Yehuda's tubercular condition endangered the lives of the fifteen condemned murderers and ordered him put in a cell by himself.

Hemda and Nissim Behar arranged to have a painter whitewash the walls of the new cell to rid them of insects. They also sent Ben Yehuda a straw rug, a bed, a mattress, a chair, and a worktable, as well as bed linen, a lamp, books, ink, paper, and a small oilstove on which to make tea.

In her excitement Hemda mislaid the grating for the stove and as a substitute sent two large oriental keys to hold up the teapot.

Hemda wanted to take Eliezer's two oldest children to the prison to see him, but Ben Zion was visiting the Yonases, who some time ago had taken quarters of their own, so Hemda was able to take only Yemeemah.

They arrived at the hour of the midday meal. As they entered the prison they saw the other inmates wash their feet and then join in a prayer for their own delivery, to which they added a postscript to the Almighty "for the man with the little beard."

Hemda, describing the visit later, said:

"The courtyard looked like a melting pot of East and West."

On the way home Hemda and her stepdaughter came upon a scene which shocked them. In a narrow street they saw Ben Zion, then only eleven, surrounded by a crowd of older boys, most of them students in the Yeshiva, who danced around the child, pointing their fingers and shouting in Hebrew so he would surely understand (because he still spoke no other language):

"Your father is in prison. Your father is getting what he deserves. Your father, the Heretic, is in jail. Your father is behind bars with murderers where he belongs."

When Ben Zion saw his stepmother he ran to her with tears streaming down his face.

Later in the evening, after he had grown calm, he suddenly said to Hemda:

"One thing Father will be happy about, anyway. Every word they shouted at me was in Hebrew. In his language!"

On the third day the prison director called at Ben Yehuda's cell to pay an official visit. The two got along amazingly well, for the director was interested in astronomy, and Ben Yehuda could converse intelligently on the subject because he had studied it at the university. They were in friendly astronomical conversation when the director suddenly looked down and saw the two oriental keys beside the teapot on Ben Yehuda's table.

The warden examined the keys carefully. By an odd coincidence they were almost exactly the size and shape of the keys to the prison gate. That ended a happy friendship between two astronomy enthusiasts.

The next morning Hemda was allowed to have breakfast with her husband in the prison courtyard, at the cost of another bribe. This time the other prisoners included her in their prayers. On each succeeding visit Hemda found Eliezer more calm. He even grew philosophical.

"It does not matter," he told his wife, "what they do to me. If they condemn me to stay in prison for a long time, at least I shall be able to work on my dictionary here."

27

On Bail

ON THE EIGHTH DAY AFTER THE ARREST THERE appeared at the cell of Eliezer Ben Yehuda two guards who announced that they had come to take him to the Palace of Justice to stand trial for treason.

One of them carried a pair of handcuffs.

Passively the young editor held out his hands so they could be fastened together with the links of steel. But at this moment something caused the guard to drop the handcuffs to the floor. The other guard, his superior, cursed and said:

"Idiot! Surely you know that now we must take him without his hands bound together, for it is written that if the circles of iron drop to the ground they must not be used again."

Thus Eliezer Ben Yehuda walked through the doors of the Palace of Justice for his own trial with his hands hanging free.

Outside the building a great crowd was gathered. It was about equally divided between those who shouted the Hebrew equivalent of "Hurrah for Ben Yehuda!" and those who cried in a babel of Yiddish, Ladino, Russian, German, French, and other languages, "Condemn the heretic!"

It was worthy of note that Ben Yehuda's supporters were mostly young people, while his opponents were nearly all of the older generation.

The prisoner's defense counsel was a Dominican monk, Father LaGrange, Ben Yehuda's close friend, who had always been eager to have Eliezer enter the monastery.

The judges were a Sephardic Jew and two Arabs.

The entire case was prejudiced just before the trial began by the arrival in Jerusalem from Constantinople of a cable signed by the religious leader of the entire Jewish community of Turkey proclaiming against Ben Yehuda a ban or *herem,* as grave a punishment as excommunication of a Catholic by a decree from Rome.

Following Jewish religious procedure, the ceremony of the herem was carried out in the principal synagogue of Jerusalem, with the blowing of the shofar and the burning of black candles. Throughout the rest of Palestine the fact was widely advertised that henceforth and forever this man who had defied the ecclesiastical authorities was an unclean and evil person, beyond the realm of salvation.

According to custom, no one but members of the immediate family could have anything to do with a person placed under such a ban. It therefore amounted to a virtual business and professional boycott. Among Orthodox Jews it was the most feared of all punishments.

It later developed that the excommunication had been arranged by the rabbis of Jerusalem, who had argued with their spiritual leader that if he failed to take such action it would be a virtual announcement to the world that he and they favored the proposed overthrow by force of the Ottoman Empire.

So when the case of the Ottoman Empire vs. Eliezer Ben Yehuda came to trial it was already an established fact that his own people, the Jews, had officially, through proper ecclesiastical channels, issued their own condemnation of him.

Father LaGrange presented to the court a translation into Arabic of the disputed editorial, arguing that it contained nothing at all rebellious.

The prosecutor retorted:

"The Jewish rabbis are better able to judge than you!"

The one pregnant phrase, "Let us collect our forces and move forward," contained an old Hebrew expression, *laassot hayil,* which figuratively means "to progress, to go ahead," but literally can be translated, "to form an army."

Mr. Yonas had used it in its purely metaphorical sense, but that was not easy to prove in a court of law.

The judges were in a difficult predicament. The Jew was afraid to compromise himself and therefore held out for a verdict of guilty.

The two Arabs had been bribed by both sides and were therefore in a quandary.

Finally the bench handed down its verdict. It took a "happy" middle course. The opinion was expressed that Eliezer Ben Yehuda was not a dangerous rebel. On the other hand, said the opinion, it was clear that he was a troublemaker who should be punished. Therefore, he was hereby sentenced to one year in prison.

The newspaper, the verdict said, was certainly the cause of all the trouble, and so it was hereby suspended indefinitely.

The judges then ruled that Ben Yehuda could take an appeal to a higher court if he wished, meanwhile going free on bail, if such bail were provided on the spot. Otherwise he would go back to prison and lose his chance for temporary freedom, even if a satisfactory bond were to be forthcoming later.

The court set bail at three hundred Turkish pounds (about fifteen hundred dollars).

Nissim Behar jumped up and offered to sign the required bond, but his offer was rejected because he was not a property owner.

After an audible gasp of disappointment from Ben Yehuda's friends the guards started to take the prisoner back to his cell.

At this dramatic moment a Sephardic Jew, Shlomoh Amiel, who had emigrated from Morocco years ago and now was a wealthy Palestinian landowner, stepped forward and agreed to put his signature to a bond, which was accepted.

Flanked by his two most loyal friends, Nissim Behar and David Yellin, Ben Yehuda walked from the building a temporarily free man.

The crowd, assuming that he had been found innocent, broke into an uproar, the cheers interspersed with almost equally vehement shouts of disapproval.

Jerusalem that winter was plagued by heavy rains, fierce storms, great winds, and bitter cold weather.

It was a gloomy winter for everyone, most of all for the newspaper editor without a newspaper.

Eliezer Ben Yehuda, by the terms of the bond under which he had been liberated, was not allowed to leave the country or to move about freely. Even when he walked in the darkness of Jerusalem's narrow, twisting streets he had the feeling that he was being watched and followed. Most of the time he was a prisoner within his own four walls, although he did occasionally spend long hours in Nissim Behar's home, planning the appeal.

In these months both sides were preparing for the new trial, which was to take place in the Syrian city of Beirut.

The prosecution sought to postpone the rehearing of the case to as late a date as possible, for as long as the lower court's sentence hung over the editor's head he was under a stigma and could be controlled. Also, the case could remain a continuing source of revenue to officials who were not above subtly suggesting the payment of more bribes when they were not voluntarily forthcoming.

Ben Yehuda's advisers naturally wished to have the trial as soon as possible, because the editor was without a voice as long as his paper was banned.

Nissim Behar wrote to prominent Jews the world over for their moral and financial assistance.

The opposition followed his example, so a battle of letters ensued.

Both sides knew that the trump card in this game of strategy was held by Baron Rothschild; that whichever side he supported would have victory within its grasp. So the French millionaire was deluged with cables and letters.

For a long time there was complete silence from Paris. Then finally the Orthodox rabbis received one of the most succinct cables on record. It read merely:

EXERCEZ VOS PRIÈRES. BARON ROTHSCHILD.

It took no great astuteness to realize that behind this admonition to "look to your prayers" was the implication that they were outside their proper sphere when they interfered in political and judicial matters.

It was undoubtedly this cable which prompted them to try to back out of the case in as face-saving a manner as possible to avoid the wrath of their benefactor.

Accordingly a message was sent to Ben Yehuda that the Hacham Bashi wished to see him.

With understandable pride the editor refused to present himself.

One day Nissim Behar invited Hemda and Eliezer to his home for tea. When they arrived they found a large assemblage of guests, and from the expressions on the faces realized that this was no ordinary social affair.

After their host had greeted them he waved his hand toward a black curtain which hung over a doorway, and through the curtain came the splendid figure of the Hacham Bashi, Rabbi Jacob Saul Elyashar, with his hands outstretched.

As he approached Ben Yehuda he said in Hebrew:

"*Ahenu atah* [You are our brother]!"

Quickly Ben Yehuda was surrounded by excited well-wishers who knew that these are the words by which a herem or excommunication is formally and officially lifted.

Turning to his host, Ben Yehuda indignantly said:

"Why did you do this without my consent?"

Nissim Behar smiled.

"My friend, it is done!"

Ben Yehuda returned to his home that day full of annoyance and refused even to discuss what had happened.

It was Hemda who passed the news on to other members of the family that Eliezer was no longer technically an infidel.

The happiest of all was Feygaleh Perlman, the most Orthodox member of the household. It had grieved her that her own son, instead of becoming a conventional rabbi as she had always dreamed he would, had ended up being declared a heretic.

Ben Zion also understood what it all meant. In a burst of feeling he said:

"Now they will no longer be able to dance around me, and call me names, and shout that my father is a bad man!"

Little Yemeemah thought it meant that her father would never again be sent to a horrible place like the prison in which she had visited him, so she clapped her hands and joined in the celebration.

Later Nissim Behar arrived and convinced Ben Yehuda that he had not "lost face"; that he had actually won an important victory; that the lifting of the excommunication would help raise his stature throughout Palestine, would bring new unity in the Jewish community, and, most important of all, would pave the way for an acquittal at Beirut.

"Even if Baron Rothschild uses his influence on the judges," Behar explained, "and of course I still hope that he will, it is necessary that the high court have some excuse for an acquittal. Now the excuse has been provided, for by lifting the ban the rabbis have officially retracted their charge and have as much as admitted that they were wrong."

In the weeks which followed, Ben Yehuda devoted all his time to his dictionary, working eighteen or nineteen hours a day in his study, most of the time standing, for he preferred to work at a high desk such as bookkeepers use. He contended that he could think better standing up.

Because the winter of that year was so frigid and because the Ben Yehudas had no money for fuel, it was necessary for Eliezer to work bundled up in as many garments as he could drape on his frail body.

One day Nissim Behar arrived wearing a broad grin which heralded the good news he bore.

"The baron," he announced, "has finally thrown his full support to our side!"

Then he explained that a message had just been received by the Rothschild representative:

ACQUITTEZ BEN YEHUDA COÛTE QUE COÛTE.

That was a nice French idiom, *coûte que coûte:* "regardless of cost"!

With the message had come a check for ten thousand francs.

The defense spent three thousand francs hiring a good lawyer. Five thousand more went to bribing the prosecutor. The remainder was used for miscellaneous expenses, which of course included some minor bribes.

The appeal was heard eight months after the original trial.

Nissim Behar was unable to leave his school and Hemda was unable to leave her infant child, so Ben Yehuda went to Beirut alone.

Friend and wife waited impatiently for news of the verdict. Finally it came in a cable from Eliezer which contained just one Hebrew word:

ZAKKAY [INNOCENT].

When the exonerated editor returned home, however, he announced a detail of the decision which kept the family happiness from being complete.

The court had ruled that the ban on the *Deer* must remain in effect for a full year in all, which meant another four months of voicelessness for Eliezer Ben Yehuda.

The partial victory was hailed in the press around the world as a triumph over bigotry and persecution.

28

Words Everywhere

ALTHOUGH BEN YEHUDA WAS GLAD TO HAVE THE additional four months in which he could work without interruption on his "words," it was apparent to everyone that he was as unhappy without his paper as a professional orator or singer without the use of voice.

As the twelve months drew to a close he began counting the days. Finally, on the anniversary of the original trial, he presented himself at the office of the governor of Jerusalem and applied for the return of the *Deer's* license.

The stubborn old governor said he did not feel bound by the order of the court in Beirut. The paper would remain under the ban for a full twelve months more. If by then nothing else had happened, permission to republish might be forthcoming.

Ben Yehuda was disconsolate. He poured out his bitterness to Hemda. She tried to comfort him, saying:

"Eliezer, my dear, I am sure this is Providence's way of forcing you to concentrate on the really important task. You were happy for months working on your dictionary. Now you can continue to concentrate on it. You know that is really your lifework!"

So Ben Yehuda went back to his study and his words. For years he had been covering small pieces of paper with notations in his fine, aesthetic handwriting. The room was full of them. They overflowed from his desk and the tables onto the floor.

Whoever cleaned the room had specific instructions that no scrap of paper, however small and unimportant-looking, was ever to be thrown away or even touched.

Hemda knew that on the back of an envelope there might be notes for a word which someday would be used by millions of Jews to designate an object or idea for which no Hebrew word had previously existed. Or on such a scrap of paper there might be a few words of etymology which Ben Yehuda had spent weeks searching for in some distant library.

Hemda never forgot the day her husband "lost a word." He came to her with the expression of a child whose favorite little sailboat has just been carried out of sight by a malicious wind.

"Bitti," he said in a grieved voice, holding up a piece of paper not much larger than a postage stamp, "have you seen one of my notes about this size? I have hunted for hours and hours and cannot find it!"

Hemda shook her head. Finally she said:

"Eliezer, what was on the piece of paper?"

"It was a word, Hemda. A new Hebrew word. A very important word which we need very much. I do not know what I shall do if I fail to find it! It would take months and months of work, searching through books here and abroad, to trace that word again. It was a word which disappeared from usage long ago. I was just about to bring it back to life again when—— Where do you suppose that piece of paper went to, Hemda?"

Eventually the "lost word" was found in the cuff of Eliezer's trouser leg, but Hemda knew that this would happen over and over again until the dictionary was finally completed.

The Ben Yehuda family lived on words those days, and little else but words, for the financial situation was acute again. They had dark bread and words for breakfast. They had bread and words and olive oil for the midday meal. They had bread and words and maybe a little something else for the meal at the end of the day.

About this time the Ben Yehudas were paid a visit by an English scholar, Professor Solomon Schechter, who later was to become president of the Jewish Theological Seminary of America. He expressed great admiration for the work Ben Yehuda was doing and before he left made a suggestion which, although childishly simple, revolutionized the lexicographer's work. He advised Ben Yehuda to inaugurate a filing system; to put his notes on small cards and arrange them systematically.

This suggestion enabled Ben Yehuda to classify his material and make much speedier progress in his work.

Two young theological students, Rafalowitch and Hirschenson, were hired at ten francs apiece per month to work half of each day copying Ben Yehuda's notes in alphabetical order.

Few people in Jerusalem understood Ben Yehuda. Very few understood what he was doing eighteen or nineteen hours a day poring over so many books. But everyone knew about the books. They knew that this thin, consumptive man consumed books voraciously. So they came in a constant stream to the Ben Yehuda home laden with books.

Some came to sell their books. Others wanted to rent them at a small weekly fee. The more generous brought them as free-will offerings and presented them as gifts.

There was hardly a book they brought, no matter in what language, that Ben Yehuda did not at least skim through. He had an elaborate system of marking passages with pencils of various colors. Sometimes, however, if he happened to have a pen in his hand, in his absent-mindedness he would make marginal notes in ink, to the eventual distress of the owner of the volume.

The mountains of books that were stacked everywhere in the Ben Yehuda home bothered Hemda, who was instinctively a neat housekeeper.

The books which the people of Jerusalem brought were often anything but clean. Often worms crawled out from the bundles, or cockroaches. Sometimes moths flew out. Once she even saw a small mouse chew its way out of a package of books someone had left in the entrance hall.

It was the mouse which prompted Hemda to say at dinner one night, trying to frighten her husband into action:

"Eliezer, I am afraid these bugs and animals will breed and multiply in your study and that eventually they will eat up all your lovely Hebrew words!"

To which the husband, in an oratorical voice, replied:

"A living Hebrew word, Bitti, is stronger than any bug or insect or animal! It will fight for its life and will survive all its enemies!"

In these days there arrived in Jerusalem from Paris a representative of Baron Rothschild, who called on the Ben Yehudas and after the usual formalities said he had something interesting to show them. Out of his suitcase he produced an album of fine leather containing ten attractive pictures.

"I have the intention," he announced, "of paying a visit to the Turkish governor of your city and making him a gift of this volume with the compliments of the baron."

"I am sure he will appreciate it," Ben Yehuda said with only a mild show of interest.

But the visitor went on, with his eyes sparkling:

"We have a hope that he will be so pleased with the gift that he will make certain concessions to us."

The visitor now had the expression of a small boy in possession of a secret no one else knows and who can hardly wait to reveal it to someone. Turning to Hemda, he said:

"Do you not notice that each picture is fastened in the book quite loosely and that there is something peeking out from underneath each one?"

Hemda had not noticed. But now she looked more carefully and found that under each picture there was a one-thousand-franc-bank note, with a corner of each just barely showing.

"I think," said the baron's representative, "that our friend, the old pasha, will like the album very much. Then we shall see what concessions the old rascal will give us."

The Ben Yehudas sent the man off with their good wishes and then waited impatiently for him to return with a report.

He was gone for hours. When he came back he had a self-satisfied smile on his face.

Eliezer had difficulty remaining patient.

"Tell us quickly what concessions if any you obtained!"

"He agreed that the ban will be lifted on the right of Jews to construct new houses."

Eliezer jumped to his feet.

"That is a great victory! That will end one of the worst handicaps our people have had in the colonization of the land! You are to be greatly——"

Hemda, however, interrupted:

"Did you by any good fortune obtain any other concession?"

The man from Paris smiled.

"Yes. It was a very fruitful meeting. The old pasha also agreed to mitigate the ban against the immigration of Jews into Palestine. From now on we shall not have to smuggle our people into the country disguised as sacks of potatoes!"

"That is the way my own mother had to enter Palestine," Ben Yehuda said wistfully.

"Yes," said Hemda, "but I had hoped that maybe . . ."

The man from Paris seemed to be enjoying the little game he was playing. Now he stood up in order to make his next announcement as impressive as possible.

"Your hopes, Mrs. Ben Yehuda, were well founded. The pasha also gave his permission for a weekly newspaper known as the *Deer* to be published again, starting at once!"

In the months that followed, Ben Yehuda temporarily abandoned work on his dictionary and devoted all his energy to reviving his "favorite child" which had, for nearly a year and a half, been sleeping. Soon its voice was stronger than ever and began to be heard not only in Palestine but even beyond the borders of the country.

The interest shown in the revival of the *Deer* indicated how much it had been missed. Young aspiring journalists in the settlements began voluntarily to send in news reports.

It was Hemda who was responsible for a journalistic fraud which greatly enlivened the paper. She had resumed her column, "Letter from Jerusalem." Now she suggested:

"Why should I not also write letters from Vienna, Paris, Moscow, Berlin?"

"But, Bitti, where would you get your material? We cannot afford to send you to all those cities!"

"If I read all that the papers from those places say about art, books, politics, music, and everything else, I could get all the information I need, then if some of our friends could send us occasional short cables they could be worked into my columns and make them appear as if they had all just been cabled to us."

Eliezer at first thought this would be a violation of journalistic ethics, but Hemda had her way and soon columns were appearing each week from foreign capitals bearing the signatures of various mythical correspondents.

One week Hemda wrote a "Letter from Safed," signing it with the pseudonym Hida. A few days after it appeared Hemda, at a literary gathering in Jerusalem, met a personable young man who obviously, from his conversation, failed to realize her identity. He was making, however, a great effort to impress this attractive young woman with his own literary accomplishments.

Oh yes, he was a writer, he said. A professional writer. A great deal of his work had been published. Surely she knew the paper called the *Deer!* He was a regular correspondent. In fact, he had had a column in the *Deer* this past week entitled "Letter from Safed." She had read it? What did she think of his literary style?

That night, telling Eliezer about it, Hemda said:

"I wonder how many people in Paris, Vienna, Moscow, and Berlin are taking credit for what I write?"

Ben Yehuda's encouragement of young Jewish writers in various parts of Europe prompted them to send a flood of contributions to the revived *Deer*. Many men who later were to become celebrated in the field of Jewish literature got their start through the little Jerusalem weekly.

Nahum Slousch wrote many travel stories for the *Deer*. His *Voyage to Lithuania* was printed in weekly installments.

Saul Tshernikowski, who later became known as the "poet of paganism" and "the poet laureate of the Jews," contributed many poems which introduced a Hellenic spirit to a growing Hebrew literature.

Micah Berdyczewski wrote fiction and philosophical pieces for the paper.

Joseph Klausner contributed articles on a variety of subjects.

Each time an envelope came from any of these men there was excitement in the office of the *Deer,* for the Ben Yehudas realized there here, without a doubt, was another piece of real literature.

One day an especially fat envelope came from Berdyczewski. It contained a philosophical article entitled "The Cane." As Ben Yehuda read it his forehead was as wrinkled as it often was when he was struggling with an especially troublesome philological problem.

Finally he tossed the article onto Hemda's desk, saying:

"Read this, Bitti, and see what *you* think of it. I am afraid I do not understand exactly what he means. But I am sure there is something in it."

After Hemda had studied it she reported:

"I fail to understand its meaning either, but it is beautifully written, so let's publish it."

The day the next issue of the *Deer* came from the press Ben Yehuda and his wife went off on their first trip to the settlements since the *Deer* had reappeared. They wanted to get the reactions of their public. They were certain they would be showered with congratulations, for the *Deer* was becoming strong and robust and adventuresome.

They went from colony to colony, thanking their friends for their support during the black hours.

At Rishon Le Zion they were greeted by an elderly subscriber who pointed a finger at Ben Yehuda and shouted:

"Those letters from Paris and London and other places—you can't fool me! You write them yourself!"

Someone else expostulated:

"That man Nahun Slousch bores us with his interminable voyages and travel tales!"

Then there were the tirades against Tshernikowski by those who said he wrote only of "love and stolen kisses, sweet promises and broken hearts." In the same breath they denounced the love stories which Hemda occasionally wrote. Love, the critics said, should be confined to the bedroom and not written about; especially not in the holy language or in a publication that the young might read.

But it was the article called "The Cane" which came in for the most violent denunciations.

Judah Grazovski, one of Ben Yehuda's best friends in Jaffa, called it "nonsense."

David Idelovitch, the Hebrew teacher, could hardly wait to say:

"Ben Yehuda, why do you fill your paper with such straw and fodder? Do you think we are all donkeys and cattle unable to distinguish between such stuff and real literature? What does the writer of this article mean? I defy you to explain it!"

Hemda looked quickly at her husband. She could tell he was about to admit it had been incomprehensible to him, too, so she took a quick step forward and said rather sarcastically:

"It's just that you're too lazy to figure it out! Read it three or four times more and eventually you will comprehend it."

The only new writer who was generally approved was Klausner. Hemda said it was because "he manages all the time to say nothing but to say it beautifully, without making anyone think."

One subscriber said, "Why waste your energy on a little newspaper? You ought to be working full time on your dictionary."

"The dictionary depends on you people," Ben Yehuda replied. "You can have it whenever you wish. I am ready to commence the printing just as soon as funds are forthcoming. If you wish a Hebrew dictionary so badly, then go out and raise the money!"

As a result of that speech those within hearing promptly subscribed enough for the publication of a volume of forty pages. At that time Ben Yehuda himself thought one thousand pages would be sufficient for the kind of dictionary he had in mind, little realizing himself to how many volumes of how many thousands of pages the first real Hebrew dictionary in history would eventually run.

29

Burned Career

BY THE YEAR 1897, IN SPITE OF THE OBSTACLES which the Ottoman Empire had so often thrown along the path, a real national Jewish life had begun to develop in Palestine, partly as a result of the labors of Eliezer Ben Yehuda and his group of idealistic followers.

By this time Jaffa, so recently an almost Arab city, had become at least half Jewish.

The settlements were multiplying, and dividing, and increasing their holdings as well as their population.

Even the ancient city of Safed, so far from Jerusalem, was feeling the effects of the renaissance because of the colonies in that area.

Hebrew at last was being used as a living language by those who dared defy the reactionaries.

Nissim Behar, weary of the continuous difficulties he was having with assistants sent to him from Paris, resigned his principalship of the Alliance school about this time and started on a tour of the world. When he left, the Ben Yehudas felt they had lost their best and most loyal ally. His successor continued French as the curriculum language.

An institution for the education of Jewish girls, called the Evelina de Rothschild School, used English as its "official" language.

The Lämel School, supported by the Jews of Germany, conducted all its classes in the Teutonic language, as did a German orphanage which finally had a sizable enrollment.

Ben Yehuda wrote frequent articles demanding to know how long this absurd situation was going to be allowed to continue. He kept insisting that the "first" language in every school be Hebrew, arguing that this would create harmony and that if eventually the children spoke the language in their homes, their parents would also learn it.

But Hebrew *was* being taught as a "foreign language" in most of the schools by now, and many of Ben Yehuda's allies among the teachers encouraged their pupils to speak Hebrew on their playgrounds, in the streets, and after they reached home. Teachers and principals who co-operated in this way received special recognition in the columns of the *Deer*.

Not many months after the ban on the *Deer* had been lifted Ben Yehuda one day announced to Hemda:

"Look, Bitti! Here is the first copy to come from the press of the first real little Hebrew dictionary in two thousand years!"

Almost as proudly as he had showed off his first child years ago, he displayed to his wife a forty-page booklet which he had published with the small fund they had raised on their last trip to the colonies. It was badly printed on cheap paper with a thin yellow cover, yet it was a dictionary, put out in defiance of the Turkish decree against the publishing of books by Jews.

Later that day he said:

"One thing I realized as I prepared the copy for this little book. If there is ever going to be a real dictionary I must get to work on it in earnest. Years and years of work remain to be done, and I do not see how——"

"I have a solution, Eliezer. You must put everything else aside and——"

"But the newspaper, Bitti——"

"I shall take over the paper. From time to time you can give me a political article, and of course you must write your column about words. But leave the rest to me."

So it was that Hemda, although pregnant with her second child, became in fact if not in title the editor of the *Deer*. The day she assumed charge she took her chemistry notebooks from a trunk and burned them.

One day a group of Jewish women came to Hemda and asked for her help on a project of theirs. They had discovered that the people were hungry for music, so they had engaged a gifted young violinist from Rehovoth to come to Jerusalem and give a concert. The Alliance school would permit the use of its auditorium. The women themselves would sell tickets from door to door. But they needed some publicity. And they also needed a word. They wanted a Hebrew word for "concert"!

Hemda took up the philological matter with Eliezer.

"Yes, Bitti, there is a word, *tizmoret*. I have just recently made some notes about it. A very pleasant little word it is!"

Hemda reported to the concert committee that as his contribution to the project her husband presented them with tizmoret, but they should keep it as a surprise until the last moment.

Eliezer, however, not being informed that it was to be a surprise, launched the word on the public in his next word-column in the *Deer,* immediately precipitating a crisis in Palestinian musical circles, for at this same time, in Rishon Le Zion, a small orchestra was also planning a concert and also needed a word for it. Reading in the *Deer* about tizmoret, they put out announcements that a tizmoret would be given on such-and-such a date.

The women of Jerusalem were disconsolate. Not only was there no longer any surprise, but "their word" had been expropriated by a rival music group!

Hemda went again to her husband.

"Eliezer, you must create another word for concert, for *us!*"

So Ben Yehuda locked himself in his study and after a long time came out with a solution, a second word for concert; not a new creation, but a Hebrew word he had found in ancient literature which had disappeared from usage long ago: the word *mangina.*

That is how it happened that one evening a tizmoret was given by an orchestra in Rishon Le Zion and some nights later a mangina was given in Jerusalem.

Today, as a result of that friendly feud between two rival musical organizations more than half a century ago, anyone speaking modern idiomatic Hebrew has a choice of two words when he wishes to speak about a "concert."

Deborah Ben Yehuda was two years old when her mother gave birth to a second child, Ehud, who looked so much like the father that the mother called him "The Little Prince."

It was not Hemda's fault that Ehud died when he was one year old. Nor was it due to contracting the father's chronic disease. Ehud died of pneumonia.

It was Hemda's first intimate experience with death, and it left a cruel mark on her. She never forgot the picture of her baby lying motionless, nor how Eliezer had to drag her from the death chamber, nor how he had said:

"You must not sorrow any more, Bitti. It is all over."

Nor did she ever forget how, after Eliezer had left her alone, she had sneaked back to have a last look at her dead child and had found her husband on his knees by the bed, crying over the still, small form.

The illness which overtook Hemda after this had no connection with Ehud's death. It was a result of the Palestinian climate. Malaria and rheumatism combined to keep her frequently in bed. When she could move about she took numerous trips to Jaffa, partly for a change in atmosphere but principally so as not to inflict her busy husband with worries about her ailments.

Then tragedy struck again.

Father Yonas had shared with Eliezer and Hemda their joys and their tribulations. He had been delighted that his protégé had won so many battles against the forces of ignorance and intolerance.

But about this time he announced that he himself could no longer endure the ups and downs of this unpredictable sort of life. He was growing old. Palestine was a place for youthful souls.

"Would you and Eliezer be distressed," he asked Hemda one day, "if I left the country for a few years? I think I should like to stay in

Paris for a time. I could send you articles for the paper from there. When the children are ready for their advanced education you could send them to me one at a time."

Eliezer and Hemda were sympathetic. They even agreed that during his absence, however long it might be, they would care for his wife and two small children.

The entire family went to the railway station to see him off for Jaffa, where he was to catch a boat to Marseille. As they left for the depot the father took his daughter aside and said:

"Pola, my child, we have been close friends all our lives; closer than most fathers and daughters. But I warn you that if I see a single tear when we say good-by I shall be forced to change all my plans."

So Hemda smiled bravely and waved a small handkerchief until the train disappeared in the Judean hills.

Then fate played a strange trick.

The train was late reaching Jaffa and it missed connections with the boat.

Father Yonas discovered that he could not get another steamer for two more weeks. While he was waiting in Jaffa he contracted a contagious disease and went to Rishon Le Zion for treatment.

Hemda understood why he picked Rishon Le Zion. It was his favorite spot in Palestine because it was such a progressive settlement and he had so many friends there.

After a few days Eliezer received a message from Rishon Le Zion that he and Hemda and Mrs. Yonas had better come quickly.

Before the next steamer sailed for Marseille death claimed Shlomoh Naftaly Hirtz Yonas, the distiller of Glubokiah.

In trying to comfort Hemda, Eliezer said to her:

"Bitti, we can at least be happy that it happened at Rishon Le Zion. There is an old Hebrew proverb that says, 'A man's feet always take him to the place where he really wants to die.' "

Jews from all over Palestine trekked their way several days later to Rishon Le Zion to pay their respects to the man who years ago had found a small boy shivering one morning in a synagogue and had taken him home, and thus had started him on a career which already had affected the lives of so many thousands of Jews.

Nothing could have delighted Hemda more that autumn than Ben Yehuda's suggestion that they take a long trip through the Jewish settlements of Galilee.

She knew Eliezer was concerned about taking her mind off all that had happened, but he assured her he wanted to see whether Hebrew had taken firm root in Galilee.

Their first stop was Petach Tikvah, which charmed Hemda because of its lushness, owing to constant irrigation from great artesian wells.

Next they went to Hedera.

"I am sorry we must stop here," Eliezer said, "but I think you ought to see it. It is known as the 'Village of Death' now. It had a siege of yellow fever recently which killed every one of the original settlers. How many inhabitants we shall find left I have no idea!"

As they rode into Hedera they found the once busy village as deserted as a graveyard. There were no women's voices, no men at work in the fields, no children playing. Only two inhabitants were left. Both were ill in bed.

"I can feel death stalking up and down these streets," Hemda remarked.

One of the invalids was a young man, sole survivor of a family of seven. The other was an agronomist who, when he arrived to make a survey, had been warned to leave at once if he wanted to leave at all. He had refused. Now he was on his deathbed. Over and over again to Ben Yehuda he said:

"This place must somehow be brought back to life!"

Eliezer explained to Hemda that the trouble resulted from marshes on the edge of the village.

"Petach Tikvah had marshes and malaria, too, yet today it is one of our healthiest and most prosperous places. Hedera will be like that, too, someday. The baron plans to plant a forest here. The drainage of the swamps had already begun when the epidemic came. I am sure we will live long enough to see Hedera another Petach Tikvah!"

Hemda looked at the deserted streets and raised her eyebrows in doubt. Years later, however, she was to pay a return visit and see her husband's prediction come true, for Hedera was destined to become one of the largest Jewish settlements, free of disease, wealthy in its production of milk, butter, cereals, fruit, cattle.

The road now led up steep mountains to Zichron Yaakov, which called itself the "Little Paris of Palestine." Although only two hours from Hedera, the climate here was cool and healthy. This was a place settled principally by Rumanians, tall, broad-shouldered, jolly people, prosperous and self-satisfied.

"Why, Eliezer, the 'Little Paris'?" Hemda asked as she stared at unattractive lime-covered houses and mud-rutted streets down which humans and animals alike had to walk because there were no sidewalks.

Her husband smiled.

"Maybe because of its wonderful park. Or because they are so prosperous. There is a legend that no Zichron Yaakov farmer knows where his own fields and vineyards are because they are all worked by Arab employees. Or perhaps it is their European-looking synagogue and the miniature of a Paris department store. Or, more likely, because everyone here speaks such perfect French and the children are required to do their studies in the language of Paris in schools established by Baron Rothschild."

There were old people in Zichron Yaakov who complained bitterly about the loss of their children. They had skimped and saved to send their youth to France, and their youth, in most cases, had not returned, leaving the parents with fields they themselves were now too old to work and with no new generation to take their places in the settlement.

After they had left Zichron Yaakov, Eliezer said:

"I predicted this years ago, Bitti, when your sister and I first came to this place. I preached and wrote against what the baron was doing with his importation of French culture and insistence on the French language. I had bitter fights over it. They accused me, with my Hebrew, of trying to turn their children into ignoramuses and illiterates. They fought every additional quarter hour of Hebrew I tried to get into the school curriculum. When they bought books, they wanted French ones and not Hebrew.

"I called it the 'suicide of the younger generation' and I pleaded with our people to put a stop to it. I begged them to educate their children in our own language, teach them our own culture, encourage them to take pride in our own literature.

"I wrote that they were making cripples out of their children by letting them go abroad and putting them back voluntarily under the yoke of prejudice and persecution.

"Hemda, you know how much I admire things intellectual. But French culture could be the death of Israel, if what has happened in Zichron Yaakov were to happen everywhere.

"Did you see some of the young men who *had* returned from abroad? They are often referred to as the 'sons of the rich baron.' They behave just like typical rich men's sons. They consider themselves too good for hard labor, yet have not acquired the knowledge to do anything else. They can merely talk French in the Paris manner."

Despite the obvious truth of all this, the Ben Yehudas did meet in Zichron Yaakov a member of the younger generation who impressed them.

Aaron Aaronsohn was tall, strong, and proud that his family had been farmers. His spirit was as healthy as his body. He was still young, but he was already having the dreams which years later would lead to his discovery of a type of wild wheat which would become an important Palestinian crop and help revolutionize Jewish agriculture. This was the youth who was destined to achieve fame during World War I by guiding British troops through the desert and indicating to them where they might find water.

Aaronsohn's sister Sarah was to become the Jeanne d'Arc of Palestine in that same war, helping to found a Jewish intelligence service for the British, but finally being tortured to the point of suicide by Turks who seized her when a note she had written to General Allenby was captured.

The next day the Ben Yehudas went to Athlit, which in less than a quarter of a century was destined to play a spectacular role in war, for here Jews were to help liberate their own land from Turkish rule by sending secret signals to ships of the British navy.

Then on to Haifa, with a great bay at its feet and with Mount Carmel high above it, like a crown; Haifa, which one day would become the second city of Israel and boast of one of the finest ports in the Middle East, but which in those days was a backward and predominantly Arab town. When Ben Yehuda found that the *Deer* had many readers in Haifa he asked several people to send him news letters occasionally. From each he received the same reply. What would they write about? Nothing ever happened here. There was no Jewish life. Even tourists from abroad, if they came to Haifa, just rushed through on their way to Nazareth.

On the way to Nazareth, Hemda kept asking how much farther it was, because the heat was so great and she was so thirsty. When they finally reached Nazareth, Eliezer and the horses were also badly in need of water.

In the center of the town they found some Arab women drawing water from a well. The Ben Yehudas approached them with words of greeting spoken in Arabic, but the women picked up handfuls of stones and pelted the strangers, shouting angrily at them:

"Jews! Jews!"

"It is ironical," said Eliezer, "that this is the well, in the New Testament, from which Mary was accustomed to draw water!

"Someday, Hemda, this place and Bethlehem will be testing stones of the Jewish respect for the shrines of others. Nazareth has little significance in our own history, but to Christians it is of supreme importance. I am sure that when we become masters in our own land we shall show the world that we can watch over the shrines of others as carefully as over our own."

Now they began the long descent to Lake Tiberias, known in the New Testament as the Sea of Galilee, where in summer it is insufferably hot because it is nearly seven hundred feet below sea level. As usual, the heat in Tiberias was so intense that the Ben Yehudas were unable to sleep. For years Hemda remembered it because here everything they were offered to drink was full of small flies, and Eliezer refused each glass or cup that was extended to him because of his almost fanatical hatred of insects, for which he had a special Hebrew expression meaning "repugnant filthy creatures." The native people laughed and said he would die of thirst if he remained there long. "You drink flies here or you don't drink at all!"

The next morning at sunrise they took a boat trip around the lake where many of the New Testament incidents had taken place.

Eliezer's repetition of the parable of the fishes and loaves of bread was so graphic that Hemda, looking at the spot, felt she could almost see, in that strange early-morning light, Christ's disciples gathering up the baskets of crumbs left after the multiplication of the loaves.

The settlement of Rosh Pinah was to be the next stop. On this part of the trip they were accompanied by David Idelovitch. They were traveling in a coach drawn by three horses down a road which was hardly a road at all, when the carriage suddenly collapsed. The driver, surveying the wreckage, said it was beyond repair; they would have to continue on foot if they wished to continue at all.

The sun was hot enough, as Idelovitch seriously pointed out, to fry an egg on a flat stone. They were stranded in the middle of a desert wilderness. As they surveyed the landscape, Hemda noticed on the horizon a small building which looked like a ruin, but, she said, "at least we could get protection there from the heat and perhaps the driver could walk to the next village and find us a conveyance."

The coachman was violently opposed to this plan.

"That place," he warned them in an ominous voice, pointing to the structure Hemda had seen, "is the hiding place of the worst band of thieves and assassins in this part of the world!"

Just then, out of a cloud of dust, a number of horses appeared and everyone relaxed. The riders were young farmers from Rosh Pinah. When they told Hemda she would have to ride horseback, she protested, remembering that Nissim Behar's wife had died as the result of a fall from a horse, but one of the young farmers got her onto a saddle and walked beside her to quiet her fears.

At Rosh Pinah they were guests in the home of the baron's representative. As Hemda, travel-stained and weary from days of primitive living, wandered through the house staring at its luxurious furnishings and the table set with sparkling crystal and silver and expensive French china, she turned to Eliezer and whispered:

"This really *is* like Paris, isn't it? Yet we are still practically in the middle of the desert!"

In Hebrew the baron's representative gave Eliezer an account of progress being made at Rosh Pinah.

"We have fields and vineyards," he said, "and an abundance of fruit trees. The land flows with milk and honey, as the Bible says it should. Each man lies under his vine and his fig tree and is happy with his lot . . ."

Eliezer finally interrupted this report which made Rosh Pinah sound like a new Garden of Eden to ask:

"What about the Hebrew language?"

The administrator, looking around as a man might who was about to reveal a great military secret, finally whispered:

"Less French is spoken here than in most settlements!"

Then, looking over his shoulder again to be sure no eavesdropper had entered the room, he added in even more of a whisper:

"You must not allow this to become known, for if the baron were to hear . . . ! The baron, you know, does not believe in nationalism in any of its manifestations. He wants only settlements and simple farmers who work the land. The baron has a most negative attitude toward Zionism!"

30

Oriental Fashion

BY NOW THE BEN YEHUDAS WERE ABLE TO MAKE certain generalizations about the settlements in the north. They had found that the entire area was afflicted with malaria; that it took a long time for people from Europe to become acclimated to the intense heat; that a great percentage of Jews caught contagious skin and eye diseases from contact with their Arab neighbors, and that the biggest impediment to colonization was that the pioneers were mostly men who, in the countries of their origin, had engaged in commerce or the professions and therefore were not adapted by training or temperament to tilling the soil.

But now they heard about a new settlement that was being established which would be free of most of these handicaps. At a spot called Metulla, on a hilltop facing the white snow mountain of Hermon, a group of second-generation farmers was to found the most northerly colony in the entire "Land of Our Dreams," as Ben Yehuda so often called Palestine. Here the air would be cool and here there would be no malaria to battle.

It was a gay party that started out one evening from Rosh Pinah for Metulla. There were three carriages. Hemda was able to relax in the comfort of a real landau. They took quantities of food, and some of the young men brought musical instruments.

Hemda, who was still young, although she had borne two children already, became a carefree girl again that moonlight night and sang and made jokes with the young farmers.

It was 3 A.M. when they arrived at Metulla, but they were all so exhilarated by the clean, pure air that no one wanted to go to bed, so they stayed up to watch the rising sun gild Mount Hermon with its touches of golds, pinks, and lavenders.

There were thirty young settlers at Metulla, living in primitive mud huts which had been abandoned by the native Druses from whom the land had been purchased at an exorbitant price. Hemda was intrigued by stories of these fanatical Arab people. They belonged to a secret religious sect founded in the eleventh century by a missionary named Darazi. They had many strange convictions. They believed that the wicked became camels and dogs; that God had appeared to man exactly seventy times in the past in various disguises, and that there is a fixed number of humans on earth which never changes.

The Druses of Metulla had all left, except one family. After the man had accepted the price agreed upon for his holdings, his wife had refused to budge. It was the settlement's first real problem. Someone suggested Hemda might be able to argue the woman out of her stubbornness, but as she entered the Druse dwelling place she immediately regretted having undertaken the assignment.

In the one-room primitive abode, made of cakes of dried mud, animals and humans lived in the closest possible proximity, a cow in one corner, a donkey and chickens in a second, the children in a third, and the adults in the fourth. Even grain was stored there.

The woman, her half dozen screaming children clustered around her, refused to listen to anything Hemda said through an interpreter.

It was a real predicament. Sundown was approaching and there was fear that this woman's obstreperousness might upset the other Druses who had been invited to a celebration to solemnize the business deal and who would soon be arriving.

In desperation Hemda remembered something, so she hurried to the landau and found some sweet cakes, which she gave to the half dozen children. As their screaming stopped, the mother, no longer having her Greek chorus as an accompaniment, suddenly ceased her wailing and also accepted some of the sweets Hemda held out to her.

While the woman was eating Hemda talked softly to her about the beautiful new house her husband would be able to build with the money the Jews had given him, and what a happy life she had ahead of her.

It worked! It worked so well that Hemda had difficulty getting rid of the woman, who insisted on staying close at her side wherever she went the rest of the evening.

The only substantial building in Metulla was a brick structure occupied by the baron's representative. This was where the Ben Yehudas were to stay. There was no furniture. Hemda was told she would have to sleep on a blanket on the floor like the others. As she was thinking back to the elegant Parisian-type home she had just left in Rosh Pinah, Eliezer remarked:

"This is like a military camp. I find nothing wrong with it. We really are all soldiers. There is no reason Jews should not endure a few hardships until they can make a comfortable living for themselves. Of course it will take months of work to build chicken houses, barns, and dwellings, but work never hurt anyone."

Later, however, as he saw how the others were living in mud huts, he was a little more sympathetic to their complaints. One of the Jewish farmers had already paid a high price for this unsanitary way of life. During the night a snake came through the roof of his hut while he slept. There was no doctor within many miles and no medicine. He died in a few hours.

The party for the Druses lasted all night. Hemda left early and curled up on a blanket on the floor of the administration building, but she was not permitted to sleep, for the Druses kept shooting off rifles at frequent intervals as a sign of the importance they attached to the proceedings. It was dawn before the last Druse trekked off and left Metulla to the Jews.

But that was just a preliminary to the feast the next day. Jewish settlers from nearby colonies had been invited, and also a limited number of Arab leaders, because it was necessary to establish cordial relations immediately with all neighbors. Only the sheik of each adjoining village had received an invitation, but each sheik brought along his brothers, his sons, his sons-in-law, and even a few servants and womenfolk. Sixty in all.

Many lambs had to be killed, for the slaughtering of lambs was an outward symbol of the respect one had for one's guests, the number of lambs indicating the extent of the respect. The Arab chieftains must have no doubts about the esteem in which the Jews held them!

Also, it was necessary to prepare all the dishes in the Arab manner, else the guests would refuse to eat.

Hemda watched with fascination as the preparations were made. In addition to the lambs many fowl were killed. Vast quantities of rice were cooked in Arabic butter in large steel barrels. Watermelons had been brought from Hedera, quinces from Petach Tikvah, grapes from Rosh Pinah, and figs from a nearby village. There were Arabic sweetmeats, and to drink they had the juice of Indian date root. Wine was kept out of sight because of the Moslem ban against anything alcoholic.

One thing puzzled Hemda. She saw no tables being laid.

Late in the afternoon the sheiks started to appear, riding beautiful mares and followed by their servants on donkeys.

The administration building quickly filled up, and still Hemda saw no tables. While the servants remained outside to guard the horses, the Arab notables took their places, squatting on the floor in a great circle. The food was then brought in, not on plates, not on platters, but on immense trays. One tray was placed in front of each guest. Hands were used instead of knives, forks, and spoons. As soon as one tray was emptied another quickly appeared.

"I never saw food consumed so fast!" Hemda whispered to Eliezer. Before she herself had decided whether to try to manage with her hands or to shock everyone by calling for at least a spoon, the meal was over.

What was left of the food was taken outside for the servants and the Arab women who had trailed along.

Meanwhile the Arab men were drinking an interminable number

of cups of thick Turkish coffee and smoking their strange-looking water pipes.

Next (as after any banquet, whether on the edge of a Palestinian desert or in Paris or New York) there were speeches, including an exchange of mutual compliments, and a series of congratulations from the Arabs on the founding of the village. Then more coffee and more pipe smoking.

The visitors left with protestations of friendship which they expressed by saying:

"We shall be good neighbors and protect you, our children, from all evil."

The Jewish leader gave a sigh of relief and ordered a meal prepared for strictly Jewish consumption. Another lamb was killed and cooked, along with a few chickens and some vegetables.

"But who is going to eat all of this?" Ben Yehuda asked, for there were only half a dozen of them present.

The young Jewish leader laughed.

"After all the exercise I have had, I shall eat half of it myself and leave the rest for the remainder of you!"

During this private meal there was much singing of Jewish songs and some drinking of wine.

After they had finished they went out into the village square, where the rest of the settlers were having their own banquet. While Hemda and Eliezer watched in amazement, the young Jewish leader sat down and, as if he had not had a mouthful of food since morning, consumed enough to feed a small family for days.

Here there were more speeches, more wine, and the shooting of rifles into the air until the stars began to twinkle overhead and the less hardy ones went off to bed, among them the Ben Yehudas.

Thus Metulla, the northernmost settlement in the land of the Jews, was formally founded with prayers that she might become the "Pearl of the North," a hope which did not immediately materialize, because for a long time there was doubt that Metulla would survive. It was not until many years later that she finally did become one of the most important of the North Galilee colonies.

31

If You Will It . . .

ELIEZER BEN YEHUDA WAS EXCITED IN 1897 BY news that Israel Zangwill, the brilliant British author, was coming from London to Jerusalem for a visit, along with a delegation of the Order of Ancient Maccabaeans, headed by the grand commander, Herbert Bentwich.

"Bitti, this is an opportunity such as we seldom get!" he exclaimed to his wife. "Millions of people read what Zangwill writes. He is one of the most popular authors of the day. If we could only convince him and enlist his pen in our fight!"

So Eliezer Ben Yehuda sent a letter to Zangwill offering him the hospitality of the modest Ben Yehuda home.

When Zangwill and his Maccabaeans arrived they were received in Jerusalem with great honor, not only by leaders of the Jewish community but by British diplomats as well.

Zangwill paid the first of many visits to the Ben Yehuda home one hot afternoon. As he sat talking with Hemda and Eliezer, Deborah, who then was barely four, came running in from the garden and with a ladylike curtsy presented the celebrated visitor with a rose she had picked. Zangwill bent over and kissed the child, then tried to make conversation with her.

The parents laughed and Eliezer said:

"There is no use, Zangwill. My children speak only Hebrew."

"But I learned Hebrew myself as a child! Let me see if I can remember a few words."

So with an accent so "foreign" that Deborah could hardly understand him, the British writer tried to speak the language of his ancestors to the child of his host.

Eliezer took his guest into his shop to show him the old hand press on which the *Deer* was still being printed. To it was affixed a small statue of Gutenberg, the fifteenth-century German who, by inventing movable type, became the "patron saint" of printers all over the world.

Before he left the shop Zangwill raised his hand over the press and pronounced a Hebrew benediction, ending with the words *lazman hazeh,* meaning "having reached this time." It was a subtle play on words, for Ben Yehuda realized that Zangwill was thus comparing his little paper to the great *Times* of London.

There were many meetings between the two writers. Gradually Zangwill seemed to be catching the contagion of Israel. When Ben Yehuda suggested he deliver a public lecture on some historical Jewish subject, the British novelist promptly agreed.

The lecture was given in the Grand New Hotel of Jerusalem and was attended by Jewish, Moslem, and Christian dignitaries. Zangwill spoke on "Jews in the Holy Land" and made frequent reference to Jesus Christ, concluding his lecture with these words:

"How many injustices have been done to Jews in Thy name!"

It was after this successful public appearance that Ben Yehuda one day, talking privately to the visitor, said:

"Zangwill, you have glorified the life of Jews in the ghettos in many books. Now you have seen something of the life of Jews here in the place they really belong. Why do you not return and make your home with us and glorify our new national life in your future books?"

Zangwill did not immediately reply, but his expression indicated that the suggestion tempted him. Finally he said:

"As you know, I am leaving tomorrow. Please come down and see me off."

As Zangwill left there were tears in his eyes.

On the way home Ben Yehuda said to his wife:

"Unless I am very mistaken, we have won him to our cause!"

Ben Yehuda devoted much of the next issue of the *Deer* to the visit. For days Jerusalem talked about Zangwill, always using possessive little words about him. He was "our Zangwill" to them.

Although Zangwill had left without giving a definite answer to the invitation to come to Palestine to live, Ben Yehuda waited impatiently for his next book, certain that at least he would put into print the emotions he had so obviously experienced.

The next Zangwill book was *Dreamers of the Ghetto.* It was not about the Promised Land.

Eliezer Ben Yehuda was bitterly disappointed.

About this time Hemda happened to meet some visitors from abroad who added another chapter to an old story. They were from Sweden and knew Tshashnikov, Eliezer's Polish journalist friend, who, they said, had gone to Sweden, but at the time of Deborah's death had wanted to return to Jerusalem and offer his consolation and see Deborah's children but had not been certain how welcome he would be. Recently he had married a Swedish girl who, he said, reminded him of Deborah.

Hemda wondered whether she should tell Eliezer.

Intellectuals and liberals the world over in these days were aroused to a fever pitch by the Dreyfus case. Ben Yehuda threw his small weekly paper into the fight against the forces of bigotry and intolerance.

Article after article appeared in the *Deer* calling on the Jews of the world for their support of the Frenchman who was being persecuted because he was a Jew.

This was the sort of fight Eliezer Ben Yehuda liked. Father Yonas would have liked it too.

But now something happened which relegated the Dreyfus case to a position of relative unimportance in the *Deer* and in Ben Yehuda's mind.

In 1896, seventeen years after Ben Yehuda had issued his first appeal for a Jewish homeland and a revival of the Hebrew language, a book entitled *Der Judenstaat* (The Jewish State) had been published by a brilliant Hungarian journalist and playwright, Theodor Herzl, correspondent for *Neue Freie Presse* in Vienna.

Ben Yehuda knew of Herzl, but up to now they had been diametrically opposed on most issues. Herzl had written for his paper that the Dreyfus case was of no particular importance and that the Jewish officer was probably guilty.

Just four years before his publication of *The Jewish State* Herzl had said in a newspaper article that "the historical homeland of the Jews no longer has any value for them; it is childish [for a Jew] to go in search of the geographical location of his homeland."

This article had come out at a time when Ben Yehuda and his colleagues were fighting such lonely battles for the Zionist cause.

But now Herzl had changed his mind and in his book had argued for the creation of a Jewish state in Palestine, to be chartered by the Turkish authorities and financed by colonization companies.

There had been Zionists, although they were not called that, since the year 70, when the Temple was destroyed. In every generation there had been dreamers and visionaries who talked of a Jewish return to the homeland. George Eliot, in 1876, when Eliezer was at school in Dünaburg, had written *Daniel Deronda,* which for years was the Bible of Zionists.

Eliezer Ben Yehuda himself had written and worked for seventeen years before Herzl's book came out to give the dream substance. But Herzl was a "man of action" and now was leaping into a position of leadership which would win him the title of the "Father of Modern Zionism" and after his death would cause his name to be spoken almost with reverence by Jews in every part of the world who believed in the dream.

One of his chief contributions was to be a single sentence which was to become a slogan for Zionists the world over.

"If you will it, it is no dream!"

Herzl had followed up his book by issuing a call for a world-wide conference of Jews to take place at Basle, Switzerland, in August 1897.

Associated with him were many men Ben Yehuda knew and respected, among them Israel Zangwill and Herbert Bentwich, whom he had so recently entertained in Jerusalem, and two of the most important French Zionists, Dr. Max Nordau and Dr. Alexander Marmorek, who at that time was working on a cure for tuberculosis.

Ben Yehuda should have gone himself to Basle, for the conference had been called to discuss the idea which had been his obsession since his student days in Paris. But, as he pointed out to his wife, there were two reasons why he would have to report the proceedings from a distance. The Ben Yehuda financial situation made such a trip impossible. Besides, the Turkish officials would not permit it. He was a subject of the Ottoman Empire and had so recently been accused of "revolt against the kingdom" that the right to travel had been denied him, and there was no court of appeal.

But as he read the call for the conference, Ben Yehuda exclaimed to his wife:

"Would it not be wonderful, Bitti, if these men were to declare from their platform, for all the world to hear, that Jews should return to their own land and make it a place where they could live as free people?"

Yet Ben Yehuda, in his most excited dreams, had no idea the Basle conference would dare go as far as it did.

With firmness and clarity the leaders of world Jewry at Basle announced that their ancient homeland, Eretz Israel, must become the new abode of Jewish people. They went so far as to state their program in these words no one could misunderstand:

"Zionism aims at establishing for the Jewish people a publicly and legally assured home in Palestine."

A World Zionist Organization was created. Any Jew anywhere in the world could belong by agreeing with the Basle aims and paying one shekel, one mark, one shilling, or one American quarter.

A council of distinguished Jews was elected, with Herzl as president.

There was talk of the erection of a Hebrew university in Jerusalem, of the creation of a Jewish national fund, and the setting up of a Jewish world bank in London to finance colonization.

A song written in Hebrew was accepted as an anthem of a country yet to be born. A design was adopted for a national flag of blue and white, the colors of the traditional prayer shawl, emblazoned with the Star of David.

It was only a few days after all this news arrived that Ben Yehuda received a letter in longhand, written by Herzl himself, announcing that the editor of the *Deer* had been unanimously elected a member of the executive board.

For days Ben Yehuda went around Jerusalem as if in a trance. This was what he had been working for all these years. Now that it had happened, he was intoxicated with the news that came pouring in from Basle.

There was only one sour note. The congress had concerned itself with a flag, a song, and many more trivial matters, but no mention had been made of a national language; a revival of Hebrew. Why had not some friend of his insisted on this? They might create a nation without a flag, without an anthem, but they never could do it without a language!

It was Hemda, as usual, who tried to console her husband, arguing that there would be other Zionist congresses and plenty of time to convince the leaders of their oversight.

What was done at Basle created some immediate problems for Ben Yehuda. He was forced to write to Herzl and explain why it was out of the question for him to accept membership on the executive board. Friends in Turkish government circles had warned him that, if he were to accept, his days of activity in Palestine would quickly come to an end. He must remember, they said, how close he had come to serving a prison term. He still was not out of the shadow of the bars.

The government in Constantinople had been astonished, he was told, by the "effrontery" of the Jews. They talked of Palestine as if it were *their* country! This new movement must be stamped out before it spread. A series of new decrees was being planned as an answer to the Jews of Basle.

Then the Turkish censor, Ishmael Bey, sent for him and made it more positive.

"Not a word about this thing called 'Zionism' must be printed in your paper. The expression 'Eretz Israel' must never be used. There is no such thing as Israel. The place is Palestine. You do not have a country, you Jews, and you never shall have. Remember that!"

When he returned home from the censor's office Ben Yehuda poured out his grief to his wife.

"Bitti, how can I write about Zionism without using the word? How can I try to win support for this movement without mentioning Israel?"

Hemda reminded him that the censor had not forbidden him to write about a revival of the Hebrew language, which, after all, was his own great project.

"Now, Eliezer, you can be thankful that they did not include a national language in their program at Basle, for if they had, the censor surely would have prohibited your writing about it!"

In the days and weeks which followed, Ben Yehuda watched carefully for reaction from abroad. What stand would England, France, and Germany take? These great powers exerted considerable influence over the "Sick Man of Europe," as Turkey was often called.

And what would the reaction be in the Vatican? After all, it was Rome which put handcuffs on the Jews nearly two thousand years ago and started this long era of slavery. What would Rome now say to the announcement of the Jews that they finally were going to break loose from this bondage?

Ben Yehuda had to wait a long time to get answers to all these questions, but he found out within a few days what some people thought of the plan. Many learned and cultured Arab friends came to him and expressed their happiness. One of them put it this way:

"Through you we also will be liberated from this ruthless tyrant, the Sultan, Abdul Hamid II. We have seen what you Jews have accomplished in the desert. We favor your revival of the Hebrew language because it is so similar to our own. We must remember that Arabs and Jews are children of the same father."

Of course there were Jews in Jerusalem who thought that a great mistake had been made by even calling the Basle conference. When new decrees finally came from Constantinople banning all further Jewish immigration into Palestine, forbidding the purchase of land by Jews, and reimposing the ban on the construction of Jewish dwelling places, these timid members of the Jewish community were quick to say: "We told you so!"

But Ben Yehuda was accustomed to such opposition. Basle for him was a stimulant which inspired him to work even longer hours than usual on both his paper and his dictionary.

Often when Hemda entered his study she found him pacing up and down the long room with one hand to his head, in such deep thought that he would fail to notice her presence. Once she found him standing in front of his desk looking up at the slogan he had tacked to the wall:

THE DAY IS SO SHORT;
THE WORK TO BE DONE SO GREAT!

When he saw her he pointed to the motto and said:

"How much truer those words are now than ever before! They drive me on and keep me from sleeping, for now more than ever we need a language, now more than ever we need a real newspaper."

One result of the Zionist Congress was that Ben Yehuda, instead of having to rely now on the contributions of young, unknown writers, was able to obtain articles for his paper from such men as Zangwill and Nordau.

But Ben Yehuda wanted to make some outstanding contribution of his own to the cause, so he prepared what he called "The Second Appeal," a sequel to the first call he had issued for the resettlement of Palestine eighteen years ago in the Vienna paper, just before he himself had emigrated to the Holy Land.

In his second appeal Ben Yehuda laid stress on a point he thought had been overlooked at Basle. This new movement, he wrote, was not merely for those who had deeply religious reasons for returning to the land of their fathers. This must be a movement of all Jews, whether they were extremely Orthodox in their religious beliefs, or had adopted the assimilationist position, or even if they had embraced Christianity.

Ben Yehuda was even more specific than that. He called on Jews abroad who had married non-Jewish women and were the fathers of half-Jewish children to turn their eyes toward the Promised Land. All of them, he wrote, would be welcome.

Then, raising a point which would become a bone of contention in future years, when the dream turned into an actuality, he argued that the fate of this land must not be dictated only by those who were Orthodox in their beliefs.

This second appeal, although avoiding the technical pitfalls the censor had warned about, was unpleasing to the Turkish authorities, but it was received with acclaim by most Jews, except those who were already lining up as confirmed opponents of Zionism.

32

Garden of Eden

THE EXCITEMENT OF THE BASLE CONFERENCE WAS quickly followed by another development which affected the Ben Yehudas' personal future as much as the decisions taken at the meeting in Switzerland were ultimately to affect the future lives of so many millions of Jews.

The Jewish Colonization Association, organized by Jewish philanthropists in England to help transplant Jews, came to Eliezer's assistance by advancing him the sum of five thousand francs to use as he saw fit.

It was typical that he spent the money in this order:

First he wiped a considerable number of debts from his books.

Next he bought some new type for his printing shop which not only would give the *Deer* a fresh and more attractive appearance but also could be used, when the time came, to set his dictionary into print.

Finally he turned what was left over to his wife, saying:

"Bitti, you have struggled along with me in these inadequate old quarters long enough. You have been a good soldier about it. But now we are going to have a real home."

It took Hemda only a short time to find what she considered a "dream house." It was a stone building, large and roomy, set in the middle of an immense garden. At the same time she succeeded in renting from a neighbor a two-story structure adjoining the property to house the printing shop. There was a caretaker's lodge which Hemda made into a real bathroom by leading water from a nearby cistern through a rubber hose which stretched across the garden and through the lodge window. This improvised bathroom soon became one of Jerusalem's showpieces. Hotels in those days had bathrooms, but not private homes, so visitors from abroad, after they had seen the other sights of the ancient city, were often taken to the Ben Yehuda place to see what Hemda called "Jerusalem's first private bathroom."

Eliezer Ben Yehuda was happy in his new home. Now at last he had an adequately large study and the privacy he had always needed, for the nursery was on the other side of the house instead of being next door to his room.

He enjoyed working in the garden. There were forty flower beds to be cared for, and almond, fig, and olive trees, as well as grapevines. At the entrance stood two tall rose laurels with a bench between them. There, in summer, Ben Yehuda took his afternoon tea and in winter his ten o'clock morning refreshment.

In the garden there was an old Roman ruin consisting of two low stone arches which the children loved to climb. In the interior of one arch they installed their small dog; in the other, the family cat.

Life was idyllic for a time in the Ben Yehuda Garden of Eden. It was in this period that Hemda gave birth to another child, a robust boy who inherited the name of Ehud, Hemda's second child, who had died. Ehud II was the eighth child to be born to the man who had been told by doctors nearly twenty years ago that his days were numbered and that he would soon be living on borrowed time.

There were many reasons why this should have been the most serene period in Eliezer Ben Yehuda's life.

His newspaper was prospering; he had adequate quarters in which to work on his dictionary; for once his family did not have to worry about whether there was money enough for the daily bread, and all the forces which had fought him so bitterly for so many years at least temporarily had been routed.

But now a new worry arose to plague him. Hemda had grown pale and thin. The malaria she had contracted had destroyed her vitality, and frequent attacks of rheumatism also caused her great pain. The Jerusalem doctors said a trip to Europe might help, and so Eliezer, still suffering from self-accusations about the death of Deborah, bought two steamship tickets and one day casually handed them to his wife, saying:

"The boat sails from Jaffa tomorrow. I hope you can get ready in time."

Hemda became panicky. Her latest child, Ehud II, was only six months old and she was still nursing him. There were five other children to think about. She had few clothes for a trip to Europe. Why were men so thoughtless and inconsiderate?

Ben Yehuda listened calmly and then, picking up the tickets, said:

"As you please, but it will be too bad to lose all the money I have spent on these tickets."

So they sailed the next day.

Hemda made her mother promise never to go farther away from the house than into the garden. She tried to pacify her daughter Deborah, who then was just five, by saying she would bring her back a talking doll from Paris and some pretty dresses. Ben Zion, Yemeemah, and Hemda's brother and sister promised to help take care of the younger children.

They sailed second-class on a French ship called the *Orenoc,* and as soon as land was out of sight Hemda relaxed and her husband swore to her that for the first time in months color had returned to her cheeks.

Eliezer was as bubbling with excitement as a small boy on his way to a circus.

"Bitti, in Paris we will find good doctors for you. And wonderful food. You have no idea what the food in Paris is like! In seven or eight days we will be in the most exciting city in the world. I shall take you to places which will fascinate you, and after you get to know Paris, I shall work while you play."

Hemda smiled. She had never seen her husband like this.

"There are many people to be seen in Europe. I wish to meet some of the great Orientalist scholars and discuss the dictionary with them. I need their help if I am to succeed in making it a popular dictionary for the everyday use of everyday people and also a scholarly work valuable for scientific men and students of languages.

"I wish to visit many libraries and institutions and go through hundreds of books which cannot be obtained at home.

"I wish to talk with Baron Rothschild and thank him for all he has done. We must meet Dr. Max Nordau, and perhaps Emile Zola.

"We must see Narcisse Leven and other officers of the Alliance Israélite and thank them for their support. And then we must find Herzl. Maybe through Zangwill. It is necessary to persuade him to make Jerusalem the heart of Zionist activities."

33

Eliezer's Paris

IT WAS SPRING IN PARIS, AND ELIEZER BEN YEHUDA was a boy again.

The horse chestnuts along the Champs Elysées were in bloom, filling the air with their heady perfume.

The cafés, great and small, had put their thousands of steel tables and chairs out onto the sidewalks so people could see and be seen as they drank their coffee or *apéritifs*.

There were elegant ladies riding up and down the Rue du Faubourg St. Honoré in shiny black carriages.

Boulevard St. Michel was teeming with students whose *joie de vivre* infected the entire Left Bank.

The great pillared church at the end of Rue Royale called the Madeleine had had its spring bath; its white stones glistened in the morning sun.

The Ben Yehudas had sat up all night in the train from Marseille, but when they reached Paris, Eliezer was suddenly no longer tired.

They went from the railway station directly to the small Hôtel de Cologne on a side street just off the Boulevard des Italiens which was patronized by so many visitors from Palestine that it was known even to hack drivers as the "Hôtel des Palestiniens."

Hemda suggested that they rest before starting out to explore the city, but Eliezer refused to allow her even to unpack a bag.

He was like an old graduate returning to a college reunion.

"We can sleep any time," he ejaculated. "But Paris won't wait!"

So he hired a fiacre drawn by a horse which was so full of the spirit of spring that Hemda was terrified it would leave the pavement and go galloping across the grass and into the trees.

After a half hour Eliezer said in the voice of a small boy who has just suffered a grievous disappointment:

"You do not seem a bit excited about Paris!"

His wife shrugged her shoulders and replied:

"Such streets as these I have seen before, in Moscow. What is so wonderful about Paris?"

Eliezer never tried harder to convince anyone of anything.

"Bitti, it was here that I had my dream. Everyone dreams in Paris, of something or someone. Here a man may grow old in wisdom and learning, but at the same time he grows younger and younger in spirit.

"But what is more important than anything else, Bitti, is that this is the country which has given the world three of the most wonderful words in any language: *liberté, egalité, fraternité*. They are stamped indelibly on the minds and hearts of the French people. Liberty, equality, fraternity! It is those things we want for our own people."

Despite his exuberance, Eliezer was tired now, so when they reached the hotel he lay down for a nap, and his wife went off on a little expedition of her own.

Although she was wearing a costume which had been made for her by the best tailor in Jerusalem, she realized that people in the streets had been staring at her. She had even been able to tell by his glances that the concierge at their hotel thought her appearance odd. Knowing that something must be done about it, she wandered around the Right Bank until she found a department store called the Louvre. Maybe here she could get some clothes which would make her look as French as the paintings in the museum which bore the same name.

As fast as she made her purchases she insisted, to the bewilderment of the salesgirls, on putting them on. When she finally returned to the hotel she was carrying in bundles under her arms most of the Palestinian clothes she had been wearing when she started out.

She was rewarded when the concierge beamed and said:

"Now you look like a *grande dame!*"

Eliezer also liked the purchases and, following her example, he went on a shopping spree, returning with a pair of elegant gloves and a *chapeau à haute forme,* one of those cylindrical silk hats which fold up as flat as a pancake but can be extended to a height of more than a foot by virtue of a set of concealed springs. This, he explained, was an indispensable article for a gentleman in Paris, and he was going to be a gentleman in Paris this time!

Each evening, after a day of sight-seeing, the Ben Yehudas made their way to the Café Soufflé, where they would sit by the hour summarizing their impressions, or talking with writers and artists who frequented the place.

One evening Eliezer announced that as soon as possible he wanted to call on Dr. Max Nordau, the Jewish writer and scientist who had played such an important part in the Basle congress. Hemda quickly said:

"When you go to see him, you go alone. I heard in Jerusalem that he is a violent woman hater; that he detests all members of the opposite sex!"

"But, Bitti, what if he is? He can't bite you! If he hates women, the worst he can do is to ignore you."

A letter was written to Max Nordau, and back, quickly, came an invitation to call.

The two men had never met before and yet such was their admiration of each other that they kissed in French fashion and threw their arms around each other's shoulders. Hemda stood at a discreet distance studying this man who was supposed to be such a misogynist. His hair and beard were white, but he had a young and handsome face, with soft, intelligent eyes. Hemda knew that he had come to Paris from Germany, where he had studied medicine; that he now not only was a practicing physician, but had established a reputation as an authority on art, literature, and social questions. He had written several excellent books and had been the "golden-voiced orator" at the Basle congress.

While he was greeting Eliezer there was a knock at the door.

"Entrez!" he shouted over his shoulder, and in came a tall blond young woman whom he introduced as his wife.

"One more proof," Hemda later said to her husband, "that one must never believe Jerusalem gossip."

Hemda took an immediate fancy to Mrs. Nordau and to her infant daughter, Maxa, whom she carried in her arms. Although Mrs. Nordau was Danish, she had a warmth which Hemda had never associated with Scandinavians. She once had been a celebrated opera singer.

After a short time she kissed her husband good-by, excused herself to the Ben Yehudas, and said:

"I'm sorry I must go home now, but I would like all of you to have dinner with me some night soon. You can arrange a date with my husband."

After she had left Dr. Nordau explained. He lived here in this house with his mother and sister, both of whom had been opposed to his romance with the Danish girl, not because she had previously been married, nor because she had had several children by her first husband, but because she was a Christian. He had begged for his mother's understanding, but she had remained firm in her opposition. So they had been secretly married and Mrs. Nordau still lived in her own home with her children by the previous marriage and with little Maxa, their own child, while he still lived in this house with his mother and sister.

"And now that I am taking a leading part in the Zionist movement, I wonder what others will say."

Then he shrugged his shoulders and added:

"However, my wife and I are very much in love and, as you saw, we have a wonderful child!"

During the visit Eliezer received much encouragement from Dr. Nordau, Hemda received some pills he thought might help her regain the strength to fight off the malaria, and they both received an invitation to dinner.

On the way back to their hotel Eliezer said:

"Perhaps your sickness has been a blessing in disguise. I feel that this trip is going to be profitable to us in many ways. Just meeting Nordau has been worth the journey!"

Ben Yehuda's conference with Narcisse Leven, founder of the Alliance Israélite, was even more successful. Although in principle the Alliance Israélite was not in favor of a Hebrew revival in Palestine, Leven declared that he and his associates were interested in the dictionary project and would provide additional financing. A limited sum would be forthcoming immediately to enable Ben Yehuda to remain in Paris for a few weeks and work in the National Library gathering material. This meant that the small monthly allowance from Baron Rothschild could be sent to Jerusalem to finance the rest of the family.

Leven even promised Hemda to take care of the children's education in Paris as fast as they grew old enough to be sent abroad, so that night Hemda wrote to her mother to send her sister Peninnah to Paris at once.

Although Hemda gave no indication of having become "infected" with Paris, she was excited by the theater. Now that a living allowance had been granted to them, she took what was left of the money they had brought from Jerusalem and bought tickets for a number of plays and operas, fearing that unless she did the money would go for "more practical things."

Once Hemda bought two tickets for Meyerbeer's *Le Prophète* and was looking forward to her first evening at the Paris opera with great anticipation. She had already begun to dress when Eliezer returned to their hotel room and said:

"You must look very pretty for the dinner tonight!"

"Dinner?"

"Yes, I am sure I told you that tonight we dine with the Nordaus."

Mrs. Nordau's apartment was small but furnished in impeccable taste. The salon was lined with books. There was great excitement when the Ben Yehudas arrived; their hostess had a surprise for them.

Israel Zangwill, who was on his way back to London from a visit in Italy, had heard that his Jerusalem friends were in town and said he wanted to see them and accepted an invitation to the Nordau dinner with the understanding that the Ben Yehudas not be told in advance.

With the British writer came a lovely Englishwoman, a painter, Miss Stewart. An American artist, Louis Loeb, was also a guest.

As they were drinking coffee Hemda remarked to her host:

"I am enjoying the evening so much that I do not even mind having missed the opera."

When she was asked what she meant, she told about having tickets for *Le Prophète,* whereupon Dr. Nordau looked at his watch, ran out and got the Ben Yehudas' wraps, and insisted that they still had time to get there before the end of the second act.

"One does not give up a first night at the opera even for a Zangwill!" he said with a laugh, and then went out into the street to find a carriage for them.

Hemda knew the works of Meyerbeer by heart. For Eliezer it was enough that the composer was a Jew who had achieved top rank in the field of music, competing successfully with the best of Italian, German, and French composers. They both greatly enjoyed the performance, even though it was based on a Christian theme.

As they were leaving the opera house Hemda turned around to look at the crowd.

"Such a staircase as that one I have never seen! I thought one found such staircases only in royal palaces! Look, Eliezer, at the people descending! Did you ever see so much jewelry? Now I understand what they mean when they say that a first night at the Paris opera is not the music, not the singing! No, nothing in Moscow was ever like this!"

The Ben Yehudas spent four weeks in Paris. Not once were they plagued by such worries as they both had known for so long a time. They played like children, and Hemda was almost cured of her malaria, yet Eliezer did considerable serious work.

He saw Baron Rothschild, whose generosity had saved his life when he was so ill and had to go to Algiers, and whose beneficence since then had helped so much with the financing of the paper and work on the dictionary.

When Eliezer thanked the wealthy banker for all his kindness, Baron Rothschild, who had a reputation for a good memory, replied:

"What do you thank me for? I do not quite understand, young man. Have I ever done anything for you?"

Eliezer smiled.

"Yes, sir. You have contributed about fifty thousand gold francs to my work!"

"Indeed!" replied the baron, and that was all.

Then they discussed Palestine and the baron's colonies. It was obvious that the great Jewish philanthropist was far from being a Zionist. In a kind but firm voice he said as Eliezer left:

"I saved you once. Be careful now not to annoy the Turks with your nationalistic writings!"

Ben Yehuda was not able to see Emile Zola because he had gone abroad, but he did have a brief interview with Georges Clemenceau, who was deeply interested in all he had to say. But the great French statesman remarked that he could not understand how a person of intelligence could possibly be interested in Zionism, which he himself considered a retrogressive movement. He spoke bitterly of Palestine, calling it a country from which three religions had issued which he disliked in equal measure. He ended the interview with these words:

"Voulez-vous la Palestine, Monsieur Ben Yehuda? Prenez-la, elle ne nous intéresse pas [Mr. Ben Yehuda, you wish Palestine? Then take it, for it does not interest us]!"

When Ben Yehuda made a final call on Narcisse Leven, the Alliance Israélite founder promised to consider allowing more Hebrew to be taught in the schools the organization sponsored in Palestine. He pointed out, however, that the Jewish Colonization Association, which he also headed, was favoring the settlement of Jews in Argentina rather than in Palestine.

This was the worst news Ben Yehuda had heard and he tried to argue about it. The answer he got was:

"We are afraid of the rabbis of Palestine. We are afraid of their interference. They insist that we follow all the Orthodox rules in our institutions. They themselves wish to run everything."

The other big disappointment was that Ben Yehuda missed Herzl, who had been called back from Paris to Vienna by his newspaper. No one was certain when he would return.

But Dr. Nordau promised that he would use his influence with the president of the Zionist Organization, and Ben Yehuda was certain that with Dr. Nordau on his side the Viennese journalist could be won over to a consideration of the point of view of those in Jerusalem who had been working for a reborn Israel for so many years before the congress at Basle had even been a dream.

34

Hemda's London

IT WAS RAINING WHEN THEY REACHED LONDON, ONE of those dismal, mentally dampening rains. Besides, the Channel crossing had been the roughest voyage either of them had ever taken.

Some acquaintance had suggested a small hotel in Houndsditch Street. It turned out to be a depressing place in the East End, patronized almost exclusively by Jewish traveling salesmen with limited expense accounts. It smelled from morning until night of herring, and its lobby was loud at all hours with noise and vulgarity, everyone speaking Yiddish and everyone speaking at once.

"What a terrible contrast to Paris!" Eliezer said, and in his heart regretted there had been the necessity of coming to London.

The next day they telephoned Israel Zangwill. In Paris they had told him they expected to arrive in London on a certain Saturday and he had said, with an appearance of casualness:

"If you do get to London on Saturday, then come out to my place for dinner on Sunday."

They had stayed in Paris one week longer than they had expected to. Now it was another Saturday.

Zangwill sounded annoyed with them on the telephone. When he arrived at the hotel he made it clear why.

"What have you two done to me?" he began.

Eliezer became panicky. He considered Zangwill one of the best friends he had ever made. Now Zangwill was angry.

"What *have* we done? Tell us."

Then the British writer explained. Thinking that the Ben Yehudas were definitely arriving on the previous Saturday, he had arranged a reception for them the following day. He had invited to his home to meet them sixty of his most celebrated friends: writers, scholars, journalists, and artists. They had stood around for hours waiting impatiently for the guest of honor.

"Quite embarrassing! Quite embarrassing, old fellow! Now they think Ben Yehuda is just a character I invented!"

Then, suddenly changing mood, he added:

"But you shall be punished for your lack of punctuality! Tomorrow you two shall dine with me, and there will be no reception, no other guests, just the family."

Then, looking around the hotel, he said:

"How on earth, my dear chap, did you ever land in this place? You must get out of here at once!"

So the Ben Yehudas moved to a hotel in Kilburn, which was clean, respectable, and did not smell of fish.

The Zangwill dinner was one party they never forgot. The family consisted of the writer's mother, whom Eliezer called "intelligent" and Hemda later described as "brilliant"; two brothers, one a collector of antiques, the other a cartoonist of ability, and two sisters, a musician and a dress designer.

Before dinner, when Zangwill heard about Clemenceau's acrid comment on Zionism, he smiled and said:

"Despite Clemenceau, Ben Yehuda, I think it will be a jolly lot easier to get support for our movement from non-Jews than from Jews. I have already found much opposition among our own people. Jews here in my country are strong for assimilation. The argument they use most against us is that if we do succeed in establishing Israel as a land of our own the day will come when non-Jews in various parts of the world will say to us:

" 'All right, now you have a country, so go to it!'

"How do we answer such timid souls, Ben Yehuda?"

The man from Jerusalem replied that the Italians have a country, yet Italians who live in a place like New York are not told to go back to Italy, even though they had actually emigrated from Italy.

Zangwill shook his head.

"Even if someday we do achieve the dream, it will be used against us by Jews who are satisfied where they are and have little interest in the plight of fellow Jews not so happily off."

In a more optimistic tone Zangwill went on to say that plans were already being made for a second Zionist congress at Basle.

"I hope this time, Ben Yehuda, you will be present."

But the man from Jerusalem shook his head.

"I am more handicapped than you would ever believe by being an Ottoman subject. I had great difficulty getting permission to travel even to France and England. They would never give me permission to go abroad to attend a Zionist meeting.

"Baron Rothschild has implied that I cannot count on his further assistance if I get in trouble with the Turkish authorities. He himself is not enthusiastic for our Zionist cause. So again I probably shall have to watch the proceedings from afar."

At dinner Zangwill was in a jovial mood and told many stories which Eliezer said were even more amusing than those he had narrated in such books as *Children of the Ghetto* and *The King of Schnorrers*. The room echoed and re-echoed with laughter during the entire meal.

As they were going to the library for coffee, Eliezer whispered to his wife:

"He's wonderful, isn't he, Bitti!"

Hemda replied:

"Yes, but he was so entertaining that I laughed instead of eating, and now I am hungry! I think he was the only one who consumed a good meal!"

Another dinner party they always remembered was at the sumptuous home near Regent's Park of Herbert Bentwich, who had come to Jerusalem with Zangwill. There they met a son, Norman, who in later years was to become British Attorney General in Palestine and help revise the laws under which the British would rule the country. But at that time Norman was a boy of fifteen and his interest was music, not law. He was a violinist, and with his mother and two sisters gave a concert for the guests after dinner.

Mrs. Bentwich won a place in Eliezer's heart by telling how she had had nine children (two more were born later), and as fast as they were old enough to learn, she was having them study Hebrew under the distinguished scholar, Ephraim Ish-Kishor.

In later years the Ben Yehudas were to see this love of Hebrew implanted in the Bentwich children in their youth come to fruition when most of them decided to emigrate to Palestine and make their homes there.

At a dinner party given by Mrs. Herbert Samuel, whom they had once entertained in Jerusalem, the Ben Yehudas met her nephew, Herbert, who years later would become British High Commissioner of Palestine and later a viscount, but at that time he was just a curious youth interested in stories of their life in the Promised Land.

The Ben Yehudas spent two months in London, and not one evening were they without an invitation of some sort.

Lord Lionel Rothschild made it possible for Ben Yehuda to work during those two months in the British Museum, where he found traces of many "lost" words.

Ben Yehuda found considerable interest on the part of the British in his revival of Hebrew, but hardly any in his newspaper. They told him they had Jewish papers printed in English and also Yiddish papers. What did they want with one in Hebrew?

As the Ben Yehudas prepared to leave the British capital Eliezer asked his wife how, after two months, she liked London contrasted with Paris.

"Very much, Eliezer! It is all so neat and orderly. It has a confidence in itself which makes a visitor feel confidence also."

"But, Bitti, it is such a cold city; cold in every way. Paris is a gay city, so hospitable, so easy to live in, so——"

"I still like London better, Eliezer!"

Eliezer refused to drop the subject.

"I have observed over here that the Jews have been swallowed up. They have become more British than the British; cooler, more reserved, more phlegmatic.

"I have been in some of their private clubs. Do you know what you find inside of them? Boredom! One gets bored to death here."

Hemda dropped the argument, deciding that it was principally a matter of language. In Paris Eliezer felt at home because he spoke fluent French and could express any thought that came to his mind. He could read and write English perfectly, but he was timid about speaking the language and had difficulty expressing himself.

So it was "her" London and "his" Paris!

35

Hide-and-Seek

FOR ONE MONTH ELIEZER BEN YEHUDA WORKED IN the National Library at Paris, checking and rechecking the material he had obtained in London, covering thousands of additional pieces of paper with notes in his almost feminine handwriting. He also conferred with many celebrated philologists and scholars of oriental languages.

Hemda, meanwhile, cured of malaria, fell victim to a new contagion which she would never be able to shake off for the rest of her life. She was finally "bitten" by Paris. Before the month was up she wrote to a friend:

"I begin to love Paris, the life of the boulevards, the small twisting streets, the light and gay French way of saying things, the cafés and their habitués, the modesty of the writers, journalists, scholars, artists, and diplomats.

"The Frenchwomen I now find charming. I like to watch the faces of those who pass by, for there is life in their smiles and the joy of living in their eyes."

As the month drew to a close she made the great confession to her husband.

"I feel now," she admitted, "that I am like a woman in love with two men at the same time, one an intelligent scholar, serious-minded, an explorer of the depths of the soul; the other an artist, light-hearted, a teacher of the love of life above everything else, who possesses the art of always making the best of any situation."

Eliezer smiled and took her hand.

"Bitti, I knew this would happen. I am glad it happened. I would have been greatly disappointed in you if you had not caught the spirit of Paris as well as you did the spirit of London!"

Before they left, Eliezer arranged for his eldest son, Ben Zion, to enter the Alliance Israélite school in Paris, with the idea that he would eventually return to Jerusalem and become a teacher of Hebrew in one of the schools.

While the Ben Yehudas had been in London, Dr. Nordau had gone to his summer home in the country, so Eliezer went there to see him and summarize his own ideas for the renaissance of Israel.

He advanced his old argument that there never could be a Jewish state without a common language. That was basic. A Hebrew dictionary must be published as soon as possible, for how could a language be properly taught if there were no standards of pronunciation and meaning?

Next, plans must be made for the purchase of land from individual Arab owners, land on which new colonies could be founded. Baron Rothschild could not be expected to finance such projects indefinitely alone.

Third, there must be a definite program of fostering amicable relations with the Arabs. There should be, for example, schools where Jewish and Arab children would study side by side and learn the art of living peacefully together.

Fourth, there must be a definite program of adult education so the older generation already in Palestine could be enthused with the spirit of the new Zionist movement.

Fifth, schoolbooks were needed in Hebrew. It was foolish to try to bring children up entirely on oral instruction, which was too easily forgotten.

Ben Yehuda argued that he himself, for seventeen years, had been working almost singlehanded on many of these projects. But now, with the acceleration of the Zionist movement resulting from the

Basle congress, others must help. He wanted to get back to Jerusalem as quickly as possible and begin publishing his paper again, enlarging it to meet the needs of a growing Jewish population and adding an Arabic supplement to help carry out Point Three and to convince the Arabs of the advantages of a Jewish settlement of the wasteland.

Dr. Nordau listened attentively, then said:

"Ben Yehuda, as worthy as this program is, I must point out that I am only a soldier in the ranks. You shall have to see the commander in chief. Already preparations are being made in Basle for the Second Zionist Congress. I understand why you cannot attend, but there is no reason why you should not go to Basle immediately and see Herzl, who is already there."

Eliezer was disappointed. He had anticipated that Nordau would offer to help in convincing Herzl. It was with a weary voice that he said:

"I shall do as you suggest. I, too, am only a soldier. I shall go to Basle."

This was the first time either of them had ever been in Switzerland, but it was not a happy visit.

At Basle they went directly to the Casino, where preparations for the Second Zionist Congress were already being made. When they asked for Herzl one of his friends said:

"But didn't you know? Herzl left yesterday for Vienna!"

Then, noticing how disappointed Ben Yehuda was. the man added:

"Wait a few minutes. I shall be back."

When he returned he announced he had sent a telegram to Herzl saying that the Ben Yehudas were on their way to Vienna to see him.

And so, without having a chance to debate the wisdom of continuing the chase, the Ben Yehudas found themselves again on a train, this time heading for the Austrian capital.

Because their funds were getting low they traveled third-class, and when they arrived in Vienna they were physically as well as mentally exhausted. They washed their faces at the depot and went out to look for a carriage. By the time they reached the small garden of the

Herzl home, breathing fresh clean air for a change, their spirits had somewhat revived. But now they received another blow. The woman who greeted them introduced herself as Madame Herzl and said:

"My husband left last night for the Austrian summer resort of Ischl for an important interview with Emperor Francis Joseph. He regretted exceedingly having to go, but he had no alternative. He told me to urge you to meet him in Ischl. You will find him at the Hotel of the Three Kings."

Back at the railway station, the Ben Yehudas just missed a train and had to wait several hours for the next one. When they got to Ischl they went directly to the Hotel of the Three Kings.

"You are looking for Herzl, the man with the long beard, yes?" the manager announced rather than asked. "Without a doubt you are the people he was expecting. He went to the station some hours ago to meet you, and you were not on the train. He said that if you eventually arrived I was to express his regrets, but he has gone back to Vienna and then to Basle."

Hemda counted the money they had left. It was not enough, they decided, to finance any more of a chase, so they "submitted to fate," as Eliezer put it, and left Ischl for Constantinople.

In the Turkish capital Ben Yehuda had a Herculean labor to perform. He had received word, just before they left Paris, that he would not be able to resume publication of the *Deer* unless he obtained a new permit from the Turkish authorities.

When they reached Constantinople, Ben Yehuda was told that if he sought a permit in his own name the old matter of his imprisonment and his "revolt against the authorities" would be brought up. That difficulty could be circumvented by applying in his wife's name.

So the application was made in Hemda's name, but it was immediately rejected on the ground that the request for the *firman,* as it was called, must first be filed with the Turkish authorities in the city where the newspaper was to be published.

The night after they received this news Eliezer and Hemda decided that the course of wisdom would be for her to go to Jerusalem and file the application, while he remained in Constantinople to "apply the necessary pressures." But before Hemda left, something happened which made their first separation more difficult than they had anticipated.

The strain of all the traveling, the emotional upsets, and the changes of climate combined to bring on the sort of attack Eliezer had had when he was a student in Paris. He coughed violently from morning until night and had serious internal hemorrhages which confined him to his bed.

And at this precise time Herzl, whom they had chased all over Europe, came to Constantinople, but Ben Yehuda was too ill to try to see him.

Ostensibly Herzl came as a correspondent for his Vienna paper, "covering" a visit of Kaiser Wilhelm to the Sultan, but behind the scenes there had been months of subtle negotiations.

Turkey at this time had an enormous foreign debt, and Herzl hoped that the Sultan might be persuaded to accept some financial help in return for a charter permitting the Jewish colonization of Palestine. With this in mind Herzl had conferred with some of the Kaiser's intimates and had offered the argument that the Jews would need a "protector," and why not Germany?

Word finally trickled back to Herzl that the Kaiser was extremely interested and would try to persuade the Sultan to open negotiations with the Zionists. Herzl should go to Constantinople and meet the Kaiser there.

At their Constantinople conference the German Emperor said he wanted to see Palestine for himself and would meet Herzl in Jerusalem.

Meanwhile Hemda Ben Yehuda had gone home. The warmest welcome she received, after her four-month absence, was from her daughter Deborah.

"Now I am like other little girls because I have a mother again just like they do!"

All Palestine was excited over news that Kaiser Wilhelm was going to pay the Holy Land a visit, but the Jews attached even more importance to the visit of the famous Viennese journalist, Theodor Herzl, president of the Zionist Organization.

Herzl was anathema to the Turkish officials of Palestine, because they were convinced that somehow he was going to try to "steal" this piece of territory from them, but knowing that he was on speaking terms with the Kaiser, they took no steps to stop him from coming.

The Jews of Palestine prepared an elaborate reception for Herzl, and the Ottoman officials could do nothing about it, for if any questions were asked, the answer was that the decorations, the spectacles, the triumphal arches, and the processions were, of course, in honor of the Kaiser.

The German monarch and the Zionist leader met, by previous arrangement, at the Mikveh Israel agricultural school, where they saw an exhibit put on by the students. Herzl got down from his horse, responded to the salute of the reception committee, then approached the Kaiser's carriage and saluted the German monarch. Wilhelm extended his hand, a gesture of friendship in which he rarely indulged.

Eliezer had not yet come home, and so once again he missed meeting Herzl. Hemda was prevented from attending any of the receptions because she was now confined to her bed awaiting the birth of her fourth child, so she sent Ben Zion to greet Herzl and to welcome him to Israel in the name of the Ben Yehuda family and to invite him to call on her.

Ben Zion, then just sixteen, introduced himself as "Ben Zion ben Ben Yehuda."

Herzl received him with cordiality and laughingly called him the "Triple Ben." He sent word back by the boy that he would be charmed to call on Mrs. Ben Yehuda.

When Hemda received the message she suddenly wondered whether she had made a mistake. She had heard that Ottoman detectives were checking up on all of Herzl's movements. If he came to the Ben Yehuda home, a search of the house would undoubtedly be made later. So she left her bed long enough to ransack Eliezer's study and burn any letters or papers which might, to suspicious Turkish officials, seem to have a nationalistic tone.

But Herzl never came. Friends convinced him that such a visit might result in Ben Yehuda's being imprisoned again. Thus, once more, direct contact between the Zionist leader and either Ben Yehuda or his wife was postponed.

When Hemda applied for the newspaper permit she was first told it was out of the question.

"A woman editor? Unheard of!"

She cited the precedent of a woman newspaper owner in Constantinople. Then they asked her age.

"Twenty-six."

The answer was that no permit could be issued to anyone under thirty.

"If I could grow four years older in a hurry, would that be all right?" she asked, winking.

The Turkish official, suddenly showing a sense of humor, replied that if she could bring papers proving such an age her application would be forwarded to Constantinople.

Through the conniving of friends Hemda obtained the necessary documents and one night wrote Eliezer a letter telling him the application finally was on its way. Jokingly she added:

"In connection with the application, I today became thirty years old."

Eliezer absent-mindedly replied:

"You say you have just had your thirtieth birthday. I thought that you were much younger."

Weeks went by, and every time Ben Yehuda called at government offices he was told the application from Jerusalem had not yet arrived, but friends advised him that someone was simply waiting for a bribe.

After Ben Yehuda had raised the necessary money and paid all the proper officials, the application suddenly was found. Now, he was told, there would be a delay while it was given consideration.

Ben Yehuda spent eight unhappy months in Constantinople. During that time he interviewed influential Turks, trying to ascertain the official reaction to Herzl's attempt to "buy" Palestine. He was told from every source that Herzl was wasting his time.

In a letter dated January 21, 1899, he wrote to Hemda:

"The more I think over the state of affairs, the more clear it becomes that there is hardly any hope for us to settle now in the land of our fathers. I have had an interview with Oscar Straus, an outstanding Jew who is Envoy Extraordinary and Minister Plenipotentiary from Washington to Constantinople. He says the Turkish government is determined not to permit the Jews the foundation of any colony and, in general, not to allow us to increase our numbers in the country. I am also told that Russia and France are backing up Turkey in this resolution. . . .

"I have already written Herzl about this state of affairs."

36

Two Bearded Crusaders

DURING THE ABSENCE OF ELIEZER HEMDA GAVE birth to her fourth child. She sent her husband a telegram telling him he was the father of a girl with intelligent dark eyes and black hair; they were both quite well; she suggested they name the child Ada.

The telegram reached Eliezer in Vienna. After sitting impatiently in Constantinople for eight months, ill most of the time, he had suddenly decided it was imperative to see Herzl, even if he had to chase him halfway across Europe again. It was important, he felt, that they discuss all he had learned in the Turkish capital.

He had tried by letter to point out to Herzl that his idea of "buying" Jewish colonization rights was an idle dream.

The reply he received from Herzl had read merely:

"We are trying to arrange it."

Ben Yehuda admired Herzl and had stoutly defended him since he had become a champion of Zionism, but now he feared that Herzl was being blind and deaf as well.

So Eliezer Ben Yehuda took the Orient Express to Vienna, and there the two men finally met; two men of letters, two men burning with Zionist zeal; two bearded journalists, and yet unlike in so many other ways.

In his own diary Herzl told of the meeting in one sentence: "There came to me a young enthusiast, Ben Yehuda."

The "young enthusiast," who was two years older than Herzl, started out by congratulating his host and saying that without doubt history would write that the state of Israel acually was created by the First Zionist Congress, when Jews publicly declared their wish to re-establish themselves in their own ancient land.

"But why, Herzl, did you say 'it will come to pass in five or fifty years'?"

Herzl smiled and explained that during the next five years, in his opinion, one of the great powers would take possession of Palestine and give the land to the Jews for their own national state. (A prediction not borne out by subsequent events.)

"Then why fifty years?"

Herzl went on that if his first prediction did not materialize, then it would take fifty years for Turkey to collapse. (A prediction which was about thirty years off in its timing.) Then, he added, the Ottoman Empire would be divided up and the Jews would get Palestine as their share. In either case, he concluded, the Jews should now be preparing, on their own soil, to take advantage of whatever situation developed.

"I heartily agree!" Ben Yehuda declared intently. "But if that is your belief, then political Zionism should be supporting the pioneering movement we have already begun in Palestine."

Herzl half evaded by answering that the important problem at this time was political rights.

Ben Yehuda then told of his conversation with the American Minister and said all his talks in Constantinople buttressed his opinion that the Ottoman Empire would never sell the Jews any colonization rights in Palestine.

"If you concentrate all the efforts of Zionism on raising money for that purpose," Ben Yehuda argued, "and neglect the tender roots we have already planted, not only will our efforts bear no fruit, but practical Zionism will die!"

Herzl disagreed.

Ben Yehuda then presented, in even greater detail than he had to Dr. Nordau, his own five-point program. As for the creation of a national language, Herzl said:

"Let the Jews go to Palestine and live there for a few generations. After that they will decide themselves what language they wish to speak."

"But if there is no language ready for them, if there is no modern Hebrew, then what language could they possibly speak?" Ben Yehuda asked, spreading his hands out in an empty gesture.

As for better relations with the Arabs, Herzl apparently considered Jewish-Arab relations relatively unimportant at this stage in Jewish history. He also showed little enthusiasm for Ben Yehuda's ideas about the political education of those Jews already in Palestine.

The talk was without a single positive result. Herzl ended it by saying that he still hoped to win the Sultan over to the colonization idea and in the meantime was going to dedicate his efforts to raising the money to solve Turkey's national indebtedness, which he felt was a bribe the Sultan would not be able to resist.

From Vienna, Ben Yehuda went to Paris, hoping to make a new impression on Herzl's chief lieutenant, but that meeting was also futile. Dr. Nordau seemed more sympathetic, but again he had the I-am-only-a-soldier attitude.

From Paris, Hemda received the blackest letter Eliezer had ever written to her:

"The situation is desperate. Herzl is convinced he will succeed in buying the charter from the Turks and will not think or talk of anything else. He has no interest in either the paper or the dictionary. Nordau is of no help. We will not get support from anyone. We are indeed an unfortunate people."

As Hemda read the letter she was lying in bed nursing her newborn baby. With the letter had come a clipping from a Vienna paper. She unfolded it and spread it out on the bed. It was a cartoon showing Herzl and Ben Yehuda in conference. She studied the face of her husband, then suddenly put the baby down on the bed and burst into tears. The look of suffering and despair on Ben Yehuda's face told better than a thousand words might have done what the result of their conference had been.

Eliezer Ben Yehuda returned to "his" Jerusalem a disillusioned man with a heart full of sorrow. His shoulders were more stooped than usual, his eyes lacked any trace of sparkle. It was obvious that he had neither slept nor eaten properly in a long time.

But Hemda had a surprise for him which she hoped would revive his spirits.

"You must treat me with great respect now, Eliezer," she said after they had greeted each other, "for I am the second woman in history ever to be given a permit by the Ottoman Empire to run a newspaper!"

It worked!

Ben Yehuda, who had labored so long in Constantinople for the firman, had bribed so many officials, had pulled so many strings, forgot for the moment his defeats in Vienna and Paris.

"It is difficult to believe, Bitti! After eighteen years, at last we have the right to a paper of our own! We must start work at once! I wonder how quickly we can get out the first issue."

As he talked he was on the way to his study. Hemda had to remind him that he had still not greeted all the members of his family; that he had not yet met his own youngest child; that he still had on his hat and coat, and that dinner was waiting.

In applying for the permit they had used the name *Hashkafah* (The Review), hoping that such an innocuous title would convince the Turks that the paper would not have a subversive political complexion.

But whatever the name of the paper was to be, it was being awaited eagerly by the former readers of the *Deer*. Much had happened lately. Another Zionist congress had met. Hostilities had broken out between the British and the Boers of South Africa. Here in Palestine the followers of Ahad Haam, the Russian intellectual who had read Pines out of his secret society, were conducting a relentless campaign against the political Zionism of Herzl and what they called "the Basle crowd." Also, there was a new campaign under way for the elevation of the liberal Sephardic rabbi, Jacob Meir, to the post of Hacham Bashi.

After a full year without the *Deer,* the Jews of Palestine were hungry for news and opinions. Besides, many had paid-up subscriptions to the *Deer* and they wanted a paper every week or their money back.

The second day after Ben Yehuda's return his wife had another surprise for him.

"You know, Eliezer, how much you have talked about putting out supplements to the paper in various languages? I have an Arab writer who will edit our Arabic supplement. You, of course, can do the German one yourself. And for the French supplement . . .

"In your absence I saw a great deal of a wonderful young French couple, the Duc Quercis. They have been most kind. I told them so much about you that they talk of you almost in religious whispers! They are both writers, Eliezer; brilliant writers! They have agreed to edit the French section, and without pay, Eliezer!"

The first issue of the *Review* gave the Jews of Palestine enough controversial material to keep them arguing for weeks. Ben Yehuda took bold sides on every one of the questions of the day.

He threw his paper behind Rabbi Meir again, thus antagonizing the reactionaries.

He heaped scorn and denunciation on the followers of Ahad Haam and stoutly defended the organized Zionists, despite the rebuffs he had had from Herzl himself. He wrote that in his opinion Ahad Haam wished to make Palestine a spiritual rather than a political center, which would mean only a small community of Jews, content with their lot, a high-class ghetto.

It was difficult to take a stand on the Boer War because the South Africans were fighting for their freedom, and instinctively Ben Yehuda was on the side of any people trying to get out from under a yoke. But in this case Ben Yehuda felt that the future of Israel was more important than any other considerations. He had evidence that France and Russia were both taking anti-Zionist positions. In this situation England was the one great hope. Therefore, it was to the Jews' interest to be on England's side, so the *Review* came out for England.

Jerusalem buzzed like an overcrowded beehive with excited talk after the first issue appeared. It was the old story all over again. Ben Yehuda was denounced and vilified; defended and eulogized. There were few neutrals. But he had made more enemies than new friends. There were few who agreed with his stand on all the big controversies. If they saw eye to eye with him on the Boer War, they were in violent disagreement on the Rabbi Meir controversy. If they approved of the *Review's* stand on those questions, they disapproved of Zionism.

But the greatest conflict developed within the office of the *Review* itself.

Ben Yehuda paced his study in great agitation when he read the French supplement and found that the Duc Quercis had supported the Boers. He called them in and argued. A paper must have a policy. One page cannot contradict another.

But his French editors were adamant. They were socialists. They were on the side of the Boers because these people were fighting for their independence. How could Ben Yehuda, a Jew, possibly oppose other people struggling for freedom?

Later, when the Russo-Japanese War began, the editor and his assistants split again, Ben Yehuda taking the side of the Japanese because of his hatred of the evils perpetrated by the czarist regime. The French section supported Russia. The Duc Quercis explained that they had a hope that out of Russia someday would come a great socialist uprising which would change the history of all the world and that as a result all oppressed peoples, including Jews, would benefit.

The feud with the Duc Quercis was a continuous one. Ben Yehuda often accused the French couple of falsifying the meaning of dispatches published in the French supplement, giving them the opposite meaning they had in the Hebrew part of the paper. The Duc Quercis rebutted by saying that Ben Yehuda exaggerated British victories and minimized the gains of the Boers.

When Ben Yehuda for a second time lost his fight to elevate Rabbi Jacob Meir to the post of Hacham Bashi, the Duc Quercis said:

"I told you so!"

It was seven years before Rabbi Meir obtained that post, but even then the victory was Pyrrhic, for the Sultan refused to ratify Rabbi Meir because of his "too advanced ideas."

This fight was like so many in which Ben Yehuda engaged; constant defeats, which the slow inevitable progress of events finally turned into victories. Rabbi Meir, just before Ben Yehuda's death, finally did become Chief Rabbi of the Sephardic Jews of Palestine.

Despite the acrimony of the debates with the Duc Quercis, they and the Ben Yehudas became deep friends. There would be hours of argument, then they would eat and drink together, or sit by a fire and enjoy pleasant social intercourse, discussing culture, literature, and the arts. Often instructors from the schools and young Jews interested in progressive thought would join the circle. The Ben Yehuda home was a meeting place for those unafraid of the clash of ideas.

It was the progress of Hebrew in the schools which gave Ben Yehuda the most encouragement in this period. Although Hebrew was still not the "official" language of any one school, more and more courses in Hebrew were being given; more and more children were speaking the language in the streets; more and more pupils from the villages were coming to Jerusalem to attend classes in schools infinitely more advanced than the old Talmudic institutions.

When Ben Yehuda, not long after his return from abroad, called Ben Zion to him and told the boy he was to be sent to Paris to enter the Alliance's Ecole Normale, the child became defiant.

"I prefer," he said boldly, "to be a shoemaker or blacksmith here in our own land than to study in Paris. I refuse to go!"

Ben Yehuda knew how closely friends and enemies alike had been watching Ben Zion since the day of his birth. If this "first Hebrew child" became a failure it would hurt his own cause more than anything else. He tried to explain this to the boy, adding:

"With you, Ben Zion, I started a great experiment. I beg you to allow me to carry it to its conclusion!"

So reluctantly Ben Zion went to Paris.

Some time later Dr. Nordau wrote to the father:

"Your son tells me that as soon as he feels he has learned enough he is going back to Jerusalem to become a journalist. Here is the curse of our people, that a boy of extraordinary talents like your son must return to a country where there are no real newspapers and no readers!"

"I hope the day will come," Ben Yehuda replied, "when our sons will no longer have to leave the land of their birth to receive the education they need. As for our not having newspapers and readers, why do you not come to Israel and find out the truth about us yourself?"

Ben Yehuda added that if Nordau came he would be treated like a king. But Nordau never accepted the invitation. Today his bones rest in Israel, but while alive he never visited the country for which he did so much work.

With Ben Zion gone, the father made Deborah his favorite child. He called her the "Happy Little Prophetess," but in her babyhood she herself had chosen the nickname "Dola," which was what everyone else called her. She was now almost seven and had begun to read Hebrew as well as to speak the language fluently.

When Ada, the youngest, was less that two years old, Hemda gave birth to her fifth child, Eliezer's tenth, who was named Shlomit after one of Deborah's daughters who had died. Soon after that Deborah, Ehud, and Ada were all stricken with typhoid fever. Then the mother caught it too. Finally the newborn baby also became ill.

The home became a hospital. Barricades were put up in the street covered with posters announcing a stringent quarantine. Doctors came and went. Word soon spread through Jerusalem that there was no chance of saving the mother's life, although some of the children might recover.

Ben Yehuda's adversaries said again what they had said each time calamity came: this affliction was heaven-sent, his retribution because he was a heretic and a rebel.

But one by one the typhoid victims all recovered. When the siege was over and the barricades and posters removed, the Ben Yehuda home seemed like a battlefield just after the shooting has stopped. Eliezer was a haggard skeleton. The other members of the family showed the physical scars of what they had been through. But they had all lived. The *Review* had lived too. Ben Yehuda had not failed to put out a single issue on time. Now, perhaps, God willing, he could settle down and try to re-establish life as it had been before the epidemic.

But real tragedy stalked through the doors of the house less than six months later. Deborah, called Dola, caught pneumonia.

From the start of her illness the child seemed to know she was going to die.

Once, when Hemda laid a cool hand on the hot small forehead, Dola whimperingly said:

"Mother, I never again shall see the stars! I never again shall see the blue sky!"

Then one early evening, as she lay clutching a doll to her cheek, she suddenly cried out with fright:

"Mother, what is the matter? Mother, I do not see you! I do not see you!"

Her body writhed for an instant in agony. Then death came and ended the suffering.

Duc Querci and his wife went out into the garden, picked an armload of flowers, and laid them lovingly over the body of the dead child, unaware, not being Jews, of the Orthodox attitude toward flowers and the dead.

Eliezer was more bowed down with grief than he had ever been. He had centered his hopes on Ben Zion, but his deepest affection had been for Deborah.

When the undertakers arrived and were shown into the death chamber, the "spectacle," as they called it, revolted them. This was sacrilege! Did not the Ben Yehudas know that it was contamination of the dead to have flowers anywhere near the body? Now the sanctity of burial could not be accorded the child.

Ben Yehuda stood it as long as he could. He was slow to wrath, but finally he exploded:

"Be silent in the presence of my daughter! Silent, I tell you!"

The undertakers suddenly stopped their chattering.

"Now leave quickly! Tell whoever wishes to know that I shall bury my own child in my own garden with my own hands. That is how much respect I have for you and your customs!"

Then, stumbling out into the garden, he found a spade and furiously started to dig.

Meanwhile the Duc Quercis promised the undertakers that they would put the "scandal" on the front page of every newspaper in Europe unless they relented. So the undertakers held a whispered conference and at last agreed that if someone would remove the flowers they would take the body.

Ben Yehuda and Duc Querci accompanied Deborah, called Dola, to her last resting place.

A heavy stone, according to ancient custom, was placed upon her breast. As this was being done Ben Yehuda gave a sharp cry of inner torture and shouted:

"Why? Why so *large* a stone?"

37

Three Iron Chests

ONE DAY IN THE SUMMER OF 1901 ELIEZER BEN Yehuda said to his wife:

"Bitti, do you realize it was just 20 years ago this month that I arrived in Jerusalem?"

In twenty years he had fathered ten children. Five had died, but five still lived. Two of them spoke fluently the language he had spent so much of these twenty years trying to bring back to life. More important, the streets of Jerusalem, the market places, the villages scattered over the desert were thronged with other Jews who spoke this same revived language.

Through all the vicissitudes and in face of all the opposition, he had managed to keep alive a real Hebrew newspaper which could help popularize the words he kept adding to the language for an only half-receptive public.

Today there was a Hebrew literature. True, most of the books which came out in the new language were translations, but the day was approaching when men would write books directly in Hebrew.

There was already an amateur dramatic group which gave plays in Hebrew, and this might be the forerunner of a real Hebrew theater.

Now it was no longer unusual for lectures and speeches to be delivered in Hebrew.

Progress had certainly been made in these twenty years. But on the debit side of the ledger one must make entries too.

There was no uniformity to Hebrew as one heard it spoken in the streets. One man pronounced a word this way, his neighbor or even his wife pronounced it some other way.

And their vocabularies were still too limited. The language was feeble in many respects, and inadequate.

As for the Hebrew books which were published, their style was heavy and ponderous, lacking in elasticity. Often the sense was unclear because different people had different ideas about the meanings.

But, Ben Yehuda kept telling himself, when his dictionary finally came out all these problems would disappear. The dictionary would be a stimulus in many ways. Most important of all, it would help to accelerate the development of the Jewish state.

The only celebration of the twentieth anniversary of Ben Yehuda's arrival in Jerusalem was this little self-summation, but it served a purpose. That day Ben Yehuda went back into his study, took a red pencil, and drew heavy lines under the words of the motto which hung on the wall over his desk:

THE DAY IS SHORT;
THE WORK TO BE DONE SO GREAT!

Then he returned to his scholarly labors with a new determination. It must not take another twenty years to finish the task!

So he went back to a schedule of working seventeen or eighteen hours a day. He was older now and grew tired more easily, but he found that if he worked for one or two hours standing up at his bookkeeper-type desk and then one or two hours sitting down he could keep going long into the night without a break.

In these twenty years he had read through thousands of volumes; the works of many forgotten poets and writers of little fame. He had even perused countless private manuscripts.

He had had to become a master not only of written English,

French, German, Russian, and Hebrew itself, but also of the "sister languages" of Arabic, Coptic, Assyrian, Aramaic, and Ethiopian.

Work of this sort required concentration. He needed peace, solitude, and quiet. Yet Ben Yehuda rarely in these twenty years had had any peace, solitude, and quiet.

It was difficult to go from a room in which your favorite child had just died back to a roomful of dead words and try to bring some of them back to life.

It was difficult for a man who, these twenty years, had been trying to fight off the ravages of what medical science then called an incurable disease to work seventeen or eighteen hours a day, whether he stood or sat.

It was difficult to keep the mind on scholarly matters when the body announced that it was not being properly fed.

Yet Ben Yehuda had, there in his study, tens of thousands of file cards covered with his own fine handwriting and a mountain of odd pieces of paper to prove that he had succeeded, during these two decades, in rising above temporal distractions.

There were some who wondered why it was taking Ben Yehuda so long to put out his dictionary. If they had understood something about his method they might not have been so perplexed and so impatient.

Ben Yehuda's self-imposed task was to take a language which had not been commonly spoken for two thousand years and popularize it for modern usage, and at the same time to make it adequate for the needs of a complex group of people. It must be made sufficient for intellectuals as well as tillers of the soil. It must be flexible enough for artists, scientists, engineers, and for literary people who wanted all the little nuances and shadings of expression. It must be adequate for ordering groceries, shouting at cattle, and making love.

But Ben Yehuda wanted to keep Hebrew pure. He wanted to help make modern Hebrew a consistent and beautiful language, without harsh sounds; without words which grated on the ear because they were inconsistent with the ancient music of the language.

That was the basic theory on which he worked.

In 1881, the year he began his philological labors, Jews were using Hebrew principally as a language in which to pray. It had been kept alive in the Talmudic schools where students were taught to read ancient Hebrew and argue over the meanings of obscure passages in books on biblical law.

To make this musty language adequate for common usage it was necessary to add thousands of words to the vocabulary. It would have been simple for Ben Yehuda or anyone else, when a word was needed, to steal it bodily from some other language. But this would have violated his own rule about keeping Hebrew pure. This would have been "bastardization," and bastardization was exactly what Ben Yehuda was trying to avoid.

His first task, therefore, when he was looking for a combination of letters to express a certain object, concept, or idea, was to go back and see if perhaps the word had once existed in Hebrew and had been in common usage but had disappeared from the language.

Such searches required infinite patience. Ben Yehuda would comb the pages of hundreds of books, sometimes feeling as if he were a little man with a magnifying glass looking on a great sandy beach for something the size of an ant egg. But often these searches were rewarding and he would return with exactly the right word, pure and consistent, all ready to be put back into the common vocabulary.

When he found such a word Ben Yehuda would handle his discovery as tenderly as if it were some priceless relic of ancient times.

Sometimes Ben Yehuda would find words almost by accident. While he was working in the British Museum he came upon some yellowed pieces of parchment and on them discovered a number of words which had been "lost" for hundreds of years and which he himself had given up any hope of finding. On that occasion he was as excited as, years later, the archaeologists would be when they suddenly uncovered the ancient wealth of King Tutankhamen.

Hebrew, when it ceased being a spoken language, ceased increasing its vocabulary. That meant there would be no Hebrew word for any idea, object, or conception which had evolved, been created, or been invented in the past two thousand years. In such cases Ben Yehuda had a more difficult problem.

He then would go to the "sister languages." If one of them "had a word for it," he could "borrow" it and graft it onto Hebrew. This would not violate his own rule against bastardization, because Arabic, Assyrian, Egyptian, Ethiopian, and Coptic were languages akin to Hebrew in sound and form.

Arabic provided many of the words he needed, because it was the only Semitic language which had remained alive, vigorous, and in current usage down through the ages. But here he was handicapped by the fact that the Arabs, for so many centuries, had led a primitive life far removed from modern civilization. As a result, they had retained in their vocabulary only the words which a simple people needs. So often even Arabic was of little help, and then the task of word-birth became even more difficult.

One of Ben Yehuda's constant and almost fruitless searches, as he went from city to city and from library to library, was for some trace of the ancient Canaanite and Moabite languages. They had been closer to Hebrew than any other, and Ben Yehuda was certain that in them he would be able to find thousands of "lost words." But in ancient times the Canaanite and Moabite languages had died completely, leaving little trace of their once healthy existence.

If the word he wanted did not exist in any Semitic language, and if he could find no trace of its ever having existed, then Ben Yehuda would have to do a job of actual word creating. But here again he would never just put together a combination of sounds which were pleasing to the ear. Instead he would first look for a Hebrew base, and from that base would evolve the word.

For example, as he had once pointed out to his wife, there was no real Hebrew word for "dictionary." The expression which people had been using as a substitute was *sefer millim,* which merely meant "book of words." So Ben Yehuda, failing to find an adequate word in ancient Hebrew books or in sister languages, took as a base the Hebrew word *millah* ("word") and from it created *millon,* which he offered as one of his first contributions to the new language. Today when Jews speak of a dictionary they use this Ben Yehuda word.

Another example was the need of a word for "journal" or "newspaper." Lacking such a word, Hebrew-speaking people were using the expression *michtav-et,* which literally meant "a letter of the time." Ben Yehuda, as a journalist himself, decided that that was clumsy; they needed a more succinct way of saying it. So he took the Hebrew word for "time" and, improvising a bit, came from his study with the new word *itton,* which quickly won popular acceptance.

Although a pacifist, Ben Yehuda was bothered that there was no real Hebrew word for "soldier." The closest was *ish-tsavah,* "man of the army." So he manufactured *hayal* and even gave it a feminine form, *hayellet,* which would come in handy half a century later when an Israeli army was formed with girls fighting alongside men for the preservation of their new Jewish state.

Sometimes a word which Ben Yehuda had created from a purely Hebrew base turned out to resemble its European equivalent, and some people surmised he had stolen the word from one of the European languages.

For example, in most ancient languages there had been no word for a machine which flies through the air. When such a machine was finally invented, English-speaking people decided to call it an airplane. The French named it an *avion.* Ben Yehuda took the base *aveer* (Hebrew for "air") and added *on.* So *aveeron* is an example of a purely Hebrew word which appears as if it had been stolen, because it sounds a little like the English word and very much like its French equivalent.

In his research Ben Yehuda often found pure Hebrew words which had been taken bodily into Western languages. "Shibboleth" was an example of one which English-speaking people had stolen. In Hebrew it meant "ear of grain." There is a curious story of how it came to be used in English for "password."

In ancient times the Gileadites were fighting the Ephraimites. One night the Ephraimites tried to infiltrate the lines of the enemy disguised as Gileadites, but a suspicious sentry tested them by requiring their leader to pronounce the Hebrew word for "ear of grain."

"Sibboleth," the Ephraimite said, omitting the *h* sound from the first syllable, as was the Ephraimite custom.

Thus the enemy soldiers were identified as Ephraimites. Thus the Gileadites avoided defeat. Thus "shibboleth" came into use, even in English, to mean "password" instead of "ear of grain."

Whenever he returned from working in a library somewhere, Ben Yehuda would copy his notes onto separate filing cards. There was a card for each word.

Anochiuth, the Hebrew word for "egoism," had been difficult to trace, but finally, in old volumes somewhere, he found some examples of its early use and had copied his findings onto the master card. But now the master card had been lost. This created a major crisis. Ben Yehuda had no idea in what books, in what libraries, in what distant cities he had found the traces of "egoism." Without the card how could he ever do justice to "egoism" in his dictionary? If he must start the research all over again, where would he commence? Was it in Moscow, or Constantinople, or Paris, or London that he had found the word quite by chance?

After the entire family had searched without success for the card, Ben Yehuda wrote a pathetic letter to the Hungarian scholar, Wilhelm Bacher, which Professor Bacher mentioned in a tribute to Ben Yehuda many years after his death. In the letter the unhappy lexicographer wrote:

"I am so sorry, but I have not the possibility to reread all the books to find this word again. This is why I ask you, very esteemed sir, whether you possess any notes showing where this word 'anochiuth,' with its meaning of 'egoism,' is first mentioned. Please let me know about it and I shall be most grateful."

Professor Bacher fortunately was able to supply some clues to the missing word and the crisis ended.

Having revived or created a word, or having borrowed it from a sister language, Ben Yehuda's next task was to introduce it to a new generation of Hebrew-speaking people in need of just that word to fill a gap in their vocabularies. But he soon found that people are basically conservative, slow to change, reluctant to accept something new and better in place of the old and shabby but familiar.

His newspaper was his principal vehicle of introduction. Each week's new words were incorporated in articles on agriculture, literature, education and the arts, and in the children's corner.

Immediately they became the subjects of stormy debates. The critics referred sarcastically to "Ben Yehuda's word factory." His friends called it his "language laboratory."

The more enterprising schoolteachers looked forward to the enlargement of the Hebrew language; lazy ones fought it, for it meant that unless they were alert and kept up with the new words themselves, their pupils might embarrass them by using words which they themselves did not know.

Having launched a word through the newspaper, Ben Yehuda then considered that it was up to the public to accept or reject it.

There were those who, in Ben Yehuda's lifetime, accused him of being arbitrary and asked why this one man should have the power to decide what words they should use in speaking or writing.

The answer he always gave was that he was merely the excavator. He dug out a word and put it on display; if they were pleased with it and felt a need for it, the word was there for them to use. If they rejected it, the word died a-borning. It was pure democracy. The final decision, regardless of what Ben Yehuda might say or do, was up to the mass of the people.

However, it was natural that Ben Yehuda, having played the role of midwife, did everything he could to win acceptance of his "baby." The paper always remained his most effective instrument of propaganda. But there was also his own large family.

Each word, as it came from the "factory," was given to Hemda and the children, with instructions to get to work with it. This meant they were to sprinkle it liberally through their conversations, and if the word were ever questioned they were to explain its meaning.

"The army," as the family was called, often was the deciding factor in getting a word accepted.

There were those people in Palestine who vied with each other in trying to get the new words as fast as they came out and using them first, just as a woman in Paris or New York might try to be the first to have a hat or gown in the latest style. There was a certain amount of snob appeal about being the first with the latest word.

But there were others who went to the opposite extreme and built up a sales resistance to Ben Yehuda's creations, which they said were sacrilegious. The language without these improvisations had been good enough for the prophets; it was good enough for them.

Generally the Ben Yehuda "army" won its word battles, and most of the father's creations or discoveries were accepted, but some few words were so completely rejected that as years went by the only people who ever used them were the lexicographer himself and members of his own family. One such word was the one he introduced for "tomato." The common word already in use was *agbanit,* from a root which meant "to love sensuously." Ben Yehuda felt that a better word was needed, so he went back to colloquial Arabic and coined the word *badurah.*

After it had been announced in the paper, "the army" received its marching orders. Henceforth, if any Ben Yehuda went into a shop to purchase this vegetable, he was to ask for a badurah, and if the shopkeeper seemed perplexed, he was to be given a little lesson in modern Hebrew and was to be introduced formally to badurah.

Such tactics generally succeeded, but after many years of proselytizing, the only shoppers in Jerusalem who ever called a tomato a badurah were members of the Ben Yehuda family.

Then there was the story about the most expensive word in the Hebrew language.

A friend in London, knowing of Ben Yehuda's need of financial help with his dictionary, approached a wealthy English Jew, explained the project, stressed how Ben Yehuda was bringing the language up to date, filling it with practical, modern words, and then asked for a contribution.

The wealthy Englishman, who was greatly interested in sports, quickly replied:

"If what you say is true I will make out a sizable check for this man. But to prove it, you must telegraph him at once and ask if he has a Hebrew noun for 'sport,' and if so, to telegraph it back to you."

When the telegram arrived in Jerusalem, Eliezer read it, then shook his head.

"That is one of the many words which is not ready yet!"

Hemda was impatient with him.

"Eliezer, you cannot allow one little word to stand in the way of financial assistance, which we need so badly. If you don't have a word, create one quickly so we can telegraph it to him today!"

But Eliezer Ben Yehuda, the scholar, would not be hurried. He still had additional research to do in this field.

It was years before he finally announced that the Hebrew noun for "sport" would be *mil'ab,* based on an Arabic root meaning "to play."

Knowing that the Englishman's financial assistance had been lost because mil'ab had not been ready earlier, the Ben Yehuda family always referred to it as "the most expensive word in our language."

Then there was the story of the day one of the Ben Yehuda daughters came home from school and resolutely announced she was not going back to the *gymnasia* any more. Her parents were distressed. Why not?

"Because you tell us that we must speak only Hebrew, yet you send us to the gymnasia! Why must we call a school by a Russian name? Why can't we have a Hebrew word instead of gymnasia? When Father gives it a Hebrew name I shall go back to whatever he calls it!"

In that case, fortunately for the education of the child, Father was ready. He had already decided on *midrashah,* which was based on an Arabic root. And so his small daughter went back to school and announced to her fellow students that they might be attending a gymnasia, but she was different; she was attending a midrashah!

But this was another word the people refused to accept, and so for years even Hebrew-speaking Jews in Palestine continued to send their children to the gymnasia; only the Ben Yehuda young went to a midrashah.

One of Ben Yehuda's dreams was that someday there would be a great Hebrew university, preferably in Jerusalem, of course, which would become the intellectual center of the new Israel, and that in it there would be incorporated a body of language scholars similar to the French Academy which would pass on all linguistic matters and keep the language pure and uncorrupted, yet still permit it to be fluid.

In the meantime some substitute must be created; some board or body to say "yes" and "no."

Accordingly, soon after he began work on the dictionary Ben Yehuda founded what was called in Hebrew *Vaad Halashon,* an Academy of the Language. This was to be the supreme tribunal to pass on words and settle disputes which might arise as the result of philological rivalries.

However, few men could be found to serve on such a board who had the crusading zeal of Eliezer Ben Yehuda. One of those finally chosen was partially blind. A second was totally blind. A third liked to make speeches. A fourth vociferously opposed everything the majority favored.

Whenever a meeting was called, a number of the members would appear one or even two hours late. Some would send excuses, saying that the day was too hot or that they feared to go out in the rain. If the meeting were at night there were always those who worried about breaking a leg in the dark streets. Others in cold weather refused to attend unless they were guaranteed a heated meeting place.

Ben Yehuda tried to appease them all. Often when he called a meeting, impatient to lay before the council a number of new words that were ready, he would send the members a message in advance that hot tea would be served, hoping thus to bribe them into attending. If the meeting were to be at night he would tell the reluctant ones that if they came he would see that they were accompanied back to their homes by his own Yemenite watchman, with a lantern to light their path.

Protests began to come from Jaffa. Why should this council be composed of the learned men of just Jerusalem? Why should Jaffa not also have some representation? Did Jerusalem think it had a monopoly on brains? If Jaffa were not given recognition she would set up a rival council!

To avoid the confusions which would have resulted from the creation of a second council, it was decided that alternate meetings would be held in Jaffa.

Then protests came from the settlements. Why was Rishon Le Zion being ignored? And how about Petach Tikvah? It took great patience to appease everyone.

Two of the most helpful members of the council were Dr. David Yellin and Joseph Meyouhas, both of whom spoke fluent Arabic and made invaluable contributions to the new language through their own research and advice.

In addition to the filing cabinets full of cards, Ben Yehuda had a mountainous collection of pieces of paper on which there was additional material he intended to use when the day came to correlate and compile. He kept most of this mass of "raw material" in a wooden chest which was so full that pieces of paper dribbled out onto the floor.

One night, as was his habit when he was searching for notes he wished to consult, Ben Yehuda put an oil lamp on the lid of the opened chest while he rummaged inside. Just then an old friend came into the study, Jacob Shertok, for whom Ben Yehuda had found a job in a carpenter shop when he arrived in Palestine twenty years before.

"Is this the way you treat the treasury of our Hebrew language?" the visitor asked in dismay. "This is terribly dangerous! You might start a fire which would not only destroy you and your home and your family, but would reduce to ashes our language as well!"

So the next day Jacob Shertok ordered ironsmiths to make three great fireproof chests. When they were delivered he personally helped Ben Yehuda transfer all his papers into them.

It was some months later that the Ben Yehudas had as a visitor in their home Z. D. Levontin, one of the pioneers in the colonization of Palestine, one of the founders of the Rishon Le Zion settlement, and now manager of the Anglo-Palestine Bank. With him was Dr. Isaac Levy, manager of the bank's Jerusalem branch. During the evening Eliezer brought up the delicate subject of a loan.

"For what purpose, and what is your security?" Levontin asked, suddenly putting on his office manner.

"To print my dictionary," Ben Yehuda replied. Then, waving a hand toward the iron chests, he added:

"My dictionary which is now imprisoned in those vaults."

It was Dr. Levy who spoke up next, saying:

"I do not understand. What do the chests contain?"

Ben Yehuda opened them. He said that if he could get a loan of five thousand francs it would be sufficient. When the bankers asked for more details, he explained his plan.

He now figured that he had material enough to fill four volumes. Five thousand francs would enable him to have the first volume printed. The proceeds from the sale of the first would cover the cost of printing the second. The proceeds from the second would cover the cost of printing the third. The proceeds from the third would cover the cost of the fourth. The proceeds of the fourth would be used to repay the original loan.

The answer the bankers finally gave Ben Yehuda was a loan of one thousand francs, which he accepted, although with this limited amount of credit he knew he would be able to put out only three small booklets containing less than one third of the material which eventually was to comprise the first volume of the dictionary, which was to run to many, many more volumes than he or anyone else even imagined at this point.

Hemda later went to Levontin and asked him to increase the credit. When the banker hesitated, in a typical burst of self-confidence she said:

"Maybe you will laugh, but I tell you that if you help finance the dictionary the day will come when Ben Yehuda will be one of the most important clients of your bank, for we will deposit all the funds we receive from the sale of the dictionary with you!"

This piece of salesmanship failed to impress Levontin. Then Hemda offered to have the iron chests full of notes put in the bank's vault as security. He laughed at this suggestion, saying:

"We take solid collateral as security for loans, but not iron chests full of pieces of worthless paper covered with Hebrew handwriting intelligible to only one man in the world, and a sick man at that!"

About this time the Ben Yehudas were visited by a celebrated oriental-language scholar from Budapest, Professor Samuel Krauss, who spent days going over the dictionary material, analyzing, perusing, criticizing.

Dr. Krauss gave Ben Yehuda more encouragement than anyone else had ever given him. The Hungarian scholar complimented him on his careful research and on his scientific methods. He expressed amazement at the amount of heretofore undiscovered philological material he had unearthed. He called the project a "Herculean task which no one but a man with tremendous enterprise and boundless energy could ever have undertaken." He said that if Ben Yehuda's work had no other results, it had been worth while because of the new light it threw on many obscure passages in the Bible.

Professor Krauss wanted to see Jericho, so the Ben Yehudas took him to the ancient biblical city, where they saw the oldest and one of the most modern modes of travel side by side, the camel and the bicycle.

"I know the Hebrew word for 'camel,' " the professor said with a smile, "but have you coined a word yet for 'bicycle'?"

It was Ben Yehuda's turn to smile.

"Yes, and it is already in common usage. The word is *offnayim,* coming from the word for 'wheel' and the word for 'two.' "

Hemda added:

"If you visit us thirty years from now, Professor, we shall bring you to Jericho again and your eyes will behold airplanes, automobiles, and trolley cars, and in your ears will resound the Hebrew words for all of them."

38

Overnight Hotel—Jews Only

IT WAS PROBABLY THE DEATH OF DEBORAH WHICH caused the nervous breakdown that Eliezer Ben Yehuda suffered about this time, but a doctor in Jerusalem suggested he had an incurable cancer and so he went to Berlin to consult specialists.

While he was away a handsome young man in a blue uniform with polished brass buttons walked through the door of the Ben Yehuda home one morning and greeted the family as casually as if he had come from around the corner instead of from Paris, thousands of miles away.

"What has happened, Ben Zion?" Hemda gasped.

"Oh, nothing!" the boy replied casually. "There was a little strike of students against the principal of the Ecole Normale, and of course I was in it. I had to be loyal to my friends, the revolutionaries of the school."

"You mean you were dismissed for taking part in the strike?"

"That was not the reason they gave. They had me looked at by a doctor who said I had tuberculosis. But Dr. Nordau says I am healthy and normal."

With Eliezer away, Hemda was perplexed over what to do with

her stepson. He was much more independent with her than with his father.

"At least," she finally said, "you must take off the school uniform. You no longer have any right to wear it."

But Ben Zion refused to obey any of her commands. Instead he kept on the uniform and left for Jaffa. Some days later Hemda received a letter of apology. He said he had a job teaching school. Yemeemah also received a letter that she could make a living in Jaffa giving private lessons. Over Hemda's protests she left too.

Meanwhile, in Berlin, Eliezer had been told he did not have cancer; he was merely suffering from nervous exhaustion. When he returned to Jerusalem his two rebellious children came home from Jaffa to take part in the welcome for him.

Ben Yehuda told them how impressed he had been in Berlin with the high standards of the schools. With the assistance of Professor Otto Warburg, member of a family prominent in both Berlin and New York, he had made arrangements for Ben Zion to enter the oriental-language section of the university, to equip himself to help later on the dictionary. Yemeemah would be admitted to the teachers' seminary.

The children finally agreed to go to Berlin. Before long, however, the parents began receiving letters that Ben Zion was neglecting his language studies and had become infected with the virus of journalism, for which there is no cure. Then Ben Zion himself wrote that he had become assistant to the Berlin correspondent of a Paris newspaper. In the same letter he sent his first article from abroad for Ben Yehuda's paper.

In this period, in the first years of the twentieth century, little progress was being made toward the establishment of the Jewish state. Herzl's plan to "buy" Palestine had failed of achievement, and the first of his predictions had not come to pass. The year 1902 had come and gone. Still no great power had taken over Palestine and given it to the Jews.

More and more anti-Jewish regulations were being promulgated by the Turks. Jewish immigration had to be effected illegally. No new colonization was permitted. And there seemed to be no hope that the situation would ever change for the better.

It was no wonder, then, that there was excitement when the Colonial Secretary of England, Joseph Chamberlain, proposed that six thousand square miles in the Guas Ngishu or Uasin Gishu Plateau of British East Africa be turned over to the Jews for the establishment of their own state under British protection. The spot was not in Uganda proper, but the scheme came to be known, anyway, as the Uganda Plan.

Seldom in the two thousand years of the Jews' dispersal had any announcement precipitated such an immediate taking of sides. Eliezer Ben Yehuda was one of the first to come out in favor of the plan.

"This is a great ray of sudden light!" he said. "At last we shall have a shelter, free from persecution; a home where England, at least, will protect us in our yearning for self-government and peace. Even though it is far away, we will be able to gather there from the four corners of our exile, and there we will be able to learn statehood and prepare ourselves for the time when we shall receive our ancient heritage, the land of Israel, for which we have prayed these two thousand years."

To Hemda he said:

"At last I shall be free to write openly about Zionism. This development surely will calm the fears of the Turks that Palestine will be snatched from their empire."

The older Orthodox Jews took the attitude that this was fine. Now Ben Yehuda and the young settlers and the other rebels and heretics would go off to Uganda, and Palestine would belong again to the religious who spent their days at the Wailing Wall praying for the arrival of the Messiah to save them. So strangely enough, they, too, became ardent supporters of Chamberlain's Uganda Plan.

But the younger generation in the settlements did no rejoicing. They had planted their roots here and had grown to love the land. Were all the sacrifices they had made going to count for nothing? Must they renounce their dreams of a new Israel on the site of the old?

Ben Yehuda tried to answer them, saying that nothing would be renounced. This would be just a period of preparation for a brilliant future. It might take two or three generations to gather together all the exiles, to foster in them a national ideal, and to prepare them for the day of their final victory. Uganda might not be an ideal preparation ground, but no other place had been offered.

In private conversations he went so far as to argue that in Uganda they would be able to build a military force which might someday return and take the Holy Land at the point of guns.

A few were convinced by such arguments, but many continued to rebel.

"Has Ben Yehuda become a traitor to all his own ideals?" they would ask. "He wants to settle Jews among Negroes. What a future for the Hebrew race!"

Hemda, when the controversy was at its height, injected a personal note one night, asking her husband:

"What will be your attitude, Eliezer, if you are told to go yourself to Uganda?"

A strange look came over his face. For a long moment he said nothing. Then almost painfully he answered:

"There would be nothing in the world more difficult to do than leave Jerusalem, Bitti. But, if our national life should demand it, I am ready to make the sacrifice."

The reply did not make Hemda happy. She had finally acclimatized herself to this strange place. She had made all the necessary adjustments to the primitiveness, the prejudices, the provinciality of Palestine. Now she must contemplate moving to a torrid place called Uganda, in the unfathomable wilderness of Africa!

"It overwhelms me," she burst out, "with apprehension and alarm. I see a vision of our children becoming victims of that terrible disease they call sleeping sickness. A hundred thousand have died of it in the past year or two."

The Ben Yehuda conflict between husband and wife was being repeated at firesides all over Palestine. In general the women were against the scheme. Their most emotional argument, but one which the men found difficult to answer, was that the blood stream of Jews and Africans would unavoidably become blended, and a race of Negro Jews would evolve which might not be a credit to either Jews or Africans.

Reports from abroad indicated that the controversy had no geographical limits. Theodor Herzl had taken exactly the stand Ben Yehuda had. Israel Zangwill joined the Uganda ranks. So did Dr. Nordau, who coined an expression everyone began to use. He called Uganda "our overnight hotel." But Russian, Rumanian, and Galician Jews rose up in arms against the plan.

Then a letter came from Ben Zion, who had celebrated his twenty-first birthday by changing his name. At his birth Ben Yehuda had been persuaded to drop the name of Ittamar which he had at first given him. Now the boy had reassumed that name, adding to it "Ben Avi" (Son of My Father). A letter came in which the son of his father said he must express himself without equivocation about Uganda. He was against the plan.

Many other fathers and sons split over the issue. In London, Norman Bentwich opposed his own father's championship of the Uganda Plan.

Ben Yehuda devoted all his waking hours to turning out literary arguments for Uganda. Seeing him work, no one would have thought that he had ever been ill. He glowed now with enthusiasm. An inner fire seemed to be driving him on. He wrote articles which were reprinted in papers all over Europe. He, Herzl, and Nordau exchanged frequent letters. All three were being condemned as "destroyers of Israel, no longer worthy to be respected."

As feelings in Palestine reached fever pitch (it was August, when the temperature was also at its highest) there arrived in Jerusalem unannounced a member of the Zionist Organization's executive committee, Menahem Ben Mosche Ussishkin, who had come to Palestine "to get inspiration to take to the Sixth Zionist Congress with me."

It soon came out, however, that he was violently opposed to Uganda and hoped to "convert" Ben Yehuda and others. There were many arguments, but no one budged from his previous position. Finally Ussishkin declared to Ben Yehuda:

"Let us forget Uganda. Whatever is done about it, the time has come for an organization of Palestinian Jews whose voices can be heard at the congress and who will strengthen the Zionist cause."

Ben Yehuda wrote an editorial calling for a convention to form such an organization. The meeting took place at Zichron Yaakov.

Delegates came from all corners of the country. It was the first convention of Jews in two thousand years conducted entirely in Hebrew.

Ben Yehuda arranged it so that Ussishkin received most of the limelight and full credit for having brought the meeting about. Ussishkin knew what to do with the limelight when he got it. He made such an impression on the delegates that he attained immediately a sort of immortality. The street on which the convention hall stood was renamed in his honor. Trees were planted "to perpetuate for centuries the memory of the man we today applaud."

The meeting developed no serious controversy. Uganda was hardly mentioned.

Ussishkin went from Zichron Yaakov almost immediately to Kharkov, Russia, where he called a secret meeting of Herzl's opponents for the purpose, it was reported, of lining up opposition to Uganda at the forthcoming Sixth Zionist Congress. Ben Yehuda received a message that at this meeting Ussishkin, speaking as an official representative of the new Palestinian organization, had stated that this large body of Palestinians was against Uganda.

Ben Yehuda promptly wrote an editorial he called "A Confession," in which he pleaded guilty to having allowed himself to be used as a dupe in a political ruse. He accused Ussishkin of having organized the Palestinians merely to use them as weapons against Herzl.

Most Palestinians were revolted. The signs on the street named after Ussishkin were torn down. The trees planted in his honor were dug up before they had had time to take root. The table on which the group's constitution had been written was burned.

Then the Sixth Zionist Congress convened and the effects of Ussishkin's conniving were seen.

Herzl dramatically stated the case for Uganda. Nordau made a brilliant speech. But Ussishkin, although not present, had lined up the opposition. The Russian delegates bitterly attacked Herzl. It was a war between East and West, the West represented by delegates from Germany, Austria, England, and France; the East being the Polish-Russian bloc.

So much emotion was displayed that this session of the Zionists was referred to by historians as "the Crying Congress." Herzl succeeded in getting a resolution passed merely calling for a commission to investigate conditions in Uganda, but it was a victory which soon turned to defeat. The Russian delegates walked out of the Congress, talking of secession. Others followed them.

Not long afterward Ussishkin called a conference of his followers at Kharkov and demanded that Uganda be dropped. Herzl knew that in the face of such opposition it had better be dropped. The Russians had paralyzed the movement. Besides, British non-Jews in East Africa had now become belligerent.

Herzl had gone from the Basle congress aware of his eventual defeat on the issue. His health in the weeks that followed deteriorated rapidly. Although he was only forty-four, his figure was stooped, his eyes had grown darkened, and his mouth was drawn in pain.

In April 1904 he called a meeting of the Zionist Actions Committee in Vienna, and after two hours of debate Uganda was given its *coup de grâce.*

Thus the Jews of the world turned a cold shoulder to the British offer of a temporary homeland and left the doors open for nearly half a century more of struggle, war, bloodshed, and tears, but they also left the doors open for the eventual establishment of the Jewish state on the soil where it really belonged.

Many since then have speculated on what a difference it would have made in Jewish history, perhaps even in the history of the world, if Ussishkin and his followers had not fought Herzl and if Uganda, deep in the heart of Africa, had become a Jewish place.

Uganda left scars.

Theodor Herzl became seriously ill and isolated himself in the cloistered quiet of a sanitarium.

Max Nordau, while attending a Zionist ball in Paris, was shot at twice by a Jewish fanatic. Fortunately he was not hit.

Eliezer Ben Yehuda tried to go back to his dictionary, but for the first time in his life work was no palliative for defeat.

One evening he said to Hemda:

"I cannot understand what has happened to me. I pick up my

pen, dip it in ink, put the point on paper, but nothing happens. The ink will not flow. The words refuse to be written. I wonder what it is, Bitti."

Hemda knew. Eliezer's heart had been broken. He was like an ardent young lover whose fiancée is taken by death on the eve of the wedding. He seldom ate any more. He tossed on his bed at night. He was like a man with apoplexy, only it was his spirit which had been stricken, not his body.

Ussishkin, taking advantage of his victory, sent two of his disciples to Palestine to organize the anti-Herzl, anti-Ben Yehuda forces. This was not difficult. Few remained loyal.

The Ashkenazic Jews and the extremely Orthodox group, now that there was no longer a possibility of Ben Yehuda's taking his new language and his radical ideas off to Africa, went after him again.

Turkish officials, who for a brief moment had relaxed their antagonism, thinking they might soon be rid of the Jews, now clamped down with even more stringent regulations. Henceforth no Jew would be allowed to enter Palestine without a red passport indicating he was a tourist on a limited visit.

And the baron? Whenever the mail arrived Ben Yehuda was certain it would contain a letter from Paris announcing that there would be no more Rothschild financial aid.

The circulation of the *Review,* built up slowly and painfully, tumbled to such a low point its editor wondered whether it was worth printing any more.

No longer, now, was the Ben Yehuda home a meeting place for those eager to exchange bright new ideas. Even close personal friends hesitated to call until after dark, fearing they might be seen by gossips who would revile them too.

Then one day as Ben Yehuda was standing in the doorway of his home, hoping that a breath of fresh air might make his head feel better, a boy arrived with a cable.

At this moment Hemda came from the house with Ehud, who then was nearly seven.

"What is it, Eliezer?"

Her husband's fingers trembled as he tried to open the cable.

"I imagine from Paris. From the baron. Probably telling——"

But it was not from Paris. It was from Ben Avi in Berlin.

HERZL IS DEAD.

Eliezer dropped the paper and put both hands to his head.

Half to himself he mumbled:

"Herzl dead! It really was Ussishkin who killed him."

As Hemda led her husband into the house Ehud ran to the nursery and shouted to the other children:

"Herzl is dead! Father just got a message that Ussishkin killed him!"

Then with the bravado of a boy of seven he shouted:

"Now I am going to kill Ussishkin!"

That remark by an excited child was soon to be repeated all over Jerusalem. Then in Jaffa. Finally it spread to the settlements. Eventually it reached Europe. In its repetition it became distorted. By the time Ussishkin himself heard it, it was Mrs. Ben Yehuda who was reported to have made the threat.

Years later Ussishkin, encountering Hemda on a Berlin street, threw open his coat with a dramatic gesture, saying:

"I hear you once expressed a desire to kill me. Here is your chance!"

Ben Yehuda was certain that all differences would at least temporarily be forgotten, so he at once set about organizing a memorial service and national day of mourning.

"But, Eliezer," his wife said, "what about the Turkish government? They hated him so!"

"The Turks persecute life," he replied, "but like us Jews, they are respectful of the holiness of death."

Ben Yehuda himself wrote the placards announcing the death and helped set them in type. Then the Ben Yehuda home was turned into a factory for the making of black ribbons to be worn on the arm.

The posters were distributed even to the schools. With each went a personal letter from Ben Yehuda, saying:

"Whatever your convictions about Zionism, a great Jew has died, a man of deep integrity and unparalleled sincerity. We ask you to assist in a memorial service for him."

All Jerusalem streamed silently and respectfully to the ancient synagogue in the Old City where the service was held. School children marched behind black-draped banners. The crowd was so great that only a small percentage could get into the building.

Many young people accompanied the Ben Yehudas back to their home. The house was too small for the number, so they assembled in the garden and asked the editor to address them, which he did.

The next day Hemda found Eliezer standing beside the iron chests in his study. On the top of one chest was the almost completed manuscript for the first volume of the dictionary. There was a strange glassy look in Eliezer's eyes. In his left hand he held a box of matches.

"Eliezer!" she screamed.

Startled, he dropped the matchbox, stared at her blankly for an instant, then slumped into a chair.

"What were you going to do?"

"Burn it all!"

"Why?"

"I know now I have made a mistake ever trying to do it. If it were not a mistake, the opposition would not have been so great."

"Eliezer! You have never indulged in self-pity before!"

"Call it what you will, but I am finished. I cannot think any more. I find it impossible to work. I prefer to die, and when I die I do not wish to leave all this behind."

As he said it he made a listless gesture toward the chests.

"But when you die, Eliezer, this will be your great heritage."

"No! I shall never permit that another shall come and obtain glory and fortune from the blood of my body and the tortures of my soul, while you and the children live in misery. I wish to die, and I wish my work to die with me. Ashes, together."

"Eliezer, do you not remember your own words to the people who came to our garden after the Herzl service? You said to them: 'The living are persecuted, but the dead are sanctified!' "

"Maybe that is why I wish to die. What is life worth if I cannot serve my people? They refuse to be served! What is a new Hebrew language for if no one wants it? What is a dictionary for? Who will use it?"

Hemda dug the nails of her fingers into the palms of her hands and tried a new approach.

"Eliezer, I agree with you about death. I, too, am tired and discouraged. But our children . . ."

"I have thought of them. They will grow up like all the other orphans of the world. They might even benefit by our death."

"But, Eliezer, we are deeply in debt. How can we betray those who have helped us? I have an idea! I shall borrow money and travel to Europe and sell your manuscript to the British Museum or to some other institution. With the money we will pay our debts and then together we can move on to the next world. But I beg you, Eliezer, do not go without me!"

39

"Is This Reality?"

HEMDA SET OFF ON THE PROMISED TRIP SOON after she gave birth to Eliezer's eleventh child, a girl named Zaza. She left Jerusalem with little money and with a battered suitcase full of pieces of paper which constituted the manuscript of the first volume of the Ben Yehuda dictionary.

She was in her early thirties. She had been living for many years an almost primitive life in one of the most backward parts of the world. In that time she had borne six children, two of whom had died. She had had the responsibility for two stepchildren as well as a brother and sister. She had nursed her husband through numerous almost fatal illnesses. She herself had had typhoid fever and repeated attacks of malaria.

Yet despite all this she had a physical attractiveness and a twinkle in her eye which she hoped would serve as allies when it came time to beg for the assistance needed to save Eliezer and his work from matches and oblivion.

Hemda had little money to finance her trip, but Eliezer had less to keep the family going. There were four small children to look after, a paper to edit, and a household to be managed by a man who was not very practical. Unless someone reminded him, he was never aware it was time for a meal. Only fatigue ever drove him to bed.

Knowing that his wife was going steerage, he made her promise she would try, after the ship sailed, to find some place to sleep. She did. She bribed the ship's cook to allow her to use his bed for eight of the hours when he was not using it himself.

When she was not in the cabin sleeping she sat on a packing case on the deck and read. One day she inadvertently left a book by Schopenhauer behind when she went to dinner. When she returned it was gone. A little later the ship's captain sent for her. Holding out the book, he asked her if it was hers. A ship's officer had found it and had brought it to him, knowing his interest in philosophy. So the woman from Jerusalem and the captain became friends, and he asked her what cabin she had.

Hemda blushed and admitted she had bribed the cook for a bed.

"No lady who respects herself can use the bed of a cook!" the captain growled, then gave her a cabin in second class. So it was that Mrs. Ben Yehuda arrived in Trieste looking as fresh and rested as any passenger on the ship.

Her first destination was Budapest, then the center of the greatest Orientalist scholars in Europe. First she called on Professor Wilhelm Bacher, with whom Eliezer had had the correspondence about the "lost word." Opening the battered suitcase and pointing to the voluminous manuscript, she said:

"I have come to ask you to glance over my husband's work and give me a frank opinion of it."

The professor threw up his hands.

"It will take a week to give you even a casual analysis of it!"

Hemda smiled bewitchingly.

"For this my husband has devoted an entire life. I have the temerity to hope that you will give it a week of your time."

With typical Hungarian gallantry he replied:

"I could not refuse your request, even if I would. I shall submit my opinion to you one week from today."

During the next week Hemda obtained eulogistic reports from

Professor Bacher and three of his colleagues, Professors Ignaz Goldziher, Samuel Krauss, and Lajos Blau. They said Ben Yehuda was making the most important contribution of his generation to the science of languages.

Armed with these recommendations, Hemda took a train for Berlin, where she began her search for a publisher. By a stroke of luck a friend introduced her to officials of the firm of Langenscheidtsche Verlagsbuchhandlung, a long-established house specializing in publishing dictionaries.

No salesman ever worked harder trying to sell his product than Hemda did during that first interview. But all her arguments and even the letters from the Budapest scholars seemed to make little impression. They would give her a definite answer in five days.

Hemda waited as nervously as a criminal awaits the verdict. When the answer came it stated that there were certain conditions under which the firm *might* be interested.

At the next meeting Hemda was told that it would be impossible for Langenscheidtsche Verlagsbuchhandlung to set the manuscript into type. They could make the plates, do the printing, bind the book, but the type would have to be set elsewhere. Without knowing whether it were even possible, Hemda said the type could be set in the Ben Yehuda shop and "mats" shipped to Berlin.

Then a more delicate matter came up. Payment would be required in advance. Hemda would have to raise the funds herself.

At the fourth meeting Hemda was given a long legal document which contained a clause stating that if Ben Yehuda died before the entire dictionary was completed his widow must carry on the work, from his notes, until it was finished. At the fifth meeting the contract was finally signed.

Hemda wanted to let Eliezer know immediately, but she feared to raise his hopes and then have them collapse if she was unable to raise the funds. Without communicating with him she took a train for Paris and went directly to see Narcisse Leven of the Alliance Israélite. After one month of pleading she obtained the backing of his organization. Then back to Berlin, to go through the same procedure with Professor Otto Warburg, Dr. Paul Nathan, Professor Martin Phillipson, and other leaders of the German Jews.

Four and a half months after her departure from Jerusalem she finally succeeded in her mission. The financial backing needed for the first volume was guaranteed by Hilfsverein der Deutschen Juden, several scientific societies, the Zionist Organization, and Alliance Israélite. Her accomplishment was significant to those who knew that this was the first time these ordinarily antagonistic groups had ever combined to further a single project.

Knowing the mental and physical condition Eliezer was in, she was afraid that even good news might literally kill him with joy.

So she composed a series of cables, which she sent at intervals. In the first she reported the publishing house *might* consider the project. In the second she said they had definitely agreed, but it depended on financing. In others she built up to the final news that it was now definite; his lifework would soon be coming out in handsome bound volumes.

Hemda never forgot the reply she received. It read:

"Is this reality, or shall I awaken to find that I have been dreaming?"

Soon after Hemda returned to Jerusalem a celebration was held in the Ben Yehuda home. It commemorated three events, the twenty-fifth anniversary of Eliezer's arrival in the Holy Land, which had passed some months before without fitting festivities; his fiftieth birthday, which was still some months off but which they decided might as well be observed at the same time, and the turning point in the saga of the dictionary, its acceptance by the house of Langenscheidtsche Verlagsbuchhandlung.

Eliezer Ben Yehuda was the guest of honor, but less attention was paid to him than to a small package Hemda had brought from Berlin and which she had never let out of her sight until she had placed it, as lovingly and tenderly as if it were a newborn baby, in her husband's hands. It contained a "dummy" of the book. It looked just as the first volume of the dictionary would look when it finally came out, except that the pages were blank.

"But this is the way it will be bound," she would explain to each new guest. "See how beautiful the leather is!"

Then Eliezer, excited, too, would point to the gold letters embossed on the front:

THESAURUS TOTIUS HEBRAITATIS
ET VETERIS ET RECENTIORIS
AUCTORE ELIESER BEN JEHUDA
HIEROSOLYMITANO

He did not have to explain to most of the teachers, who knew some Latin, that these impressive ancient words meant:

"A Complete Dictionary of Ancient and Modern Hebrew, by Eliezer Ben Yehuda of Jerusalem."

Eliezer was exhausted with emotion by the time the last guest had left. Sitting in his favorite chair, half to himself and half to his wife, who was putting things in order, he said:

"Someday soon our language, after all, may really begin to grow into something rich and beautiful. But the day is so short; the work to be done so great! I think I should go to my study now and commence. The printers must have the first pages this week to start setting type. I only hope my strength holds out!"

In these days the Ben Yehudas had their first proof of an old adage, common even in biblical times, that nothing is as influential as success. Well-wishers came streaming to the Ben Yehuda home. Friends who had hesitated about being seen calling in daylight were no longer afraid that their names might be linked with that of the "rebel."

With pride, many who had been lukewarm toward the Hebrew revival now boasted that "their" language, the language of the Jews, would soon, thanks to Ben Yehuda, take its proper place among the important languages of the world.

"The great house of Langenscheidtsche Verlagsbuchhandlung is printing it!" They whispered it as if it were a state secret, and while they whispered Eliezer Ben Yehuda went to work.

The first word in the first volume was to be *av* (father).

It was Hemda who sentimentally suggested that Eliezer himself should set the first few lines of type. It was Hemda who, when the printers finished setting the first column and brought the heavy mass of type to Eliezer for inspection, said:

"This first column of the first volume is set in lead type. But when we get to the last column of the last volume I shall see that it is set in gold for you!"

For months Ben Yehuda worked as if on fire. The print shop was like a furnace consuming fuel faster than it could be shoveled in. Often one of the printers would stand over Eliezer's shoulder waiting for the next page.

For nearly a quarter of a century he had been doing his research, collecting notes. Only recently had he begun actually writing the text of the book. And being a scholar, he was forever making additions, corrections, new annotations; crossing out a word here, polishing a phrase, clarifying an explanation, striving always for perfection.

Those who thought that his dictionary was going to be a mere list of Hebrew words with brief definitions were in for a great surprise. Except for the few who had seen the manuscript, no one was aware that this was to be unlike any dictionary ever compiled.

There were pages and pages of type, for example, on that first word alone, *av*. The word *kee* (because) would have twenty-four columns.

After each Hebrew word would come the translation into French, German, and English. This made the work unique; a multilingual dictionary with translations into three languages, besides references in Arabic, Assyrian, Aramaic, Greek, and Latin.

Moreover, it was a thesaurus as well as a book of definitions. After each word Ben Yehuda listed all the other words which were in any way connected with it. Following *even* (stone), for example, one would find the names of various stones and innumerable words pertaining to or suggested by "stone"; synonyms, antonyms, related words. The reader was given the origin of each word, an explanation of its construction, a comparison with its sister words in other Semitic languages, the changes it had undergone down through the ages, and all its nuances, shades, forms, inflections, and uses.

After each word were examples of its usage, which Ben Yehuda called "witnesses." With a language as old as Hebrew there were bound to be many more shadings and colorations of meaning, and even conflicting uses of a word, than in a younger language. This had given him one of his greatest problems of research; to find in ancient, medieval, and modern literature as many different "witnesses" or uses of each word as possible.

He had dug out and listed 335 different ways in which it was possible to use the Hebrew word *lo,* meaning "no" or "not." There were 210 "witnesses" for *ken* (yes).

Unlike the ordinary lexicographer, Ben Yehuda was never satisfied to explain the meaning of a word by listing several synonyms. His illustrations of meaning were sometimes whole paragraphs. He once explained why he did this by saying:

"A word when standing alone does not impress the memory. It means little unless given to the reader as part of a complete thought. Only then will it be preserved in memory."

Many of his "witnesses" were quotations from the Bible and other religious books, but there were often long passages from secular literature, from the works of little-known poets, or from manuscripts he had found somewhere in a distant library. These quotations were interesting reading in themselves. They gave pictures of the life of early Jews in their homes, market places, fields, and ghettos. For as a critic wrote later, Ben Yehuda never examined words, but thoughts; he did not accumulate sentences, but whole ideas.

To anyone reading even a single page of the dictionary it was obvious that Ben Yehuda, in selecting a passage as a "witness," was guided not only by a philological desire to clarify the word's meaning, but also by a literary and moral urge to present his reader with beauty and truth.

The odd little marks which Ben Yehuda sprinkled through his manuscript were marks of his honesty. These symbols appeared alongside words which he himself had created.

"I put them in so the reader can see immediately that these are new words, and if he does not like them he should consider them as non-existent."

40

Love, Revolution, Art

DURING THE YEAR IT TOOK BEN YEHUDA TO COMplete work on his first volume many things happened in the world outside his study door.

Ben Avi, his eldest son, now a thoroughly experienced journalist, came home from Berlin and turned the paper into a daily, called *Haor* (The Light). This was the name his father had once tried to use, to the offense of the Sultan's censor.

Yemeemah also came home, in love. The man was a handsome German actor and he wanted to marry her. The father blinked.

"I give you no opinion. You must follow your heart's voice."

But when Ludwig Frankel appeared to make a formal request for the daughter's hand Ben Yehuda, in an arbitrary manner, said:

"I do not ask whether you are qualified to support a wife. But if you wish my consent you must accept certain of my principles. First, you must have a Hebrew name, because——"

The young man interrupted:

"I am ready to change my name."

"You must also adopt our Hebrew language."

The actor promised to try to learn it.

"Third, you must agree to live in Israel."

The young man smiled.

"I accept all your conditions."

About this same time Ben Avi fell in love with a Spanish Jewess, Lea Aboujdid, daughter of a celebrated doctor who had introduced scarlet fever antitoxin into Palestine. This delighted Ben Yehuda because such a union would be a symbol of the amalgamation of the Ashkenazic and Sephardic elements of the community for which he had been working since his arrival in Palestine. The girl's family, however, was violently opposed because they considered eastern European Jews inferior, because Ben Yehuda was a "freethinker," and because the family was poor. It was some years before the marriage finally took place.

A development beyond the borders of Palestine affected the Ben Yehudas almost as much as these family affairs. After Herzl's death the Zionist Organization had difficulty choosing his successor. The logical man was Nordau, but he withdrew himself from consideration because he was in disagreement with many Zionist leaders about the colonization of Palestine. He often said he wanted "a Jewish state, not a colony; a charter and not just Turkish toleration."

Nordau's friends told Ben Yehuda that he also was reluctant to take leadership because his wife was a Christian. They claimed that the real reason he had never accepted the invitation to visit Palestine was because his wife said if he ever went she wanted to accompany him so she could visit the Christian shrines. She herself was a great respecter of human rights and freedom of religion. It would have been difficult to explain to her why her husband, as a Zionist leader, might have been embarrassed if she had toured Palestine with Christian leaders while he made the rounds of the Jewish religious places.

So instead of Nordau, the Zionists had chosen David Wolffsohn, a wealthy, middle-aged Lithuanian businessman who had been extremely generous in his support of Jewish charities and had founded the bank in London designed to finance Palestinian colonization.

After his election Wolffsohn and his wife came to Palestine. They were received with great friendliness, but some complained that Wolffsohn was not a dreamer like Herzl. He prided himself on being a conservative businessman and was always advising caution at a time when many Zionists insisted on the need for bold action.

David Wolffsohn, it developed, was closely related to David Wolfson, the uncle who had driven Eliezer as a boy from his home when he caught him reading Robinson Crusoe in Hebrew, but he himself was apparently not aware of his kinship to the Jerusalem lexicographer, and Ben Yehuda never enlightened him.

There were many who were pleased, the Ben Yehudas among them, when Wolffsohn was succeeded by Professor Otto Warburg, who not only was a brilliant scholar, a millionaire, and a gentleman of great breeding, but was also one of the group in Berlin who, by responding to Hemda's appeal, were making it possible for the publication of the first volume of the dictionary.

But the event in this period which had a greater influence than anything else on the lives of the Ben Yehudas and the entire Jewish population of Palestine was the Turkish revolution, which stripped Abdul Hamid II of the power which he had held for a quarter of a century over twenty-five million people in Asia and southern Europe.

In Palestine the superstitious called it a "miracle" that this tyrant had now been brought to his knees. When a constitutional government was established by the Young Turks, all Palestine, Jews and Arabs alike, joined in rejoicing that tyranny was at an end.

Ben Avi brought the news to his father's study, shouting:

"We are free, Father! At last we are free to write and think and talk as we please! Forget your dictionary! Let's celebrate!"

Ben Avi was partly right. The pressure of tyranny was lessened, though not entirely dissipated. Censorship was abolished. Before long the Young Turks were giving out permits for the publication of new newspapers to almost anyone who could sign his name on an application.

Then the tables were turned. Ben Avi was now the one who was complaining. A new daily had been started in Jerusalem called *Heirut* (Liberty), and although it had little political significance, it was competition for the *Light*. Smaller papers also sprang into existence which were quickly nicknamed "Little Ben Yehudas"; papers which nibbled at the circulation of the parent.

But in his idealistic way the senior Ben Yehuda decided that this was all to the ultimate good. The more papers in Hebrew, the more people who would be reading and learning the language.

It was in this same period that an attractive young man appeared one day at the Ben Yehuda home and introduced himself as Professor Boris Schatz of Vilna. He had just come from Sofia, Bulgaria, by way of Berlin. He was a sculptor and with an artist friend, Efraim Lilien, was contemplating the opening of a school of arts and crafts in Jerusalem. He wanted the advice of Mr. Ben Yehuda, please.

He had made this speech of introduction in a bad mixture of Russian, French, and German. Nevertheless, Ben Yehuda sat for six hours discussing the project with him. Schatz explained that he wanted "not merely to teach arts and crafts, but to 'create' a Jewish art."

Ben Yehuda was excited by the project and agreed to give it his full co-operation on one condition.

"And what is that?" the young sculptor asked.

"The school must be conducted exclusively in Hebrew. You must remain a prisoner in our home until you yourself can speak a little of the language. My wife, in her spare time, will teach you."

Professor Schatz replied with consternation:

"But we brought our student body with us, ten enthusiastic young Jews from various European countries. I am afraid none of them knows Hebrew either."

"We shall arrange for them too," Ben Yehuda said.

So Boris Schatz, with little chance to argue, literally became an inmate in what he always afterward called "the Ben Yehuda Prison." It was six months before Hemda told him he knew enough Hebrew to be allowed his "liberty."

Meanwhile his partner, Lilien, the painter, found a room close by but took his meals with the Ben Yehudas and sat in on the Hebrew lessons, learning in quicker time than Schatz.

The ten art students were installed in a Jewish school, this being summer vacation. Mattresses were spread on the floor and a communal kitchen was established, in charge of a teacher of Hebrew who cooked as well as conducted classes.

Thus the Bezalel School of Fine Arts was established, with Hemda as secretary without pay, so she could make certain the Hebrew-language promise was kept.

While the twelve "immigrants" were mastering the ancient language they also kept busy painting and sculpting. Finally it was decided to open the school to the public with as much fanfare as possible.

A building had been rented across the street from the Ben Yehuda home. Invitations were sent out for an "open house."

Jerusalem had had nothing to gossip about for a long time. But now it seethed with a new controversy. The young and rebellious spirits were excited over the entrance of art into their lives, but the reactionaries were shocked.

A school of art? Images on canvas and stone which violated the second commandment! Infidel things! Idolatry! More of the machinations of that heretic, Ben Yehuda!

Yet crowds came, some out of genuine interest, many out of plain curiosity; some prepared to admire, many merely to get ammunition to use in their denunciations. They came in their Sabbath dress, the young in semi-European clothes, others in blue, green, and yellow velvet, some even wearing the fur-trimmed hats which were the mark of ultra-religious Jews.

What they saw first as they streamed through the doors was a large statue of the Messiah by Glicenstein. There was a painting by Reuben Lifschitz, who was to distinguish himself in later years as an artist; a bust of Ben Yehuda by Joseph Hebroni; a bust of Nietzsche by Max Kruse, and even a copy of Michelangelo's Moses.

The building buzzed with the excitement of it. The adversaries denounced with vehemence; the young progressives were loud in their praise. In between these two groups were people who had never seen art before and were confused about what to think.

Those who had come on purpose to criticize saw in the head of the lexicographer a perfect object of their pent-up scorn. Some even spat at it. Others seemed so eager to destroy it that finally the two directors decided that until Jerusalem became more art-conscious and more tolerant of Ben Yehuda, it would be well to place a guard over Mr. Hebroni's creation.

The Ben Yehuda head, regardless of what some of Jerusalem thought of it, later won Hebroni a scholarship to the Berlin Academy of Arts.

With that open house as a start, the Bezalel School quickly became a pulsating influence in Jerusalem.

Ben Yehuda took time off from his dictionary work to instruct the students in Hebrew history and to teach them where to find old Jewish motifs to incorporate into their work.

Lilien, through Ben Yehuda's influence, conceived the idea of an illustrated Bible and began making sketches and looking for a publisher.

Craftsmen came to the school for help in improving the style and design of their work. The school's influence even reached into Jewish homes. Pictures now began to appear on walls. Housewives, learning about "taste," began replacing "atrocities" with attractive furniture and tried to make their homes attractive.

Thus art began to lose her status as a vagrant in the Holy Land.

When the first copy of the first volume of the first real Hebrew dictionary ever published arrived in Jerusalem from Berlin there was great excitement in the Ben Yehuda home.

Although no one made the comparison at the time, it is doubtful whether the arrival of any one of the eleven children that had been borne to Eliezer Ben Yehuda stirred within him quite the feelings he had on this occasion.

On the page following the title page there was a dedication to Baron Edmond de Rothschild, in gratitude for all he had done to make possible the work which this book represented.

It was typical of Ben Yehuda that he began worrying about the second volume the very day the first one came from the press.

The funds which had come from Paris and Berlin were now exhausted. The experience with the first volume proved that it took at least one year and the equivalent of two thousand dollars to put a single volume into print. And now it seemed certain that it would require eight or ten volumes to get through the alphabet, for the first volume covered only two letters, *aleph* and *beth*.

"Why don't we worry about one volume at a time?" Hemda said.

"The first is out. We need money for the second, so I think I had better go up to Berlin and see our committee there."

"If you feel you must go to Berlin, Bitti, I think I shall go with you. After all, it would be profitable to me, because I could work in the libraries there while you were doing something about money matters."

The man who walked timidly through the doors of the great German publishing house of Langenscheidtsche Verlagsbuchhandlung still had the build of an adolescent boy. Whenever he removed his hat his close-cropped hair stood straight up like so many soldiers at attention. His Vandyke beard and mustache were also trimmed short. But it was his eyes that commanded attention. A fire seemed always to be burning just back of them.

The woman at his side was much healthier in appearance, with a good figure, brown hair of an attractive shade showing from under her hat, and with none of the nervousness her husband had. She was almost fourteen years his junior and looked it. Her eyes also commanded attention, but for a different reason. There was a coquettish quality to them which years of struggle and suffering had not dimmed.

Together they walked through the doors of the publishing house. Officials of the firm of Langenscheidtsche Verlagsbuchhandlung bowed low and treated Ben Yehuda in the manner that a great publishing house reserves for one of its celebrated authors. Before the visit was over, however, they impressed upon him that he must live up to the agreement that material for subsequent volumes would be rapidly forthcoming.

Hemda took Eliezer to visit the Berlin Jews who had raised the money for the first volume and had formed themselves into a committee, with Dr. Abraham Shalom Yahuda, whom Ben Yehuda had taught as a child in Jerusalem, as secretary, and Martin Phillipson as chairman. They all congratulated Eliezer and told him he had justified their confidence in him. Later, meeting alone with Hemda, they agreed to raise the money needed for Volume Two. It would be sent in regular installments to them.

After the meeting Professor Warburg, who had made the largest personal pledge on this and the previous occasion, took Hemda aside and said that while they were in Berlin they were to consider themselves as his guests; he would pay all their expenses.

There were tears in Hemda's eyes as she thanked him and then rushed off to tell Eliezer the good news.

From Berlin they went to Paris. There Hemda received a long letter from David Yonas, her eldest brother. He was a lawyer and had recently moved from Russia to Finland. He had been one of the few Jews allowed to practice in St. Petersburg and had built up enough of a fortune to retire in comfort. Hemda had written him about her husband's dictionary, thinking she might get him financially interested.

He replied that if the Jews of Palestine wanted a dictionary it was all right with him. But let them pay for it. However, if she and her family needed a vacation, she should send for the children and all of them should come to his new home in Finland. He would send railway tickets. Everything would be paid.

As Yemeemah and her actor husband were about to leave Jerusalem for Paris anyway, Hemda cabled them to bring the four small children.

When Ehud, Ada, Shlomit (now called Dola), and Zaza arrived in Paris, each child was provided with an outfit of the best clothes the French capital had to offer, by courtesy of "Uncle David."

The Ben Yehuda family spent two months in Finland. Hemda and the children had never been so happy and carefree, but Eliezer was restless. He seemed almost relieved when a letter came from the Berlin publishing house asking why none of the second volume had been received.

41
Hats in Hand

UNDER THE YOUNG TURKS, CONDITIONS WERE IMproving in Palestine for the Jews. The ban against construction of homes by Jews was relaxed; also the prohibition against Jewish immigration.

New colonies were being established. On the shore of the Mediterranean, close beside Jaffa, a new city was taking form on what had been wasteland. It was going to be called Tel Aviv (Hill of Spring), a name inspired by one of Herzl's books. Tel Aviv would be the first really Jewish city in two thousand years.

After Hemda and Eliezer returned they were instrumental in organizing a parade of pupils of Jerusalem schools who could speak Hebrew. It reached from Machney Yehuda Street to the suburb of Motza. As Eliezer rubbed his eyes and stared he exclaimed:

"This is the living Hebrew language. Four miles of it!"

By this time Eliezer had completed work on the letter *gimel.* But as he tackled *daleth* his strength and spirit began to ebb.

"I feel like a mountain climber all the time, Bitti. I just get over one difficult peak, and before I can catch my breath, there ahead is another peak to be scaled. Each peak, each letter, has its dangers, its problems. And I get so tired these days!"

Hemda tried to get him to rest each seventh day to regain his strength. He refused. She tried to get him to take a nap each afternoon. He argued he had no right to "waste" time. She tried to get him to pause at sunset for a cup of tea. He said he had lost his taste for tea. When she invited some of his old friends in for the evening, he would greet them in friendly manner, then, excusing himself, would go back to his study to work.

While Eliezer was still struggling with daleth, the monthly payments from Berlin stopped. The Ben Yehuda debts began to mount. The printers wanted their pay. Money was needed for additional type.

At first Hemda kept Eliezer ignorant of the difficulties, hoping the payments from Berlin would be resumed soon. But getting no reply to letters and cables, she finally told him that no more words could be set into type.

Eliezer put a hand to his tired head and merely said:

"I do not understand. I do not understand."

Then he went back to his study again.

Next time he came out he collapsed in a chair and said:

"I wonder why I am so tired. I never used to get tired, Bitti, did I? And my fingers! Sometimes they get so cramped I can no longer hold the pen!"

Hemda knew there was nothing she could do about his fatigue, but she could do something about the lack of funds. Obviously there was no more hope from Berlin. She would have to go to Paris. But Eliezer could not be left behind in his condition, so she finally persuaded him to go with her, although he loudly complained:

"Why must we keep going places? Always and always it seems that we have to be wandering Jews, with our hats in our hands! From door to door. Country to country. Continent to continent.

"I suppose it will never end. We go now to get money for the second volume. Then for the third. Then the fourth. The fifth. The sixth. The seventh. The eighth. And I am so tired!"

From an unexpected quarter they obtained a loan of enough to permit them to travel third-class to Paris. When they reached Jaffa, Eliezer was so exhausted that Hemda took him to the hotel and left him, saying:

"Lie on the bed and rest. I shall be back soon."

She had no idea where she was going. As she walked down a narrow street, letting her feet take her where they would, she glanced up at a second-story window and saw a sign which read:

PALÄSTINA
AMT

She had heard about the "Palestine Office." It had been founded by the same Professor Warburg who had been so kind up in Berlin. It was under the direction of Dr. Arthur Ruppin.

Without any specific idea in mind Hemda mounted the stairs. The office was the tiniest she had ever seen, hardly six feet square, with a table and two chairs.

She had to talk to Dr. Ruppin in German, for he knew no Hebrew. She talked to him about the dictionary and the problem of money. He shrugged his shoulders and said:

"But why come to me? I do not even know the language."

Then Hemda, having spontaneously gotten the idea, asked him to call a meeting of the most influential Jews in Jaffa and see what he could do. Dr. Ruppin tried to beg off. But Hemda, feeling that she was fighting to keep alive the flame of her husband's passion, finally had her way and a meeting was called.

Z. D. Levontin, the banker, was there, and Judah Grazovski, who by now had collaborated on a pocket dictionary himself and had translated Dickens and Mark Twain into Hebrew. Dr. Shemarya Levin, an enthusiast for the Hebrew language, came, and also Dr. Meyer Berlin, a prominent social worker, and others.

Hemda did all the talking, in Hebrew. Exactly what she said she was later never able to remember. When she finished there were few questions, because many of the men had only a slight knowledge of Hebrew, yet were embarrassed not to speak Ben Yehuda's language to his wife.

Finally a sheet of paper was passed around and each man put down his name and an amount. In a short time enough was subscribed to assure the completion of the second volume, and Hemda rushed back to the hotel to tell her husband.

Hats in Hand

After their return to Jerusalem, Eliezer set to work again while Hemda went to Berlin to find out what had gone wrong there. It was Dr. Nathan who explained. As one of the founders and chief supporters of the German-Jewish schools in Palestine, he was indignant that the Ben Yehudas were trying to substitute the teaching of Hebrew for German in those schools. He frankly advised Mr. Ben Yehuda not to count on any more assistance from Berlin.

So Hemda proceeded to Switzerland, hoping to borrow enough money from her lawyer-brother, who had moved from Finland to a suburb of Geneva, to go on to Paris or even New York. But David Yonas was more unsympathetic than ever.

"Either there is or there is not a Jewish nation," he said in a queer attempt at logic. "If there is, then it should not have to go begging. If not, then why do you stay there? How can there be any need for a dictionary if no one wants to speak Hebrew?"

In Switzerland, Hemda received news from Jerusalem which made her realize she must get home quickly.

It was Ben Avi, this time, who was in trouble. He had been desperately in need of financing for his daily paper and had had what he thought was the good fortune to meet a man of wealth who agreed to provide enough financing not only to continue the paper but also to expand it in size and to put on a campaign for more circulation which would smother out its rivals. The prospective backer would pay Ben Avi a fixed salary and would demand no voice in editorial matters. When and if there was profit, he would take it.

Ben Avi had jumped at the offer. But he had ignored the fact that his new associate was a Jew who had renounced his religion and become a Christian.

When the news spread through Jerusalem the storm broke.

The Ben Yehudas going into partnership with an infidel! What depths would that family sink to next?

Fortunately, the financial "angel" broke his contract a short time after Hemda's return and renounced his support of the paper, to everyone's relief.

In the months which followed, the setting into type of the second volume was finally completed and the book went to press. It was dedicated to Professor Otto Warburg, scholar, philanthropist, man of kindly heart.

Never within the memory of living man had Jerusalem seen as much snow as fell on her sharp-pointed minarets, on her golden domes, and into her twisting streets that winter.

It was during this season that the mayor of Bradford, England, a wealthy Jew, Jacob Moser, arrived in Jerusalem on a tour of Palestine. It was Hemda who got the idea that Mayor Moser undoubtedly would understand the importance of a dictionary. (The time had come to start raising money for Volume Three.)

"I am sure everyone has been to see him for all manner of assistance since the day he came," Eliezer remarked pessimistically.

Saying nothing to her husband of her plans, Hemda conferred with Professor Richard James Horatio Gottheil, director of the American School for Oriental Research, which was across the street from the Ben Yehuda home. She showed him the first two volumes of the dictionary and some of the material for the third. Then she told him the financial problem.

The professor looked critically at the two printed books.

"Why do you make such a large dictionary? Even a tailor cuts his pattern according to the amount of material he has!"

Hemda smiled and quickly retorted:

"That is our misfortune. We have so much material that we are compelled to make a beautiful garment!"

Then Hemda asked the professor to invite Mr. Moser to luncheon and try to interest him in the dictionary.

Three days later Professor Gottheil came through the snow to report that Mrs. Ben Yehuda's hopes had been in vain. The Englishman was not a bit interested.

"I told you so, Bitti, didn't I?" was all Eliezer said.

"Well, sometimes I am right!" his wife responded.

That afternoon, without telling anyone, she went to the hotel where the Englishman was staying. He was away, but she talked with his wife, a charming English Jewess, who listened graciously and finally agreed to explain the entire matter to her husband and try to persuade him to grant Mrs. Ben Yehuda an interview.

Back home, Hemda began preparing her arguments.

It was only two hours after she had left the hotel that a carriage drove up and out of it came Mr. Levontin, the banker, in a highly excited state. He must see Mr. Ben Yehuda. The matter was urgent!

When he clasped the hand of Eliezer he blurted out:

"I bear good tidings, my friend!"

Eliezer blinked and rubbed a hand across his tired eyes.

"Tidings about what?"

"I come to tell you that Mr. Moser has just deposited five hundred pounds sterling in the bank in your name for Volume Three!"

Hemda, who had been eavesdropping, slipped out the door and ran through the snow without a coat to pay an unceremonious call on Professor Gottheil in the archaeology building. She wanted to tell him herself.

That evening, after Hemda had explained for the third time how she had done it, Eliezer shook his head and said:

"I still do not understand!"

"Well, then, let's just call it a miracle!"

"Bitti, there are too many miracles in our life. Always someone must produce a miracle! How many miracles do you have left? Remember, there will probably be six or seven volumes more!"

Eliezer Ben Yehuda started work on his third volume in high spirits, with more inner serenity than he had had in a long time. His wife spoke of his "wondrous quietness of soul."

The old opponents were dying off or giving way. A healthy new generation was taking over.

The success of the Bezalel School of Fine Arts was one example.

Aaron Aaronsohn was at work on his wild-wheat experiments and was gaining recognition among scientific agriculturists.

Ephraim Hareuveni had already found that plants and flowers mentioned in the Bible were still growing in Palestine, except that no one recognized them because they now had different names.

Abraham Zwi had begun his research into ancient Hebrew music which would be used as a base in building a contemporary Hebrew music.

These were only a few of the brilliant young Jews who were forging ahead in their fields, as Ben Yehuda was trying to do in his.

The lexicographer was happy when he received such reports, but once he said:

"What are all these things compared to the bright future ahead? Someday the Jews will be a nation. No one can stop it. The day will come when the importance and power of the Jews will be taken into consideration in the meeting places of the mighty. When the hour arrives for the last judgment of the nations, we shall be among them."

Prophetic words, spoken in 1910!

In these days the Ben Yehudas were living on Abyssinian Street in the New City, close by the British and Danish consulates, the Hebrew Orphanage, the Abyssinian Church, and the American archaeology school, having exchanged a small house with a large garden for a large house with a small garden.

The children liked the new home because it had windows with colored glass.

As they assembled for meals Ben Yehuda sat flanked by his two sons. At the other end of the long table sat "the Greeks," as Hemda and her daughters were called because they had taken to wearing sandals and long flowing robes of white, rose, yellow, or blue, cut along classical lines.

One day Ehud suddenly said:

"What's the matter now, Mother Worry?"

Hemda smiled. She had grown accustomed to the nickname her own children had given her. Each time they called her by that name she would unconsciously put a hand to her forehead and try to smooth out the wrinkles.

It was the old problem again. Volume Three, dedicated to Jacob Moser, was out and paid for. Now Volume Four must be financed.

The children dreaded this phase of the cycle. It always meant that one or both of the parents would pack suitcases and go off to foreign parts, sometimes not returning for months.

But this time the Ben Yehudas had a pleasant surprise. The house of Langenscheidtsche Verlagsbuchhandlung reported that a final audit of costs and receipts on Volume Two had been made and there was a small balance to the author's credit. They also offered to advance an additional one thousand marks to help with the work on Volume Four.

42

Language War

AFTER SULTAN ABDUL HAMID II ABDICATED, THE Young Turks sent Zakki Bey to Palestine as their military governor. He was a middle-aged man of education and culture who won immediate respect, especially from the Jews, who whispered that he was descended from Jews forcibly converted to Islam during the Spanish persecution. Whether or not that was true, he was responsible for the easing of many harsh restrictions.

Instead of the old-style bureaucrats, lazy and phlegmatic, new young Turkish officials arrived from Constantinople, most of them with progressive ideas. Turkish soldiers, instead of looking like tramps, now appeared in trim uniforms and with shined shoes.

Another direct result of the Turkish revolution was that all the great powers now turned their eyes toward this part of the world. France directed her attention in particular toward Syria and Lebanon. Russia ogled Constantinople. England concentrated her glances in the direction of the Suez Canal. But all took an intensified interest in Palestine.

Russia built a teachers' college at Nazareth to provide instructors for the one hundred or more secondary schools she had scattered over the country. Even Arab peasants began to speak Russian.

In the German-Jewish schools there was a constant attempt to decrease the amount of instruction in Hebrew and increase the use of the German language. It was openly stated that this was part of a plan to prepare Palestine for eventual German occupation.

The fear that Ben Yehuda had always had, that Constantinople would someday place a ban on the teaching of Hebrew, was completely dissipated, for the Young Turks imposed only one restriction: there must be instruction in every school in Turkish. If that were done, the schools were free to teach anything else they pleased.

Ben Yehuda's great objective had always been to have Hebrew the "language of the curriculum"; that all classes, whatever the subject, be conducted in Hebrew. He felt that French, German, Russian, English should be taught as "foreign languages."

In some schools he had already won this fight. In others progress was being made.

And then something very disturbing happened. A number of wealthy German Jews had financed the erection of a technical school at Haifa called Technikum. While the building had been under construction there had been discussions about what the language of the curriculum would be. Now the decision had been made. German! Hebrew would not be allowed.

A delegation which had attended the Zionist Congress at Vienna called and announced: "Ben Yehuda, you must get to work with your pen! Write editorials! Stir up public opinion!"

Ben Yehuda wondered whether the delegation realized what a sacrifice they were calling on him to make. It was not just that he would have to suspend work on the dictionary. It was not just that he had already spent part of the money advanced for the fourth volume. If he entered this new war he would become a crusading editor again and would irrevocably antagonize the Jews of Berlin who had helped him in the past and perhaps might help again.

But Ben Yehuda did not hesitate long. That same day he sent a message to Ephrayim Cohen, director of all German-supported schools in Palestine, that he wanted to see him at once. He received a curt reply. Mr. Cohen did not care to confer with Mr. Ben Yehuda.

Angered, Ben Yehuda went to see Mr. Cohen. He was told that

he was not at home. He tramped the streets and finally found the director. The conference took place on a public highway.

"I demand," said Ben Yehuda in a voice that had none of its habitual softness, "that you go immediately to Berlin and get this decision reversed. We will not allow anyone to dictate how the schools of Israel are to be run!"

Ephrayim Cohen tried to calm his opponent:

"I am sorry, but I have no influence in Berlin."

Ben Yehuda lost his temper.

"You can send word to Berlin that Ben Yehuda says blood will flow on the steps of the technical school in Haifa if this order is not changed at once! Things will happen which the entire world will hear about!"

"But, Mr. Ben Yehuda, would it change your mind if I told you that this order comes from the very top?"

"What do you mean, 'the very top'?"

"The German Kaiser has intimated that it would be most agreeable to him if German were made the official language of all schools in Palestine."

"And who is the Kaiser to us? Why must we sacrifice everything to satisfy one of his whims? This is war, Ephrayim Cohen! War, I tell you! We shall keep the technical school closed if they insist on German. No one will enter that building except over my dead body! Unless you go to Berlin, the war will start immediately. Decide now!"

At this point Ephrayim Cohen left Ben Yehuda to carry on his tirade to a crowd which had gathered.

Ephrayim Cohen did not go to Berlin. The war did start immediately.

No blood was spilled. No shots were fired. But in some ways it was as dramatic a war as the one which would be fought years later for the existence of the Jewish state.

Eliezer Ben Yehuda, the scholar, was the commander on his side. David Yellin, one of his earliest followers, came back from Vienna and took an active part in the fight.

The Ben Yehuda home on Abyssinian Street became general headquarters. Councils of war were held long into the night. Teachers from the various schools gathered there for strategy meetings. Jerusalem was tense, knowing that the "rebels" were facing powerful opposition this time.

Finally the teachers voted to abandon their classrooms, close the schools, and enlist their pupils in the fight. Ephrayim Cohen was left alone in his empty buildings.

The children and their instructors paraded through the streets shouting in Hebrew, "Down with the Germans," and "Hebrew must live." A marching song was composed with a martial air and militant Hebrew words.

The revolt spread to Jaffa, then to the settlements. More and more schools were closed because pupils and teachers had walked out, swearing to return only after the fight had been won.

From Judea and Galilee came many teachers to confer at GHQ.

Ephrayim Cohen sent for Dr. Paul Nathan, who had been responsible for stopping the Berlin contributions to the dictionary. Dr. Nathan was having a vacation in Egypt but hurried to Jerusalem for conferences. Ben Yehuda sent him an ultimatum that he had a choice between surrender or interminable war. There was no reply.

Finally the war council authorized Mrs. Ben Yehuda to confer with Dr. Nathan, thinking she might be able to hold her temper better than anyone else.

The meeting lasted for hours. Finally Dr. Nathan said:

"Maybe Mrs. Ben Yehuda ignores the fact that her husband's dictionary is in jeopardy. Has she no longer any interest in it?"

"And if I have, what should I do?"

"Persuade your husband to withdraw from this fight at once."

"He would be stoned to death if he turned traitor to the language he believes in, and rightly so!"

"Then woe to the Jews of Palestine and woe to the dictionary!"

As Hemda walked home she saw a crowd of students around a bonfire in the street in front of the German consulate.

Several hours later the elderly German consul, Dr. Schmidt, appeared at the Ben Yehuda home. There were tears in his eyes as he told his close friend, the lexicographer, that Jewish children had been burning their German schoolbooks in front of his office and had shouted at him when he tried to stop them:

"We shall never need German schoolbooks again!"

Dr. Nathan quit Palestine without capitulating. The technical school in Haifa remained closed. So did all the other German institutions.

Meanwhile, under Ben Yehuda's guidance, "emergency" schools were opened in which all the instruction was in Hebrew. In some wooden boxes had to be used for seats.

As in any civil war, families were divided; friends fought each other; those who tried to remain neutral were criticized by everyone else.

About this time there came to Jerusalem the American Ambassador to Turkey, Henry Morgenthau, whose son a generation later would play such a dominant role in raising funds for Israel. He was disturbed at the chaos he found and decided to try to make peace between the two camps.

Instead of calling a meeting, which everyone might have refused to attend, he saw to it that members of all factions were invited to a banquet to be given in his honor. Among the guests were many Christians and Moslems who had taken sides.

Ambassador Morgenthau, in the address of the evening, spoke of the need for love and peace, not only among brothers, but among Jews, Christians, and Moslems.

His oratory was effective. It served as oil to quiet the sea of seething emotions.

After that the agitation gradually subsided. Compromises were worked out. Neither side won a clear-cut victory, but the German schools eventually were reopened and Hebrew was not dropped from the curriculum.

Ben Yehuda returned to his study, picked up his pen, and resumed work on his dictionary, strangely refreshed by his activities as the battle-front commander in what Jewish history thereafter would refer to as the "War of the Languages."

Despite the bitterness engendered by the War of the Languages, Eliezer Ben Yehuda, when his fourth volume was completed, dedicated it to the committee in Berlin.

Hemda thought this was carrying fair play too far. But her

husband pointed out that without the help of the Jews in Berlin the dictionary never could have progressed this far.

"Let us give to Caesar what is Caesar's due!"

Volume Four was in many respects better than the others. It was richer in quotations. One critic said that reading Volume Four was like "taking a guided excursion through the ages."

Volume Four also showed the value of all the traveling the Ben Yehudas had done. It did more than the previous three together to establish Ben Yehuda's reputation as a thorough scholar.

The most tangible recognition came from the Zionist Organization, which, at the goading of Professor Warburg, voted Ben Yehuda an award of one thousand marks per year. This was especially welcome, because Baron Rothschild at this time cut his subsidy exactly in half as a gesture of his disapproval of Ben Yehuda's "Zionism."

When last in London Ben Yehuda had found traces in the British Museum of many words which would be included in Volume Five, but he needed to go back there to complete his philological detective work. On the way he wanted to see what language treasures he could uncover in Egypt.

A pattern by now had been established. It was clear that until the last word of the last letter of the alphabet was put into type the Ben Yehudas would wander from city to city, country to country, searching; Ben Yehuda for words, his wife for financial support. This had become so much a routine that any time money was mentioned Eliezer would smile and say:

"That, Bitti, is your department!"

Sometimes she grew weary of this need of being a one-man, twelve-month-per-year, self-perpetuating fund-raising organization, but she realized it was the role she was destined to play.

So they packed for a long trip and headed for Cairo.

Norman Bentwich, who as a boy had entertained them at his father's home in London with a violin concert, was now in the service of His Majesty's government in Cairo and helped show them Egypt.

Ben Yehuda delivered a lecture in the Arabic Academy of Science, pleasing his Arab hosts by telling them of the close relationship between their language and his, and how many words of their own, which they thought purely Arabic, had been "borrowed" from Hebrew.

While Eliezer secluded himself with manuscripts and books in the libraries and museums, Hemda began traveling along what she sometimes, in pessimistic moods, called her Via Dolorosa, seeking contributions to the dictionary.

When they left Cairo, Hemda carried with her as souvenirs of their visit a small glass bowl which had been buried in Egyptian sands for three thousand years and, as a more tangible evidence of the good will of Egyptian Jews, a check for five thousand francs to help finance Volume Five.

The morning after they arrived in London, Ben Yehuda went directly to the British Museum, saying he would not be back until late afternoon. But he returned to the hotel room in little more than an hour.

Hemda realized as he walked through the door that something was wrong. She could tell by the sag of his shoulders. He was like a small boy who needs to be mothered and told that whatever it was that had happened was not really important.

Obviously trying to be casual about it, he said:

"Does it seem strange to you, Bitti, that my dictionary is not in the library of the British Museum?"

"Impossible, Eliezer!"

"But it is so, nevertheless. I searched for a whole hour in the files and there is no listing of it!"

"Then you must look again, because it is surely there!"

So, as obedient as a small child, the great lexicographer picked up his hat and went back to the museum.

That evening when he returned his shoulders were straight again and his eyes sparkled with boyish happiness.

"You were right, Bitti! It is there! But can you imagine how stupid! It's listed under the name of Dr. Yahuda!"

(Abraham Shalom Yahuda had been secretary of the Berlin sponsoring committee.)

When they left for home Hemda was full of good spirits over having raised enough money to put out Volume Five. Her husband was bubbling with excitement because in the library at Oxford he had got on the trail of some words which had been evading him for years.

A friend arranged for them to travel from Liverpool to Port Said on a luxury ship at a greatly reduced rate. It was the first time in their lives that either of them had ever gone first-class.

While Ben Yehuda was working on Volume Five a distinguished visitor arrived in Jerusalem from America, Julius Rosenwald, who had helped found an experimental station at Athlit and had made possible Aaronsohn's scientific work in agriculture. He promised to write out a check for five hundred pounds sterling to put out the sixth volume of the dictionary.

So it was that as Ben Yehuda worked on Volume Five he was in the most serene mood of his entire life. They could look forward now to at least a short period of calm and peace. For the next two years, anyway, they would not have to pack bags, catch trains and boats, and travel from place to place, explaining, pleading, begging. Hemda could devote her energies to her family, her writing, her home. Eliezer could work in his study without interruption.

For these reasons Ben Yehuda changed the motto which hung over his desk. He took down the words:

THE DAY IS SO SHORT;
THE WORK TO BE DONE SO GREAT!

In the place of that slogan, which had been driving him for so many years, he hung up these words:

MY DAY IS LONG:
MY WORK IS BLESSÈD.

43

1914!

VOLUME FIVE WAS PUBLISHED DURING THE HEBREW month of *Tammuz,* in the summer of the Christian year 1914. It was dedicated to the Jews of London.

After the last page had gone to the printer the Ben Yehudas made plans for a vacation in Lebanon.

The children were sent to Petach Tikvah. The parents packed a trunk and went to Haifa to board a ship for Beirut. In the seaport city they found the streets full of excitement.

"What is this all about?" Ben Yehuda asked a passer-by.

"Are you joking? Have you not heard of the war?"

"War? What war?"

"Germany asks Belgium to let her through to get at France! England declares war on Germany and Austria!"

The Ben Yehudas had brought with them a letter of credit for five hundred francs to finance their holiday. They pushed their way through the crowds at the Anglo-Palestine Bank to draw part of the money. But the bank was closed. Someone in the crowd said there was a moratorium.

They counted their money and found they had just enough to get home. They sailed from Haifa on the last ship going south. In Jaffa the streets were full of Arab demonstrators. Some were running around with drawn swords, shouting:

"Our blades thirst for blood! God will protect the Sultan!"

Army officers stood in doorways watching and smiling. The uniforms of the men with the swords were so immaculate, their red fezzes so new-looking, their faces so healthy and glowing that Ben Yehuda had a suspicion, but it was not until much later that it was confirmed. The men with the swords shouting about the glory of the Sultan were not Turks, not Arabs, but German *provocateurs.*

They found, when they reached Jerusalem, that that city was also in a nervous state. Turkey had not yet joined in the war, but the foreigners were worried. Especially the British and French.

News from the battlefields those first few weeks was bad. Dark clouds settled over Israel. The Jews of Palestine were isolated from the rest of the world. Few ships touched these shores any more. No money flowed in. Shortages of necessary goods were made worse by hoarding. Sugar, rice, kerosene could no longer be bought. Prices rose astronomically.

Ben Yehuda paced his study, making no pretense at work on Volume Six. His dream, which had just been emerging from the realm of impossibility into a state of probability, was now threatened, he felt, with complete annihilation.

Many came to him to argue, to listen, to ask his opinions and advice. He told them all honestly how he felt. If Turkey entered the war on the side of Germany, and if Germany were defeated, then the Allies, without a doubt, would carve the Ottoman Empire into small pieces, and there would be a chance of the Jews asking for and receiving Palestine as their own.

If Turkey joined the Allies, and if the Allies won, then out of gratitude to Turkey the Allies would, of course, allow her to keep all the territory she now possessed, and the hope of a free Israel would be as dim as ever.

But, they would argue, what if Turkey should join the Allies and Germany should win?

That possibility Ben Yehuda would always dismiss, insisting that ultimate victory was bound to go to the Allies.

So he would conclude, they must pray that Turkey would oppose the Allies but that the Allies eventually would win. It would mean horrible days for them all.

This reasoning was very unpalatable for the German Jews, many of whom were so imbued with German nationalism that they were positive the Kaiser's armies could never be defeated and even worked openly for a German victory.

The situation was made still more complex by the attitude of the Russian Jews, who hated the czarist regime so much for its anti-Semitism that they opposed anything Russia did. And now Russia had gone to war on the side of England and France!

In this period Ben Avi ran the newspaper alone. He was young and enthusiastic. He also was reckless. He wrote as he thought and said what he pleased, ignoring the consequences. His fearlessness in arguing for an Allied victory won him many new friends. When he went down the street he was quickly surrounded by both Jews and Arabs who wanted to hear his opinions. But he also made enemies who soon would be shouting, literally, for his life.

Then came the news that Turkey had thrown in her lot with Germany.

This created a state of near panic in Jerusalem. Ben Yehuda and his son had to make a quick decision about their paper. If they continued publication they would have to support Turkey in everything they wrote. If they stopped publication it would be tantamount to an announcement that they did not wish to write pro-Turkish articles and therefore were traitors to the country whose citizenship they held. In the Ottoman Empire, as in most other countries, death was the punishment for traitors.

They tried to avoid the Scylla and Charybdis of this situation by printing an announcement that the lack of funds and shortage of newsprint forced them to close down the paper.

Then a German, Beck Bey, arrived to take over the running of Jerusalem. Zakki Bey, the Turkish governor and the Jews' friend, lost most of his authority. Each day new edicts were issued. Jewish homes were searched for Hebrew flags, and woe to him in whose house one was found! The death penalty was imposed on Jews in possession of stamps issued by the Jewish National Fund.

Up to now the Ben Yehuda home had not been ransacked, but Hemda was terrified that if it ever were, some stupid or evil officer might confiscate the manuscript and notes for the remaining volumes of the dictionary, so she took them to the American consul, who assured her that in his care they would be as safe as if in a vault in New York.

The fact that no funds were arriving from abroad left those Jews who had been supported by foreign charity in a disastrous situation. Their plight was relieved temporarily by the arrival of Maurice Wertheim, son-in-law of Henry Morgenthau, who came with fifty thousand dollars in gold to be distributed among the various Jewish organizations for the relief of their members.

A meeting of the Jewish leaders of Jerusalem was held, but a violent argument broke out as to the proportion of the fifty thousand dollars each group should get. Finally Wertheim, with Solomon-like inspiration, picked up the suitcase of gold, went into an adjoining room, locked the door from the inside, and shouted:

"I shall not come out until you gentlemen announce through the keyhole that you have reached a friendly decision!"

An agreement was quickly arrived at.

Before he left, Wertheim visited Ben Yehuda and tried to encourage him to get busy again on his dictionary. Later, on his return to the United States, he eulogized Ben Yehuda and his work in his report to American Jews.

When the forests which Jewish settlers had planted at Petach Tikvah and Hedera, tree by tree, patiently, lovingly, were ordered cut down by Turkish authorities, Ben Yehuda cried aloud with rage. When the orange groves of the settlements were seized he refused to come any more to his meals.

Sometimes he would sit for hours with his head in his hands, silently mourning. For whole days he went without food. Often in the middle of the night he would get up and pace for an hour or two.

Finally his condition worried Hemda so much that she suggested it might be well for them to try to get to America. There he could work on his dictionary in peace. What she did not add was her conviction that time was running out. His frail body could not stand many more crises. There were four or five volumes of the dictionary left to be done. If he were to finish them, there was no time to lose. But instead of bringing up that argument she said:

"Eliezer, you have often told me that someone should explain this whole situation to the Jews of America and make them see the importance of an Allied victory to the future of the Jews. If you were to go to America you could do that!"

But nothing she said seemed to have any effect. Desert Israel? Not unless they drove him away at the point of a gun!

In desperation Hemda arranged a meeting which she kept secret from her husband. His old friend, David Yellin, was there and many others who, Hemda knew, were concerned about him. She had heard that an Italian ship was due to stop at Jaffa in a few days. If they hurried they might make it.

Yellin and the others agreed to help, so they held another meeting and asked Ben Yehuda to be present. Without telling him of Hemda's part in the plot, they announced their opinion that he would serve Israel better by going to America as a propagandist than merely by dying for Israel on Israeli soil.

"It will not be easy to change the minds of many of our American brothers," someone said. "A lot of American Jews are eager to settle old accounts with Russia. You must go over, Ben Yehuda, and tell them it is their duty to Israel to forget their feelings toward Russia and support the Allies!"

The next day a number of Jewish leaders met at Tel Aviv and drew up a document addressed to the Jews of America, urging their support of the Allies. Ben Yehuda was asked to undertake the mission of delivering the communication.

This ended his wavering. This gave a *raison d'être* to his trip. So he started packing.

All the provisions stored up in the Ben Yehuda home for an emergency were distributed to the needy. Moshe Nissim, who had been serving as Ben Yehuda's secretary, was given keys to all thirteen rooms in the house and was instructed to put on the lights each night and otherwise conduct the affairs of the household as if they were all there. If anyone discovered they were gone, he was to say they had left for one of the settlements to help fight the plague of locusts which, ironically, had settled on Palestine at almost the same time as the plague of war.

Ehud was in Germany studying agriculture. Yemeemah was living with her husband in Canada. Ben Avi decided he would endanger his parents' safety if he tried to go with them; he would make an attempt later. That left just the three small children, Dola, Ada, and Zaza, who were fifteen, thirteen, and ten.

The Ben Yehudas took no baggage except a few clothes for the girls. They left at night. They were certain everything had been arranged so secretly that no one knew of their plans.

But they were unfortunately not aware of the intensity of the enmity that some of their fellow Jews bore them. The scars of the War of the Languages had not yet healed, for it later turned out that it was several German Jews who had notified Turkish officials of their departure.

They were already in the harbor of Jaffa on a barge which was to take them out to the Italian ship when the military commander of the port presented them with an order to return to Jerusalem.

The small daughters cried all the way home.

When they reached Jerusalem they were not taken into custody, and Eliezer cheered up a little. Hemda advised him to relax and wait. Somehow they would still get to America.

But it was not easy for anyone to relax in Jerusalem in those days. All Palestine was like an armed camp. The Turks were preparing to attack the British in Egypt in order to get control of the Suez Canal. Arrests were being made every day, and what happened to those arrested no one dared inquire.

Hemda tried to keep from Eliezer the news that German officers in the Turkish army were demanding that Ben Avi be executed as a traitor and that Eliezer himself be sent to Anatolia, which she knew for him would be worse than death.

She did not hide from him the news that some of his Arab friends had agreed to go to the authorities with an appeal that he, his wife, and small children be allowed to quit the country.

By some freak of luck it worked. Word came back that Eliezer, Hemda, Ada, Dola, and Zaza Ben Yehuda were granted the right to leave Jaffa by ship. The irony of it was that now there were no ships leaving Jaffa.

But one day the American consul told Hemda that as long as they had an official permit he would guarantee that they would be taken aboard the U.S.S. *Tennessee* when the warship arrived in Jaffa on Christmas Day to evacuate stranded Americans.

Although they did have the permit, the Ben Yehudas went through the same precautions again. Once more they gave Moshe Nissim the thirteen keys and instructions to keep the lights burning.

In Jaffa they spent Christmas Eve lying with other refugees on the floor of a small German hotel. In the morning, with the others, they went to the office of the military commander of Jaffa to have their passports stamped.

Ben Yehuda's was returned with Turkish handwriting scrawled on one of the blank pages:

DANGEROUS JOURNALIST
NOT PERMITTED TO
LEAVE FROM ANY PALESTINIAN PORT

Hemda took the passport to the American consul, who exploded:

"Incredible! I shall insist they allow you to leave!"

But the U.S.S. *Tennessee* sailed on Christmas Day without the Ben Yehudas.

Back on Abyssinian Street, for the second time they unlocked doors which they had expected would remain closed for years.

For two nerve-torturing months they waited again.

Finally their old friend, Zakki Bey, persuaded Jemal Pasha, commander in chief of the Turkish army in Palestine, to write a request to the military commander at Jaffa to allow the Ben Yehudas to leave.

As Zakki Bey gave them the document he whispered:

"I beg you, do not let the Germans hear about this!"

So for the third time they said their good-bys, locked the doors, gave the same old instructions, and departed with little baggage at 4 A.M. They took a carriage to Jaffa and hoped that no "enemy" would see them.

By this time Eliezer was reconciled to the failure of the mission with which the Jews of Tel Aviv had entrusted him. He also seemed reconciled to packing up, traveling to Jaffa, being turned back, then waiting again. But this time it was different.

They found a Greek cargo boat which was going to Alexandria. The owner agreed to transport them for a reasonable fee. They would sail as soon as he finished loading his cargo of Palestinian oranges. Probably late in the evening.

It was Hemda who had the foresight to advise two of Ben Yehuda's high-placed Arab friends of their sailing plans. And the two Arabs were kind enough to invite Hassan Beck, military commander of the port, to dinner that night. They took him to a place a considerable distance out of town. They ordered an elaborate meal with plenty to drink. They saw to it that the meal lasted until a late hour, hoping that by then the little Greek vessel would have sailed away with its oranges and its Ben Yehudas.

Meanwhile the family from Jerusalem and the skipper became good friends. He assured them that the minute they set foot on his decks they were "as good as on Greek soil."

"That may be the law," Hemda said nervously, "but I wonder how well you know the Turks."

The owner of the oranges, a Jew named Aboujeben, was so much more concerned about the Ben Yehudas than he was about getting the fruit to its destination that before the ship was more than half loaded he begged the skipper to leave the rest of the cargo and sail away.

"I should gladly lose a million oranges," he said dramatically, "than that Ben Yehuda should fall into the hands of the Turks again!"

So they sailed out onto the Mediterranean, from the same port to which Eliezer had come nearly thirty-four years ago as a boy with a dream; the same port to which he had brought Hemda nearly twenty-three years ago as his child bride.

The dream had not yet been fulfilled.

But half a dictionary had been written and the battle to revive a dead language had been more than half won.

The Greek vessel with half a cargo of oranges and five eighths of the Ben Yehuda family made Alexandria by the next morning.

A Jewish friend in the Anglo-Palestine Bank in Jerusalem had given Eliezer a check for five thousand French francs out of the account which Julius Rosenwald had established for the dictionary. By good fortune Z. D. Levontin, the Palestine banker, was in Alexandria when the Ben Yehudas arrived and helped them get the check cashed. Hemda was annoyed that it took a full week, but it turned out to be a stroke of luck that it did.

They had all been worried about Ben Avi, who was on the Germans' black list and who had stayed behind in Jerusalem.

Now just as they left the bank and were walking in the direction of the water front, they saw, coming toward them, Ben Avi and his wife! They greeted each other affectionately. The handsome young son was full of stories about how Zakki Bey, their friend, had also helped get him out.

Eliezer and Hemda had already made arrangements to sail on another Greek boat for Peiraeus. It took little talk to persuade Ben Avi and his wife to join them.

The ship which took them from Peiraeus to New York stopped on the way at Naples. There was excitement in Naples, for on that day Italy had entered the war on the side of the Allies.

When Eliezer heard the news he was radiant.

"This will bring an Allied victory and freedom for Israel one step nearer!"

It took two weeks for the small ship to cross the Atlantic. Halfway across Eliezer began to get nervous about the document still pinned in the lining of his coat. He talked to Hemda about it as he sat in a deck chair with a blanket bundled around him.

"I am sure, Bitti," he said, "that I am not the right man for America. I know so many languages, yet I am not able to speak English properly. The Jews over there will want to talk Yiddish, and Yiddish I shall refuse to speak. None of them will understand Hebrew, and Hebrew I shall insist on speaking. I will be small man among giants, Bitti!"

At the dock they were greeted by a brother whom Eliezer had not seen for forty-one years. They had called him Hayim Maeer Perlman when he was a boy in Luzhky, Lithuania. Then the family Seydel had adopted him to save him from Russian military service, and he had become Hayim Maeer Seydel. When he emigrated to America he changed his first name to Jacob.

It was a strange scene as they met. They greeted each other as strangers, this frightened little man with the sharp-pointed beard and the sad eyes, and his own brother, a self-assured, prosperous American businessman.

Jacob Seydel loaded them all into his automobile, which Hemda said was the biggest automobile she had ever seen. He drove them through what Dola called "a very large garden" with lakes and bridges, which he said was called Central Park.

On the way he said to Eliezer: "Do you remember the time we took the herring to the river to wash them and dropped them in? I wonder if Mother ever found out that I was the one who lost them and not you?"

At the brother's home a delegation of Zionists was waiting to greet the man from Jerusalem. It was obvious that many of his well-wishers had expected to meet a dynamic personality who would tell dramatic stories about the struggles he had been through. Instead, here was a short, frail, sad-looking man who reminded some of them of a deer that had been cornered by hunters. He answered many of their questions with a motion of his head or a simple "yes" or "no."

A few days later Ben Yehuda was told of plans for a reception for him. He was adamant in his refusal to have any part in it.

"I am an exile," he replied intently. "I left my country in blood and fire. This is not the time for receptions and festivities!"

They argued with him. A large hall had been rented. Tickets had been printed. Announcements had been sent to the newspapers. Eliezer kept shaking his head. Finally a member of the delegation said the reception was necessary to promote interest in Zionism, his dictionary, and the war. Reluctantly he agreed to attend "as long as there are not too many people present."

The night of the reception Hemda had difficulty forcing Eliezer to keep his promise. On the way to the hall she whispered to him:

"You must try to cheer up, Eliezer! You look as if you were going to a funeral instead of to a reception in your honor!"

A crowd was milling around outside the hall. This frightened the mild little man from Jerusalem. He begged Hemda to permit him to go home.

Finally they reached the entrance, but an Irish policeman who seemed at least twice Eliezer's height barred the way.

"No more in here! No more! How many times do I have to tell you people? No more in here!"

Obediently Eliezer turned around and started to walk away, looking relieved.

"But, officer," Hemda said, "this man is Ben Yehuda!"

"I don't care if he's President of the United States! I've got me orders! This here hall's full to capacity, see? Not one more person goes in until someone comes out! Get me, lady?"

Hemda finally succeeded in having a message sent to those inside and two people left the hall so the Ben Yehudas could enter.

The ovation he received frightened the guest of honor. But when it came time for him to speak, his courage returned a little and he made a plea for Israel and the Allies which those who understood Hebrew found convincing.

A few days later Ben Yehuda was invited to be the guest of honor at the Zionist convention in Boston. He declined, explaining, as he had done so many times before, that he would never attend a Zionist meeting anywhere unless it were conducted in Hebrew.

"But one of the biggest Zionists in America, Louis D. Brandeis, says it is necessary for you to come."

Eliezer finally agreed on a compromise. He would not go to this convention, but he would have a private interview with Brandeis.

When he returned from the session Hemda asked him what he had said to "the famous lawyer."

"I told him about Israel."

"What else, Eliezer?"

"I told him that the Jews of America must forget their feelings about Russia and work for the victory of England."

"And what did he say?"

"He said nothing. That man is a sphinx! He listened to me politely. Then he was silent. He just said 'Au revoir' when I left."

After a pause he added: "I am afraid my mission has failed, Bitti. I do not understand these Americans!"

Two or three days later he received an invitation to attend a conference of officers of the Federation of American Zionists. He had had some rest now and had regained a little of his old enthusiasm. He decided that this was his opportunity to deliver the message from Tel Aviv and try to convince the leaders of American Jewry that they must play a vital role in the war.

He was as nervous as a small boy giving his first recitation at school as he and his wife were led into the conference room. Seven distinguished-looking men sat around a table. Brandeis, who in a few months would become the first Jew ever appointed to the Supreme Court, was presiding. The others were introduced as Dr. Stephen S. Wise, Dr. Shemarya Levin, Dr. Harry Friedenwald, E. Lewin-Epstein, Louis Lipsky, and Jacob de Haas.

The chairman said:

"Mr. Ben Yehuda, will you please tell these gentlemen just what you told me the other day?"

Standing at the head of the table looking down into the seven faces, Ben Yehuda felt, he later told his wife, as if he were facing a court-martial. But as he began to talk he lost his nervousness. He became excited. His eyes, Hemda thought, were as they used to be when he was younger. They were bright, full of excitement.

He read them the message from Tel Aviv, then said:

"Israel demands from the Zionists of America and from Jews everywhere that they stand up like one man on the side of the Allies in this war and forget all other feelings.

"If the Germans should win . . ."

He went on to picture Israel's fate as he saw it under German or continued Turkish rule.

In concluding he said with deep intensity:

"We Jews must show ourselves worthy to be entrusted with our own destiny!"

Then he sat down. There was a dead silence. Finally Brandeis took his hand and thanked him.

At that moment Ben Yehuda lost his patience. He jumped to his feet and, facing the chairman, said:

"You have heard from me. Now I should like to hear from you. What is your opinion? What are you going to do?"

Brandeis smiled.

"Mr. Ben Yehuda, we asked you to come here to talk to us, not to have us talk to you."

A few minutes later Mr. and Mrs. Ben Yehuda were on an elevated train, accompanied by a young man who had been sent to show them the way home.

When they were finally alone, Eliezer opened the floodgates and let his pent-up feelings pour out.

"This proves, Bitti, what I tried to say on the ship. I am not the right man. I am not suited to America. Over here they need a powerful speaker who pounds the table and shouts until his throat bursts. I am a failure here, Bitti. I wish I had never come!"

Three days later, however, newspapers carried the story that the Federation of American Zionists had declared itself for the Allies.

"So, Eliezer, you have won another fight, see?" his wife said to him. "You are always so impatient! I hope all the battles you have in the future will be as easy as this one! You should be proud and happy. I am sure your friends in Tel Aviv will be grateful to you. Now you can say that your mission was successfully accomplished."

What Eliezer did not know was that before he spoke to them, the members of the Zionist executive committee had been bitterly divided. At least one of the seven men he addressed had been of the same opinion as many of the German Jews in Palestine: that their hope lay with Germany. Several others had felt that no stand of any kind should be taken. His speech, even though he had not pounded the table, had had something to do with deciding the issue.

Maurice Wertheim, who had brought the fifty thousand dollars in gold to Jerusalem, came to see the Ben Yehudas soon after their arrival, and Hemda took him aside to tell him that the money from the check they had cashed in Alexandria was almost gone. They were embarrassed about living on the generosity of Eliezer's brother.

If Mr. Wertheim could give her a list of wealthy American Jews who might be interested in sponsoring a volume of the dictionary, she would be glad, she said, to "go from door to door," as she had so often done in the past, to explain the situation and ask for their assistance.

"It would help," she said timidly, "if you could give me a letter of introduction."

Wertheim laughed.

"You are in New York now, my dear, not Jerusalem. We will arrange these matters. You must be with your husband and children. My wife has already obtained a small house for you. Now we must find schools for your daughters. But everything will be arranged so your brilliant husband can work in peace. We want him to know that we appreciate over here what he has done and what he will continue to do, God willing."

It was through the interest of Maurice Wertheim that his father, Jacob, joined with Jacob Schiff, Felix Warburg, Julius Rosenwald, and Herbert Lehman to form a small committee to "sponsor" Ben Yehuda in America.

One of the committee's first decisions was to ask the State Department in Washington to request Ambassador Morgenthau in Constantinople to get the manuscripts and notes which Hemda had left with the American consul in Jerusalem and have them shipped to New York.

The consul sent back word, however, that, conditions being what they were in Palestine, it was doubtful if the papers could be transported safely from Jerusalem to Jaffa. Ben Yehuda agreed that they should be left in Jerusalem.

Professor Gottheil, the archaeologist whose office was across the street from the Ben Yehuda home on Abyssinian Street, procured a special room in the New York Public Library in which the man from Jerusalem could work without interruption.

Jacob Schiff arranged with the library's Semitic department for Ben Yehuda to be supplied with all the books he needed.

So the lexicographer went back to work. From nine until six he locked himself in the private room in the great stone building at Fifth Avenue and Forty-second Street and began to cover thousands of fresh pieces of paper with notes for subsequent volumes of his dictionary.

Several times he went to Washington to consult books and manuscripts in the Library of Congress.

One day when he returned from Washington, Hemda said:

"While you were gone I heard that your old friend Tshashnikov is now here in the United States. He sent word in a roundabout way that if there is anything you need he stands ready to help you. Would you like to see him, or——"

Eliezer waved aside the suggestion and went back to the book he was reading. Hemda did not bring up the subject again.

The war years for Ben Yehuda were extremely productive. Although divorced from his notes in Jerusalem, he was able in the United States to complete most of the research for the remaining letters of the alphabet.

44

1917!

IN 1917 THE DREAM OF ELIEZER BEN YEHUDA BEgan to be cloaked with the garments of reality.

It was a year filled with events which would change the history of mankind, and most of them had special significance for the man from Jerusalem, who now lived for three things:

To complete his dictionary.

To see Israel reincarnated.

To return home from exile and set foot on the free soil of his own land before he died.

The first excitement of 1917 was the entry of the United States into the war.

Perhaps the Federation of American Zionists had little to do with the decision. Perhaps all the Jews in America combined had played no greater role than any other group in bringing about the climate of opinion which made the move possible. Yet Eliezer Ben Yehuda felt a personal triumph when the news was shouted in the streets on that chilly day in April.

"Now, Bitti, my mission really has been accomplished!"

Another excitement was the departure of several thousand Jewish soldiers who had volunteered for service in all-Jewish battalions. Ben Yehuda was invited to help send them off. The committee in charge gave him an armband, and there were Hebrew letters on it. It was one of the few souvenirs he ever kept.

Then there was the bright day an organization of Jewish women called Hadassah sent a contingent of doctors and nurses to the battle front. Eliezer cried, watching them go.

But the day which Ben Yehuda said no Jew in the world should ever forget was November 2, 1917.

It was on November 2 that the government of Great Britain came to the support of those Jews scattered around the world who wanted Palestine proclaimed the homeland of the Hebrew people.

The Balfour Declaration, history would call it. And Ben Yehuda called it "our charter of freedom."

It was only a statement of policy on the part of the government in London. It could be repudiated by any subsequent British government, as would actually happen many years later. It could be ignored by other Allies. It was no ironclad guarantee of anything. It was only a few sentences on a piece of white paper. But Zionists the world over, on that November day, rejoiced as they had seldom rejoiced before.

If Eliezer Ben Yehuda was more excited than the rest, it was understandable. This, finally, was something which gave substance to the dream. This was what he had been struggling for all these years with his voice and his pen. He had said all along that it was England to whom the Jews should look for their freedom. He had been ridiculed in Jerusalem for saying it. The German Jews had told him it could never happen. There had been skeptics even here in New York.

But now it *had* happened! It was there for anyone to read in the newspapers being sold in the streets.

"His Majesty's Government view with favour the establishment in Palestine of a national home for the Jewish people, and will use their best endeavours to facilitate the achievement of this objective. . . ."

At Carnegie Hall there was a celebration. Justice Brandeis presided. The men of the executive committee were there. One of them grasped Ben Yehuda's hand and said:

"I was against you that day you spoke to us. I was sure you were wrong. Now I congratulate you on having been so right!"

The flag of Israel flew that evening in Carnegie Hall, and Eliezer Ben Yehuda was as happy as a young groom.

December 11 was another day in 1917 which Eliezer Ben Yehuda never forgot. That was the day General Edmund Allenby led his British soldiers through the gates of Jerusalem, driving out the Turks who for more than four hundred years had kept the Holy City under heel. Eliezer was so excited when he ran home with the news that he could hardly talk.

"Think, Bitti, how many centuries it has been since our city was free! And there were Jewish soldiers with Allenby! Some of that Jewish Legion we helped send off!"

Another dream came true while Ben Yehuda was still in America when the cornerstone was laid on Mount Scopus for what some people would someday consider the greatest university anywhere in the Middle East.

"How often have I talked and written about this, Bitti! Remember? Now it is going to happen. Think of it! We shall be able to stand in our streets and look up and see it. Great scholars will gather there, and it will be the headquarters for the Academy of Hebrew which will take over my work on the language and will see that Hebrew is kept beautiful and pure!"

The fact that Ben Yehuda assumed that the language of the curriculum would be Hebrew was an indication of how much progress had been made. The War of the Languages was over and won.

It was in 1917 that Hemda and Eliezer Ben Yehuda celebrated their silver wedding anniversary. Mr. and Mrs. Jacob Wertheim gave a dinner party for them. As a surprise Ben Yehuda presented his wife with a bulky manuscript, explaining to her and to the others around the table:

"We often hear about the Greek and Roman classics. Even schoolboys know them by name. Since I came to America I have been working, without even Hemda knowing it, on the Hebrew classics, for we have classics too!

"I am not through yet. When I finish there will be eight volumes of about three hundred pages each. In these books there will be one hundred and forty Hebrew classics of the post-biblical period. I am calling this new work *Fathers of the Hebrew Language.* It is the best gift I could think of for my wife on this occasion."

Later such scholars as Professor Louis Ginsberg called this new Ben Yehuda undertaking a work of great significance, equal to that of the dictionary.

When Hemda got home that night and began to look over the manuscript, she found a note attached to it in her husband's delicate handwriting. It read:

"All that I have done in my life, all that I possess, has been achieved through your assistance and consequently belongs to you."

The only thing that marred the happiness of 1917 for the Ben Yehuda family was Eliezer's impatience to get home. He continued to work, but each evening when he came home from the library he would say:

"Bitti, don't you think that tomorrow, maybe, we should see some of our influential friends and get them to inquire about the possibility of our going?"

He was vaguely aware that great battles were still being fought in western Europe, but he understood little about the complexities of wartime travel; the necessity of waiting for the end of hostilities before starting.

One evening in November of the next year the Ben Yehudas went to hear Enrico Caruso at the Metropolitan Opera House. There they learned that an armistice had been signed! The war in Europe was over!

As the audience made the opera house echo with cheers and shouting, the entire cast appeared on the stage. Flags of all the Allies were displayed. The orchestra stood up and began to play the national anthem.

Turning to his wife, Eliezer Ben Yehuda whispered:

"Bitti, this means we can go home, doesn't it?"

Friends urged that they wait until ocean travel was safer and conditions in Palestine were more settled.

"I can wait no longer!" Ben Yehuda replied.

With the help of Julius Rosenwald and friends in the British Embassy, they obtained the necessary documents.

Toward the end of February 1919 a farewell dinner was given at Chaliff's in New York by the Histadruth Ivrith, an organization for the promotion of Hebrew culture, and a specially formed Ben Yehuda Jubilee Committee. In the name of the Jews of America, the treasurer, Israel Matz, presented Ben Yehuda with a check for ten thousand dollars to be used to build a house in Jerusalem in which he could work peacefully the remaining years of his life.

In his speech of thanks the lexicographer said:

"Years ago my wife suggested we try to set aside a little money occasionally so we could build a house someday. I always told her that whatever money we had must go into the dictionary. Once I said that if we were successful in helping to build a nation for our people, someday our people might help build a house for us, but that otherwise we would never have one. But now we shall!"

The first available passenger ship was reserved for diplomats and went off without the Ben Yehudas, despite all the pressure that was applied, although by an odd twist Ben Avi went on it. He was going to Versailles to represent the Zionist Organization of America at the peace conference and had semi-official status.

The rest of the family sailed on the next ship. The same brother who had been at the pier when they arrived was at the pier when they left, but this time there were hundreds of other well-wishers.

A large Jewish flag was presented to Ben Yehuda by the Zionist Organization with a request that it be flown from the house he was going to build.

The voyage was pleasant, the sea was calm, the company was strange. The Ben Yehudas were the only Jews on board.

The Americans and Britishers sang many of their own war songs.

Ben Yehuda did nothing to hide his pride when one of his daughters, without even a suggestion from him, said to a group around the piano one evening:

"We also have a country, and a language, and songs. Would you like to hear some of them?"

All went well until they landed at Naples and looked for transportation the rest of the way.

No ships to Palestine. No ships to Egypt. They almost lived in the

Cook's travel agency. That was how they had the coincidental meeting with the handsome young man who was also standing in line waiting to ask questions about ships.

"But, Ben Avi, what are you doing here? You are supposed to be in Versailles!"

After he had affectionately thrown his arms around various members of the family he explained. In Paris there had been a fight over his right to go to Versailles. The delegation from Russia insisted the people in New York had had no right to send him. It was another chapter in the old Ussishkin-Ben Yehuda feud.

The Ben Yehudas finally reached Alexandria on a British troopship. Then they crossed the desert in a sleeping car, a new sensation and the first evidence of the British occupation.

At the Palestinian frontier they met Sir Ronald Storrs, the British governor of Jerusalem, who gave Ben Yehuda one of the most heartwarming moments of his life by walking up with outstretched hand and saying with a broad smile on his face:

"Shalom alechem [Peace be unto you]!"

Ben Yehuda answered with a volley of excited Hebrew, but the governor held up his hand and laughed.

"Sorry, but those two words are all the Hebrew I know!"

Still, they were enough to bring tears of happiness into Eliezer's eyes. He turned to his wife and in a voice heavy with emotion said:

"Bitti, did you hear? I have often wondered whether I would live to see my dream come true. The Turks are gone. The British are here in their place. A distinguished gentleman taking over from a tyrant like Beck Bey.

"But I never dreamed, Bitti, of a day when a British governor of Jerusalem would greet me with Hebrew words on his lips!"

The Ben Yehudas had another serendipity at the frontier. A trim, stalwart young man came rushing up to them. No one recognized him at first.

"I'm Ehud, Father! Don't say you've forgotten me!"

They had not forgotten him, but it had been years since they had seen him. He had gone to Germany to study agriculture when he was fifteen. Now he was a man, having passed his twenty-first birthday.

On the train to Jerusalem he explained all that had happened to him. As a Turkish subject he had been liable to conscription. Not wanting to serve with the Turks, he had joined the German army with a request that he be sent to the Middle East.

Once he had been court-martialed as a suspected spy, but Ambassador Morgenthau had intervened to save him. Then he had escaped and gone over to the British. He had fought at Damascus. Finally, back in Jerusalem, he had heard his family was on the way home and had come to meet them.

It was Passover when the Ben Yehudas returned to their own soil after so long an exile. Eliezer sat in the railroad coach, staring out the window at "his " land. It seemed enough for him that he finally was back home. When they reached the Golden City he seemed happy at the sights, the sounds, the smells which had been so familiar. Only one thing bothered him. Why had no one come to meet them? Why, in the streets, when he greeted people he had known for years, did they act so queerly?

When they reached Abyssinian Street they found their home occupied by strangers. Ben Yehuda's library was intact because the door had been double-locked on his study. But there was little else of their own left in the house. Even Hemda's books were gone.

Moshe Nissim, the secretary, explained that he had had to sell some items of furniture to pay for food for his family. He would now try to buy them back. Other things had been stolen. He had done the best he could.

Ben Avi's house had fared better. His wife's family had watched over it. So Eliezer, Hemda, their three daughters, and their youngest son tried to "make house" in the one spare room at Ben Avi's. Then they attempted to learn why they had been received in such chill silence. The answer was not one that brought joy to any of them.

Jerusalem was almost unanimous in considering that Ben Yehuda had "run away." During the years that those who remained behind had suffered, they had often talked with anger about how all the Ben Yehudas except Ehud had escaped the deprivations and horrors of war. Why had the Ben Yehudas, who talked so much of sacrifice, not stayed to suffer, and to die, if necessary? Why, if they wanted to go into exile, had they not gone, as so many others had, to some miserable town in Anatolia? Real welcomes were arranged for those who returned from such exiles! But not for the Ben Yehudas, who had been safe, comfortable, warm, and well fed in America!

Hemda said they should explain about the "mission"; they should tell of what had been accomplished.

But Eliezer shook his head. His critics were right. He *had* run away. It would have been better if he had stayed. He understood how they felt. In time they might forget. Meanwhile there was work to be done.

45

Hebrew Comes of Age

IT TOOK A LAWSUIT TO GET BACK THE HOUSE ON Abyssinian Street. It took weeks of searching in Jewish and Arab homes to find all the missing pieces of furniture. But finally the Ben Yehudas were ready to receive whatever old friends would come, and to welcome the "new rulers" in as much style as they were able.

Slowly, gradually, those who had been angered by the flight of the family put in an appearance. The antagonisms melted like the snow in mountain passes in the spring; almost imperceptibly, but inevitably.

There were burning questions to be discussed. Ben Yehuda, to whom they always looked for opinions and advice, before long was taking as great a part as ever in the political, scholastic, and social life of the community.

If they reprimanded him for having gone away, he accepted their remarks in silence. But if they came with criticism of the new regime, he lashed back at them. The British must be given a chance. They must not be judged hastily. Their coming had been awaited for so long a time; now they must be treated as liberators, not as masters to be hated and fought. Gradually the Ben Yehuda home became a cultural and intellectual center again. Frenchmen, Englishmen,

Italians, and Russians came. Army officers, diplomats, members of visiting political missions. Hadassah doctors and nurses, Jewish leaders from America, scholars from all over the world.

Ben Yehuda found little time to work on the dictionary. For this Hemda often took him to task. He would reply:

"You are right, Bitti, but I have worked diligently for nearly forty years. In this hour when we prepare for our final triumph, let me take part in life for a little while. Then I shall go back to my papers and my books."

The daughters had no regrets about having returned. There were parties, dances, receptions, lectures; good company; plenty of handsome young men.

The family occasionally traveled to the settlements and to Tel Aviv, which had grown from a waste to a thriving little metropolis of thirteen thousand inhabitants and was already being called the "Miracle City of the Middle East" by people who had no idea that in another quarter of a century it would be housing nearly a quarter of a million people.

Everywhere the Ben Yehudas found a new spirit of liberty and freedom. The country was blossoming. Its gates were open. Multitudes were streaming in. Jews were buying great areas of land from the Arabs. Agricultural settlements were sprouting like grass after a summer rain. Commerce, building, education were all advancing with giant steps. A real Hebrew literature began to develop. There was a Hebrew theater now. Singers were giving concerts of Hebrew songs. There was even an opera in Hebrew. Many of the immigrants were accepting Palestinian citizenship. They were dropping names acquired in the Diaspora and taking Hebrew names.

These developments brought joy to Ben Yehuda, but he was disturbed because the house on Abyssinian Street was no longer what he had called a "Hebrew home." Foreigners who came did not speak his language. Even men of the Jewish Legion and Hadassah doctors and nurses spoke English or French.

Hemda pointed out that it was impossible now to enforce the old rule that no one should cross the threshold unless he spoke Hebrew.

"Then they must learn Hebrew!"

"Give them time, Eliezer!"

There were two questions which burned in Ben Yehuda's mind. Although France and Italy had indicated their approval of the Balfour Declaration, the Allies had taken no formal action on what was to be done with Palestine. But now a peace conference was to be held at San Remo, Italy, at which the other great powers would decide whether to give Great Britain a mandate over the Holy Land. It would be at San Remo, Ben Yehuda felt, that Israel would be given the chance to live and develop, or would be given a death sentence.

The other question was who would be the first British High Commissioner of Palestine? This, Ben Yehuda felt, would also decide much about the future. Would the man be at all sympathetic toward the Jews? Would he be a disinterested military man, or a career diplomat interested only in holding his job?

As the time for the San Remo conference of the Allies approached, Ben Yehuda went for days without food, nights without sleep. He wandered from room to room of the house on Abyssinian Street; from terrace to balcony to garden and back.

"What will they do at San Remo?"

He kept asking the question as if San Remo would decide how many hours or days he personally had yet to live.

Hemda, with all her love and respect for him, was now worried. Here was a new and different Ben Yehuda whom she had difficulty understanding.

"This is not the excitement of a normal, healthy man," she once said to Ben Avi. "He is becoming extremely eccentric. Why is he so worried?"

Ben Avi promised to keep watch over his father and try to calm him.

"There can be only one answer at San Remo, Father. Why do you fret? It is to the interests of all nations to agree about the mandate and a Jewish homeland, for in this manner they will solve once and for all what they like to call 'the Jewish problem.' "

Ben Avi was the only one who could influence his father, but as soon as Ben Avi left the house Eliezer would start pacing again, sometimes getting excited and saying:

"What if they give us a negative answer at San Remo?"

Then one morning Ben Avi came into his study.

"I have news from San Remo, Father! Fifty-two nations have just given their consent to our national home. Now will you stop worrying?"

"Are you sure?"

The father was on his feet, clutching his son by each of his shoulders.

"Who told you? Is it official? Was it unanimous?"

Ben Avi smiled and reassured his father. It was official. It had been unanimous. Israel had won her charter of freedom.

"And now," he added, "let's you and I have a glass of Jewish wine and drink a toast to our Israel!"

But the father was not listening any more.

He rushed from the house, not even stopping for a hat.

There was no telephone, so he must spread the news by word of mouth.

He went wildly from street to street, acting like the frantic fanatic his own wife had decided he had become.

Ben Avi tried to follow him, worried that he might have a heart attack.

Up one street, down the next. Rushing. Always rushing, although he was a man old beyond his sixty-two years.

Jerusalem must hear the news, so Jerusalem could rejoice with him!

He passed a schoolhouse. The children were streaming out from their classes. He gathered them around him.

"Go home! Quickly go home! Tell your parents! Tell them Israel lives! They signed!"

He rushed through the section of small shops. He stopped women on their way to market, whether they were British wives, tourists' wives, or whoever they were. Waving his arms to command their attention, he gave them the news, which few understood because his words were in Hebrew.

"They signed! Israel lives!"

He was out of breath and trembling, but he kept shouting like a devil possessed.

He met two Dominican priests who were old friends. Without any greeting of recognition he screamed at them:

"Did you hear? They signed!"

One of the priests tried to calm him.

"Ben Yehuda, my friend, what is this you are saying. Who signed what, and where?"

"San Remo! San Remo! They signed at San Remo! Can't you hear me?"

The priest smiled tolerantly.

"It is good that you won. We hope now that you will treat us better than we have treated you all these centuries."

Ben Yehuda blinked and for a moment seemed to come to his senses.

"Yes. You may be sure of that. There will be one law. One justice for us and for the stranger in our midst. We shall watch over your holy places as if they were our own."

He was still almost running when he reached his own home. Ben Avi was close behind him.

Hemda and the son put him on a couch. Each held one of his hands. They talked softly to him and begged him to lie still.

When he spoke again it was almost in a mumble.

"I cannot understand my own people."

They suggested he have a drink of water.

"Why am I the only one who is excited? Why is no one else enthusiastic?"

He looked wildly into the two faces that bent over him.

"Have Jews lost all their political sense? Does no one else comprehend the importance?"

Hemda tried to stroke his forehead.

"Do they not know that Israel has come from the dead and now lives again?"

When the answer to the second question came, Ben Yehuda became literally hysterical with excitement. Hemda was concerned about his condition and tried to keep him calm. He pushed her aside.

"Do you hear, Hemda? They have appointed a Jew! Sir Herbert Samuel, a Jew! His Hebrew name is the same as mine, Eliezer. He will become the modern King of Israel. He is a Jew, Hemda! For the first time in two thousand years a Jew will rule over Israel!"

"Yes, Eliezer," his wife said, worrying that the excitement would bring on one of his disastrous coughing spells. "I remember him. It was just twenty-two years ago that we met him at his aunt's house in London and he asked you——"

"Hemda! Do you suppose this man is—is that little boy?"

"Yes, Eliezer, 'that little boy.' I hope he remembers some of the things you told him then about our country."

On the first Sabbath after his arrival Sir Herbert Samuel went to a synagogue in the Old City and demonstrated that he had retained the faith of his forefathers. Eliezer Ben Yehuda, against whom the religious authorities had once declared a religious ban, went also that day to the synagogue.

When he returned home he was in a quiet mood, and his voice was soft again as he said to his wife:

"Our friend the High Commissioner read from the Torah, Bitti. He read those lines from Isaiah, 'Comfort ye, comfort ye, my people!' As he read them I could not control myself. I cried, Bitti, and I guess people saw me. I am sure they wondered why I was there."

After a pause he added:

"For nearly forty years I have been working to separate religion and the state, haven't I? I did it because I wanted Israel to be able to develop freely; so that those who are Orthodox and those who are freethinkers could join in the resurrection of Israel. Only in that way could our new state ever be strong.

"I suppose some people will think that now I am a traitor to my own ideas. They are always accusing me of that! I still believe we must keep our religion and our state apart, but, Bitti, it is so good a thing to see a British high commissioner standing in the synagogue reading from the Torah."

What happened next marked the real culmination of Ben Yehuda's lifework. High Commissioner Samuel announced that henceforth there would be three official languages: English, Arabic, and Hebrew.

There had been many other hard-laboring Zionists, although Ben Yehuda had exceeded most of them in the number of years he had devoted to propagandizing for a return to the Holy Land and in the number of words he had written about it.

There had been other Hebrew lexicographers, too, although none had ever even contemplated as monumental an undertaking as Ben Yehuda's multilingual, multivolumed dictionary.

There had been others who, after his death, would try to rob him of credit by saying, "I did it too!"

But there had been no one, anywhere, who had worked so hard for so long to make Hebrew an accepted language in the streets of Jerusalem, Jaffa, Haifa, and the settlements.

The proclamation of the mandatory power was like the final whistle of the referee. The game was over. The fight had been won.

One day the High Commissioner's wife, during a conversation with Mrs. Ben Yehuda about languages, said with a laugh:

"I shall stick to English. After all, the best is good enough for me!"

But less than a year later Lady Beatrice was speaking Hebrew. At Ben Yehuda's request her husband also took lessons. Their children, however, learned the language better than either of them.

After that, in the great stone palace which the Germans had named after their Empress, Augusta Victoria, and which the British had taken over as their Government House, Hebrew was heard at every state reception.

Teachers of Hebrew suddenly found themselves in great demand. American Jews, British Jews, even people who were not Jews at all, wanted to learn Hebrew. This sudden interest on the part of outsiders sent Ben Yehuda back to his study to look for new words.

"How do you say 'medicine dropper' in Hebrew?" a doctor would ask.

"What is the word for a 'policeman's club'?"

"The post office, Eliezer, has sent a man to ask if you have a word for . . ."

Many a night Ben Yehuda went without sleep, trying to satisfy these demands. He had grown old beyond his years and he was very tired and not in good health, but these were requests he could not deny.

The battle was over. But there was no rest for the winner.

If Eliezer Ben Yehuda had been younger, healthier, and not so tired, he might not have worried so much, in the early days of the British mandate, over all the "grousing," as Englishmen called it, that he began to hear. Having been the father of eleven children, he should have known about "growing pains."

The complainants came to him, knowing he was a champion of this new regime. Some even acted as if he personally were responsible for the evils to which they objected.

Vladimir Jabotinsky, nicknamed Hazeev (The Wolf), was one of the most vocal. He was the idol of the Jewish youth of Russia and Palestine alike; almost a legendary figure. During the war he had organized a Jewish military unit which fought at Gallipoli. Then he went to London and argued for the inclusion of all-Jewish units in the British army. Three battalions were formed, and the Jabotinsky idea spread to the United States, where nearly three thousand American Jews joined the Jewish Legion.

An entire battalion was recruited in Palestine and rendered efficient service in the drive which resulted in the collapse of the Turkish army in the Holy Land.

At the close of the war Jabotinsky wanted the Jewish Legion kept intact to help preserve order in Palestine, but the British insisted on disbandment.

In 1919–20 he found evidence that pogroms were being prepared in Palestine with what he called the "connivance" of the British, so he organized an underground Jewish defense force, the forerunner of Haganah, in which many former members of the Jewish Legion were enrolled.

Jabotinsky would come to Ben Yehuda complaining about the British attitude and insisting that the Jews of Palestine must prepare to fight for what they wanted with bullets and bombs.

Ben Yehuda would answer:

"The srength of the spirit is greater!"

This annoyed not only Jabotinsky but Ben Avi as well.

"When you were a young man," the son would say, "you were a rebel. You fought back, overthrowing all tradition. Now we are young. We wish to take strong measures. We are entitled to do so without interference from you and your generation!"

The father replied that concessions and sacrifices must now be made by the Jews or they would lose everything they had won.

But this was no answer to youth, and Ben Yehuda knew it and often gave evidence of doubting the soundness of his own advice.

Jabotinsky and his followers were not the only ones who had complaints. Others came to denounce the British for slighting the Jews when government jobs were given out.

Still others thought that life in Palestine had been better for the Jews under the Turks. You had to pay baksheesh, but it was possible to "buy" privileges. Now, they said, there were no privileges for anyone.

Hardly a day passed but that someone came with fresh criticism of the High Commissioner. Why was he, a Jew, so unsympathetic? Why did he do this? Why did he act in that manner?

Ben Yehuda admitted that perhaps the High Commissioner had made errors. Often he conceded that Sir Herbert might not be a perfect administrator. But, he would argue, a precedent had been established. Other high commissioners would come who might also be Jews if Herbert Samuel made a success of his job.

In these days there were the first rumblings of trouble between Jews and Arabs. Ben Yehuda pleaded for conciliation. He was a great friend of the Arabs. Through his philological work he felt more akin to these oppressed, Semitic people than most Jews. He had studied their language and knew the contributions which Hebrew had made to Arabic, and Arabic to Hebrew. He called the Arabs "our brothers." For years he had been expressing to them his belief that the day would come when both Arabs and Jews would be able to breathe the air of freedom in Palestine.

On their side, the Arabs respected Ben Yehuda as a scholar and learned man. Most of them were happy over his revival of Hebrew. They liked to hear the language spoken in the streets, regarding it as a "sister tongue," much more akin to their own than Yiddish, Ladino, or the talk of Europe.

In these days Ben Yehuda finally found personal peace.

He resigned from most of the committees he was on, except the language board, the Pro-Jerusalem Society, and several archaeological organizations.

He locked himself in his study and spent his time working on the dictionary and the manuscript for the Hebrew classics. Occasionally he wrote an editorial for his son's newspaper, which now, in the date line, gave the year in two ways: so many years after the destruction of the Temple, and so many years after the issuance of the Balfour Declaration.

In these days when Hemda and Eliezer were alone they would make plans for the home to be built with the check presented to them in New York.

When Eliezer could be persuaded to take time off from his writing they would go into the outskirts of the city looking for a suitable site. An architect drew plans for the house. It would include a real workroom which a writer like Ben Yehuda needed and which he had never had.

The prayer shawl which Ben Yehuda had worn in his early days in Jerusalem, when he was trying to win the support of the Orthodox group, he now wore for no other reason than that he wished to.

His new attitude toward his old religion perplexed many people. There were some who thought it was a pose, a new trick. There were some who questioned his sincerity.

But one of Ben Yehuda's friends one day silenced a particularly vocal doubter by saying:

"I was in the Hurva Synagogue the day the end of the Third Exile was officially pronounced. Ben Yehuda was also there. I was near enough to him so I could see the tears streaming down his face. I saw the look in his eyes.

"I knew then what I had always suspected. Down underneath it all Ben Yehuda has a deeply religious soul. He has fought superstition and bigotry and fanaticism, but that does not mean he is not a good and a humble man."

In these last days of his life Eliezer Ben Yehuda began to experience an inner serenity which all those about him observed.

46

Friend vs. Friend

ELIEZER BEN YEHUDA SELDOM INDULGED IN "FLOWery" prose, but when the Arab disorders of 1920–21 broke out he compared the thunder of that disastrous series of events to "the noise of God breaking stone walls."

Jews were dying. Arabs were killing and being killed. The soldiers of the British High Commissioner, who was a Jew, were firing on Palestinians, who were Jews. Blood was staining the soil of the newly established Jewish homeland, as had happened so often before. Blood was staining the record too. This had not been in the program. This had not been contemplated in the Balfour Declaration, nor at San Remo either.

Great Britain was being denounced from all sides.

Eliezer Ben Yehuda left the retirement of his study. He who had so stoutly defended the British and had preached the gospel of friendly co-operation with the Arabs must take a position. Whose side was he on now?

At first he defended the British High Commissioner, laying the blame at the door of Sir Ronald Storrs for not having nipped the trouble before it blossomed into a general disturbance. He also blamed anti-Semitic underlings of the High Commissioner.

Yet he sympathized with many of the arguments presented to him one evening by Vladimir (The Wolf) Jabotinsky.

"War is war, Ben Yehuda!" Jabotinsky said. "We must not shrink from fighting for what we believe. In the end, if we have the courage of our convictions, we shall come out victorious."

A short time after this conversation Jabotinsky and nineteen of his young followers were arrested by the British on a charge of storing up a secret supply of arms.

From his prison cell Jabotinsky demanded that the British give him a death sentence.

"Then perhaps my own people will see and understand the kind of a war we must fight against these people."

Instead the British shaved his head, put him in the garb of a common convict, and sentenced him to fifteen years at hard labor.

This infuriated the Jews of Palestine. Ben Yehuda, sharing their feelings, started for Acre to visit his imprisoned friend, but before he got there Jabotinsky was shipped off to Egypt "for safekeeping."

This was going too far! A clamor rose from the Jews which echoed in Whitehall and Downing Street.

Ben Yehuda sent his wife to see Mrs. Jabotinsky with a suggestion that the two of them go to England and "turn London upside down" to force the British government at least to return Jabotinsky to Palestine.

While Hemda was in conference with Mrs. Jabotinsky, London cabled Jerusalem, and Jabotinsky was returned to the prison at Acre.

Overnight he became a national hero. Jews by the hundreds streamed to Acre to see him. They sent him flowers, candy, food, books, cigarettes. Thousands of copies of his photograph were made. Many women began carrying his picture in their bosoms, close to their hearts. The rifle, helmet, revolver, and belt of the imprisoned man were declared "holy" items.

Now Jabotinsky issued an announcement that he was going on a hunger strike until the British released him.

Ben Yehuda sent him a message asking him to reconsider, because most of the Jews of Palestine would insist on going without food as long as he did, and there would be serious consequences.

Jabotinsky took Ben Yehuda's advice, but he sent word to his underground army to prepare an attack on Acre and liberate him by force of arms.

The message came one evening while his lieutenants were having dinner at the Ben Yehuda home. When their host saw their agitation he insisted they show him the message. After he read it he pleaded with them to think long before carrying out the order, because the attempt would undoubtedly cost the lives of all the young Jews involved.

Late that night some of them returned to the Ben Yehuda home, saying they had decided to take his advice.

A few weeks later Jabotinsky was released by the British.

Then the British High Commissioner made a move for which Ben Yehuda never forgave him. He ordered a halt to all immigration into Palestine. Ben Yehuda made a personal protest, but it did no good.

Regardless of the High Commissioner's order, Ben Yehuda felt it was important to bring in as many Jewish immigrants as possible, even though it had to be done illegally. On this subject he and his old friend Dr. Nordau at last saw eye to eye. Dr. Nordau was begging the Zionist Congress to bring in six hundred thousand Jews from Poland, the Ukraine, and Rumania. Had the French doctor's arguments prevailed, hundreds of thousands of Jews who were later put to death might have lived.

The trouble was that funds were lacking. Thousands of Jews were eager to come, but there was no money for transportation. So Ben Yehuda made a sensational proposal. The Jews were spending slightly more than one million dollars a year on their Palestinian schools. If they were closed for just a few months, the money saved could be used to bring in great numbers of new settlers.

The thunder of the denunciations which greeted this proposal could be heard from Dan to Beersheba.

"He is a traitor to education, to his own language, to everything he ever preached!"

"Now he wants us to sacrifice our children!"

What hurt Ben Yehuda the most was that his bitterest enemies in this new feud were the Hebrew teachers, many of whom had been his early protégés. They turned the other way when they saw him approaching on the street. They declared their own ban against him. There were no black candles this time. No blowing of the shofar. But it was a ban just the same, as emotionally imposed as the herem which the religious fanatics had declared against him so many years ago.

Brokenhearted, Ben Yehuda retired to his study. If his old friends wished to cross him off their lists again, if people chose to pass the Ben Yehuda house looking the other way, at least the dictionary would benefit.

"Bitti, the skeleton for the rest of the volumes of the dictionary is finally completed. And *tav* [the last letter of the alphabet] is even richer, I believe, than *aleph* [the first]."

About this time at Talpioth (Pretty Hillsite), on the road from Jerusalem to Bethlehem, the entire Ben Yehuda family assembled one day for the laying of the cornerstone of the new home. Eleizer was the one who picked the name for it, *Matan Am,* meaning, quite appropriately, "Gift of the People."

No one else may have noticed it, but Hemda read into the expression on her husband's face that day his own realization that others might live to make use of this symbol of America's feelings toward him but that he would never enjoy it himself.

He was only sixty-four years old, but he had been living all his adult life on what a doctor once called "borrowed time."

47

Only Ten Lines

CHAIM WEIZMANN, THEN THE UNCROWNED "KING" of the Zionists, who would become the first President of the state of Israel, was as controversial a figure in these days as Ben Yehuda.

Weizmann was only twenty-two years old when Herzl wrote *The Jewish State,* and he had been won to Zionism by the book, becoming one of the most ardent disciples of "the father of modern Zionism." For a quarter of a century he had played a large part in Zionist activities, but twice he had broken with the leadership. During the Uganda controversy he had opposed the Herzl-Ben Yehuda position, siding with the Russian bloc. More recently he and Justice Brandeis had had a "war of principle."

But now he was the "strong man" of the Zionists, and there were many Jews who tried to heap on him all the blame for all the troubles which were besetting Palestine.

The British High Commissioner, although a Jew himself, was pro-Arab in his actions, they argued, and in every compromise he made the Jews suffer. Chaim Weizmann, they insisted, must do something about this.

Then Weizmann came to Jerusalem. He had a personality before which opposition melted. He was of good appearance, tall, slim, with a winning smile.

Ben Yehuda was eager to talk to him about "grand strategy" and find out what the aim of British diplomacy here was. What about illegal immigration? Did Britain, as some people whispered, really want Arabs and Jews to keep at each other's throats?

Ben Avi gave a dinner party for Weizmann. Eliezer put on his evening clothes hours before it was time to go to his son's home. He paced his study, thinking over questions he wanted to ask.

Weizmann greeted them all warmly. He was placed between Eliezer and Hemda, who was nervous because of the disturbed state her husband was in.

After dinner, in the oriental drawing room, Weizmann and Ben Yehuda went into a corner by themselves. No one disturbed them. Each spoke with intensity and animation.

"And what did he say?" Hemda asked her husband as soon as they were alone in their own home.

"He said that England, in his opinion, will fulfill all her obligations. Yet he feels that England has some just complaints. In London they are furious over the way the Jews in Palestine are behaving, and they blame Weizmann for not exerting a stronger leadership over his people. But England, he said, is in no position to renege on her declaration."

"What else, Eliezer?"

"He says that he is disappointed that more Jews do not seem to want to leave the *Galuth* [lands of their exile] and return to their own native soil. That gets back to the disturbances again. They hear about them abroad and are afraid to come here. They say that conditions in the ghettos are bad, but there are no Arabs or British soldiers shooting at them."

"Was that all, Eliezer?"

"Oh yes, he did say he has a firm faith that if we can weather these storms the day will come when we shall have a real Jewish state."

Ben Yehuda stopped, as if this were the end, but Hemda could tell there had been something else; something that was bothering him. Finally she pried it from him.

At the end of the conversation Weizmann had said:

"What we need, Ben Yehuda, is a strong, vigorous appeal to our own people. And you are the one to write it. We have never forgotten your first and second appeals, written so many years ago. Now you must write a third.

"Write it with all your warmth and with all the magic of your pen. The situation is serious, but your words will enter the minds and hearts of our people and stir them to a realization of the crisis of the hour."

Ben Yehuda had tried to beg off. He had answered that no one could write anything more effective than the Balfour Declaration. That had been the "third appeal." If that did not impress Jews, nothing would.

When Weizmann still insisted, Ben Yehuda had finally stood up at attention, like a soldier, and had said:

"You are the leader. Your wish is a command. I shall write it for you."

That was the reason Eliezer Ben Yehuda did not go to bed that night. Still in his evening clothes, he went to his study, took up his pen, and with trembling fingers began to make marks on a piece of paper.

Hemda sat outside the study until 2 A.M. waiting for him. Finally he put down his pen and came out.

"Bitti, I do not seem able to do it. I fear I am too tired. Perhaps I shall find the right words, the strong expressions, the inspiration tomorrow. Now I think I had better go to bed."

As she turned out the lights Hemda glanced at the piece of paper. There were just five lines on it.

The next morning, early, when the rest of the family came down to breakfast, they found Eliezer standing at his high desk, with the pen in one hand and the other hand to his forehead. There were now ten lines on the piece of paper.

He would stand for an hour or two and then sit for a spell.

In midafternoon Hemda begged him to lie down for a rest. He refused.

"I *must* make the words come, Bitti! I promised the leader!"

That evening, which was the evening of the first day of Hanukkah, the eight-day candlelight festival, there was a dinner party at the Ben Yehuda home. This was an annual affair. On this day they always celebrated the anniversary of Ben Yehuda's release from prison.

After dinner the others retired to the drawing room on the second floor. Ben Yehuda excused himself, saying:

"I have some work to do in my study."

At 11 P.M. tea was served. Hemda sent one of the girls to the study to ask her husband to join them for half an hour. He sent word back that he was too busy, so Hemda sent his tea to him.

At midnight the guests left and Hemda immediately went to the study. Eliezer, standing in front of his high desk, apparently did not hear her enter. She went over to him, put one arm around his shoulder, and said:

"Give me the pen, Eliezer. You have worked long enough. Tomorrow morning you can continue. You say yourself you do your best work in the morning."

He handed her the pen just as a small boy, caught with some forbidden article, relinquishes it, not very willingly.

All he said was:

"I am afraid I shall not be able to write the third appeal."

After she had helped him to bed Hemda went back to the study and looked at the piece of paper on the desk. There were still ten lines on it.

About one hour later Eliezer called to his wife. He said he felt that something was wrong. It was difficult to breathe.

Dola, frightened by the tone of her mother's voice when she called her and by the expression on her mother's face, slipped a coat over her nightdress and with her hair still hanging down her back ran the considerable distance to Ben Avi's home.

Five doctors arrived, one after the other. An oxygen tent was sent from the Hadassah Hospital.

All the children of the family except Ada, who was in Europe, and Ehud, who was studying in California, were gathered around the bed.

The doctors shook their heads.

Hemda bent over and asked Eliezer if he wanted anything.

He said "no" with his eyes.
A moment later she said to him:
"Do you feel better now, Eliezer?"
Slowly the answer came, in that warm manner of speaking he had when he was not agitated.
"Yes, Bitti. Better."
Then he closed his eyes.
One of the doctors pulled a sheet up over his face.

Epilogue

FATE CALLED ON ELIEZER BEN YEHUDA TO PAY that penalty which true greatness is so often required to pay: he had to die to be properly acclaimed.

In life he had been fought, denounced, vilified by Sephardic Jews and Ashkenazic Jews, by Zionists and non-Zionists, by haters of Hebrew and lovers of Hebrew, the Orthodox and the un-Orthodox, Jews in Palestine and Jews out in the Diaspora.

In death thirty thousand Jews followed his body to the grave. School children with black-draped flags. Ultra-religious Jews with long side curls and garments reminiscent of the ghettos of Europe. Jewish businessmen, very Western-looking, from Tel Aviv and Haifa. Healthy young pioneers who had been streaming in for two days from remote colonies. Jewish soldiers, Jewish scholars, Jewish statesmen. There were Christians and Arabs in the procession, and British high officials. Dominican monks and Franciscan monks and Moslem leaders.

Palestine was ordered to observe three days of national mourning.

Palestine wept, knowing a man had died who had all the qualifications of greatness.

Epilogue

Eliezer Ben Yehuda had never made any "after my death" requests, except that once, perhaps thinking of the time Deborah, his wife, died, or of the trouble about burying Deborah, his daughter, he had spoken briefly to Hemda about liking the idea of cremation.

In the early hours of that Sabbath in 1922, after the doctors had gone, Hemda remembered the flag the American Jews had given her husband, so she got it and put it over the cold body.

Later that morning she made inquiries about cremation, although she knew it would be a serious violation of Orthodox practice. She was told the body would have to be shipped to Egypt. There were no crematories in Palestine.

While she was still debating the matter in her own mind, a delegation arrived at the house on Abyssinian Street to say that orders had been issued for a national funeral. This settled it. In life Eliezer had been hers. In death, she agreed, he belonged to the nation; to his people.

The entire proceedings went according to strict Orthodox practice. Members of the family were not allowed to follow the cortege.

There were many other rules which had to be adhered to. But Hemda and the rest of the family acquiesced. Eliezer was no longer theirs.

The widow was given one privilege. She could choose the place for the grave.

Hemda knew the exact spot which, as long as cremation was not possible, would have pleased her husband. It was on the Mount of Olives, where they had so often sat, looking down on the Temple area and the Golden Gate. From up there one could see the entire panorama of Jerusalem, "his" city.

The funeral was at high noon. It was conducted with solemn magnificence.

They buried Eliezer Ben Yehuda clothed in the prayer shawl which of late he had taken to wearing when he went to the synagogue. The Hebrew flag given to him in New York covered the bier.

Following Orthodox practice, members of the family were not permitted even to see the grave until the seven-day period of mourning was over.

On anniversaries of the death the family was joined in visits to the Mount of Olives by groups of young students carrying banners, who would cluster around the stone marking the spot and sing Hebrew songs to the man who had revived their language.

As for the dictionary, Hemda and her children devoted their energies during the next quarter century to organizing committees, raising funds, and putting out additional volumes.

The first committee was called the Eliezer Ben Yehuda Memorial Trust and was founded under the patronage of High Commissioner Herbert Samuel and Dr. Chaim Weizmann.

Philologists and language scholars in England, Germany, the United States, France, and Palestine, among them some of Ben Yehuda's Dominican friends, worked with his former secretary, Moshe Nissim, to complete the sixth and seventh volumes.

Later other committees helped put out other volumes. Once Ehud spent a year in South Africa, Rhodesia, and the Belgian Congo organizing a committee there.

By 1951 thirteen volumes, averaging six hundred pages each, had been put into print, and only two letters of the Hebrew alphabet remained, *shin* (the equivalent of the "sh" sound in English) and *tav,* the final letter. It was estimated that these two letters would require three more volumes, making sixteen in all.

After the state of Israel came into existence the completion of the dictionary became a state project.

The last word on which Ben Yehuda himself had done any work was *nefesh* (soul). He left, however, most of the material required for the eleven posthumous volumes.

Once, long before the Balfour Declaration was issued, Ben Yehuda had said to his wife:

"Old men talk about what is going to happen after their death. Such matters have never interested me. I only pray that I shall live long enough to see the rebirth of Israel as a nation and the use of our own language on our own soil."

After his death a British magazine, the *Palestine Weekly,* said:

"His was one of the rare cases of a life's dream fulfilled; long before he died he saw the ideal for which he had lived, labored, and suffered transformed into a solid reality, a reality which could not be disputed."

That was not technically true. In 1922 there was no Jewish state. Israel still existed only in dreams. The Jews of Palestine would have to wait another quarter century to see the flag which had been given to Eliezer Ben Yehuda in New York fly over Jerusalem as a symbol of the existence of a free and independent Israel.

But he did live to see the day when a census was taken in Palestine and virtually every Jew in the country put down on his form, under "mother tongue," the word "Hebrew."

He did live to see the language which he had had such a major part in reviving being used in all the schools without further debate. It was the language of the courts, the theater, of business, society, and public affairs, along with Arabic for the Arabs and English for officials of the mandatory power.

When Ben Yehuda started work on his dream Hebrew was only a liturgical medium, as dead as ancient Latin. It had not even breathed for two thousand years.

By the time he made his last trip up the Mount of Olives, a new and vibrant Hebrew was being spoken by a new and vibrant race of Jews.

During the forty-one years he had struggled to bring this about he had often been called a "fanatic."

After his death a eulogist added one word to that epithet, turning it into an epitaph.

The gate over his grave might well have been inscribed with the words:

HERE LIES ELIEZER BEN YEHUDA
FAITHFUL FANATIC

INDEX

INDEX

Index

Index

A PERSONAL WORD FROM MELVIN POWERS, PUBLISHER, WILSHIRE BOOK COMPANY

My goal is to publish interesting, informative, and inspirational books. You can help me to accomplish this by sending me your answers to the following questions:

Did you enjoy reading this book? Why?

What ideas in the book impressed you most? Have you applied them to your daily life? How?

Is there a chapter that could serve as a theme for an entire book? Explain.

Would you like to read similar books? What additional information would you like them to contain?

If you have an idea for a book, I would welcome discussing it with you. If you have a manuscript in progress, write or call me concerning possible publication.

Melvin Powers
12015 Sherman Road
North Hollywood, California 91605

(818) 765-8579

MELVIN POWERS SELF-IMPROVEMENT LIBRARY

ASTROLOGY

Title	Price
___ ASTROLOGY: HOW TO CHART YOUR HOROSCOPE *Max Heindel*	5.00
___ ASTROLOGY AND SEXUAL ANALYSIS *Morris C. Goodman*	5.00
___ ASTROLOGY AND YOU *Carroll Righter*	5.00
___ ASTROLOGY MADE EASY *Astarte*	7.00
___ ASTROLOGY, ROMANCE, YOU AND THE STARS *Anthony Norvell*	5.00
___ MY WORLD OF ASTROLOGY *Sydney Omarr*	7.00
___ THOUGHT DIAL *Sydney Omarr*	7.00
___ WHAT THE STARS REVEAL ABOUT THE MEN IN YOUR LIFE *Thelma White*	3.00

BRIDGE

Title	Price
___ BRIDGE BIDDING MADE EASY *Edwin B. Kantar*	10.00
___ BRIDGE CONVENTIONS *Edwin B. Kantar*	10.00
___ COMPETITIVE BIDDING IN MODERN BRIDGE *Edgar Kaplan*	7.00
___ DEFENSIVE BRIDGE PLAY COMPLETE *Edwin B. Kantar*	20.00
___ GAMESMAN BRIDGE—PLAY BETTER WITH KANTAR *Edwin B. Kantar*	7.00
___ HOW TO IMPROVE YOUR BRIDGE *Alfred Sheinwold*	7.00
___ IMPROVING YOUR BIDDING SKILLS *Edwin B. Kantar*	7.00
___ INTRODUCTION TO DECLARER'S PLAY *Edwin B. Kantar*	7.00
___ INTRODUCTION TO DEFENDER'S PLAY *Edwin B. Kantar*	7.00
___ KANTAR FOR THE DEFENSE *Edwin B. Kantar*	7.00
___ KANTAR FOR THE DEFENSE VOLUME 2 *Edwin B. Kantar*	7.00
___ TEST YOUR BRIDGE PLAY *Edwin B. Kantar*	7.00
___ VOLUME 2—TEST YOUR BRIDGE PLAY *Edwin B. Kantar*	7.00
___ WINNING DECLARER PLAY *Dorothy Hayden Truscott*	10.00

BUSINESS, STUDY & REFERENCE

Title	Price
___ BRAINSTORMING *Charles Clark*	10.00
___ CONVERSATION MADE EASY *Elliot Russell*	5.00
___ EXAM SECRET *Dennis B. Jackson*	5.00
___ FIX-IT BOOK *Arthur Symons*	2.00
___ HOW TO DEVELOP A BETTER SPEAKING VOICE *M. Hellier*	5.00
___ HOW TO SAVE 50% ON GAS & CAR EXPENSES *Ken Stansbie*	5.00
___ HOW TO SELF-PUBLISH YOUR BOOK & MAKE IT A BEST SELLER *Melvin Powers*	20.00
___ INCREASE YOUR LEARNING POWER *Geoffrey A. Dudley*	5.00
___ PRACTICAL GUIDE TO BETTER CONCENTRATION *Melvin Powers*	5.00
___ 7 DAYS TO FASTER READING *William S. Schaill*	7.00
___ SONGWRITERS' RHYMING DICTIONARY *Jane Shaw Whitfield*	10.00
___ SPELLING MADE EASY *Lester D. Basch & Dr. Milton Finkelstein*	3.00
___ STUDENT'S GUIDE TO BETTER GRADES *J. A. Rickard*	3.00
___ TEST YOURSELF—FIND YOUR HIDDEN TALENT *Jack Shafer*	3.00
___ YOUR WILL & WHAT TO DO ABOUT IT *Attorney Samuel G. Kling*	5.00

CALLIGRAPHY

Title	Price
___ ADVANCED CALLIGRAPHY *Katherine Jeffares*	7.00
___ CALLIGRAPHY—THE ART OF BEAUTIFUL WRITING *Katherine Jeffares*	7.00
___ CALLIGRAPHY FOR FUN & PROFIT *Anne Leptich & Jacque Evans*	7.00
___ CALLIGRAPHY MADE EASY *Tina Serafini*	7.00

CHESS & CHECKERS

Title	Price
___ BEGINNER'S GUIDE TO WINNING CHESS *Fred Reinfeld*	7.00
___ CHESS IN TEN EASY LESSONS *Larry Evans*	5.00
___ CHESS MADE EASY *Milton L. Hanauer*	5.00
___ CHESS PROBLEMS FOR BEGINNERS *Edited by Fred Reinfeld*	5.00
___ CHESS TACTICS FOR BEGINNERS *Edited by Fred Reinfeld*	5.00

___ HOW TO WIN AT CHECKERS *Fred Reinfeld* 5.00
___ 1001 BRILLIANT WAYS TO CHECKMATE *Fred Reinfeld* 10.00
___ 1001 WINNING CHESS SACRIFICES & COMBINATIONS *Fred Reinfeld* 7.00

COOKERY & HERBS

___ CULPEPER'S HERBAL REMEDIES *Dr. Nicholas Culpeper* 5.00
___ FAST GOURMET COOKBOOK *Poppy Cannon* 2.50
___ HEALING POWER OF HERBS *May Bethel* 5.00
___ HEALING POWER OF NATURAL FOODS *May Bethel* 7.00
___ HERBS FOR HEALTH—HOW TO GROW & USE THEM *Louise Evans Doole* 5.00
___ HOME GARDEN COOKBOOK—DELICIOUS NATURAL FOOD RECIPES *Ken Kraft* 3.00
___ MEATLESS MEAL GUIDE *Tomi Ryan & James H. Ryan, M.D.* 4.00
___ VEGETABLE GARDENING FOR BEGINNERS *Hugh Wiberg* 2.00
___ VEGETABLES FOR TODAY'S GARDENS *R. Milton Carleton* 2.00
___ VEGETARIAN COOKERY *Janet Walker* 7.00
___ VEGETARIAN COOKING MADE EASY & DELECTABLE *Veronica Vezza* 3.00
___ VEGETARIAN DELIGHTS—A HAPPY COOKBOOK FOR HEALTH *K. R. Mehta* 2.00

GAMBLING & POKER

___ HOW TO WIN AT DICE GAMES *Skip Frey* 3.00
___ HOW TO WIN AT POKER *Terence Reese & Anthony T. Watkins* 7.00
___ SCARNE ON DICE *John Scarne* 15.00
___ WINNING AT CRAPS *Dr. Lloyd T. Commins* 5.00
___ WINNING AT GIN *Chester Wander & Cy Rice* 3.00
___ WINNING AT POKER—AN EXPERT'S GUIDE *John Archer* 5.00
___ WINNING AT 21—AN EXPERT'S GUIDE *John Archer* 7.00
___ WINNING POKER SYSTEMS *Norman Zadeh* 3.00

HEALTH

___ BEE POLLEN *Lynda Lyngheim & Jack Scagnetti* 5.00
___ COPING WITH ALZHEIMER'S *Rose Oliver, Ph.D. & Francis Bock, Ph.D.* 10.00
___ DR. LINDNER'S POINT SYSTEM FOOD PROGRAM *Peter G. Lindner, M.D.* 2.00
___ HELP YOURSELF TO BETTER SIGHT *Margaret Darst Corbett* 7.00
___ HOW YOU CAN STOP SMOKING PERMANENTLY *Ernest Caldwell* 5.00
___ MIND OVER PLATTER *Peter G. Lindner, M.D.* 5.00
___ NATURE'S WAY TO NUTRITION & VIBRANT HEALTH *Robert J. Scrutton* 3.00
___ NEW CARBOHYDRATE DIET COUNTER *Patti Lopez-Pereira* 2.00
___ REFLEXOLOGY *Dr. Maybelle Segal* 5.00
___ REFLEXOLOGY FOR GOOD HEALTH *Anna Kaye & Don C. Matchan* 7.00
___ 30 DAYS TO BEAUTIFUL LEGS *Dr. Marc Selner* 3.00
___ WONDER WITHIN *Thomas F. Coyle, M.D.* 10.00
___ YOU CAN LEARN TO RELAX *Dr. Samuel Gutwirth* 5.00

HOBBIES

___ BEACHCOMBING FOR BEGINNERS *Norman Hickin* 2.00
___ BLACKSTONE'S MODERN CARD TRICKS *Harry Blackstone* 7.00
___ BLACKSTONE'S SECRETS OF MAGIC *Harry Blackstone* 5.00
___ COIN COLLECTING FOR BEGINNERS *Burton Hobson & Fred Reinfeld* 7.00
___ ENTERTAINING WITH ESP *Tony 'Doc' Shiels* 2.00
___ 400 FASCINATING MAGIC TRICKS YOU CAN DO *Howard Thurston* 7.00
___ HOW I TURN JUNK INTO FUN AND PROFIT *Sari* 3.00
___ HOW TO WRITE A HIT SONG & SELL IT *Tommy Boyce* 10.00
___ MAGIC FOR ALL AGES *Walter Gibson* 4.00
___ STAMP COLLECTING FOR BEGINNERS *Burton Hobson* 3.00

HORSE PLAYER'S WINNING GUIDES

___ BETTING HORSES TO WIN *Les Conklin* 7.00
___ ELIMINATE THE LOSERS *Bob McKnight* 5.00
___ HOW TO PICK WINNING HORSES *Bob McKnight* 5.00

___ HOW TO WIN AT THE RACES *Sam (The Genius) Lewin* 5.00
___ HOW YOU CAN BEAT THE RACES *Jack Kavanaqh* 5.00
___ MAKING MONEY AT THE RACES *David Barr* 5.00
___ PAYDAY AT THE RACES *Les Conklin* 5.00
___ SMART HANDICAPPING MADE EASY *William Bauman* 5.00
___ SUCCESS AT THE HARNESS RACES *Barry Meadow* 5.00

HUMOR

___ HOW TO FLATTEN YOUR TUSH *Coach Marge Reardon* 2.00
___ JOKE TELLER'S HANDBOOK *Bob Orben* 7.00
___ JOKES FOR ALL OCCASIONS *Al Schock* 5.00
___ 2,000 NEW LAUGHS FOR SPEAKERS *Bob Orben* 7.00
___ 2,400 JOKES TO BRIGHTEN YOUR SPEECHES *Robert Orben* 7.00
___ 2,500 JOKES TO START 'EM LAUGHING *Bob Orben* 7.00

HYPNOTISM

___ ADVANCED TECHNIQUES OF HYPNOSIS *Melvin Powers* 3.00
___ CHILDBIRTH WITH HYPNOSIS *William S. Kroger, M.D.* 5.00
___ HOW TO SOLVE YOUR SEX PROBLEMS WITH SELF-HYPNOSIS *Frank S. Caprio, M.D.* 5.00
___ HOW TO STOP SMOKING THRU SELF-HYPNOSIS *Leslie M. LeCron* 3.00
___ HOW YOU CAN BOWL BETTER USING SELF-HYPNOSIS *Jack Heise* 7.00
___ HOW YOU CAN PLAY BETTER GOLF USING SELF-HYPNOSIS *Jack Heise* 3.00
___ HYPNOSIS AND SELF-HYPNOSIS *Bernard Hollander, M.D.* 5.00
___ HYPNOTISM *(Originally published in 1893) Carl Sextus* 5.00
___ HYPNOTISM MADE EASY *Dr. Ralph Winn* 7.00
___ HYPNOTISM MADE PRACTICAL *Louis Orton* 5.00
___ HYPNOTISM REVEALED *Melvin Powers* 3.00
___ HYPNOTISM TODAY *Leslie LeCron and Jean Bordeaux, Ph.D.* 5.00
___ MODERN HYPNOSIS *Lesley Kuhn & Salvatore Russo, Ph.D.* 5.00
___ NEW CONCEPTS OF HYPNOSIS *Bernard C. Gindes, M.D.* 10.00
___ NEW SELF-HYPNOSIS *Paul Adams* 7.00
___ POST-HYPNOTIC INSTRUCTIONS—SUGGESTIONS FOR THERAPY *Arnold Furst* 10.00
___ PRACTICAL GUIDE TO SELF-HYPNOSIS *Melvin Powers* 5.00
___ PRACTICAL HYPNOTISM *Philip Magonet, M.D.* 3.00
___ SECRETS OF HYPNOTISM *S. J. Van Pelt, M.D.* 5.00
___ SELF-HYPNOSIS—A CONDITIONED-RESPONSE TECHNIQUE *Laurence Sparks* 7.00
___ SELF-HYPNOSIS—ITS THEORY, TECHNIQUE & APPLICATION *Melvin Powers* 3.00
___ THERAPY THROUGH HYPNOSIS *Edited by Raphael H. Rhodes* 5.00

JUDAICA

___ SERVICE OF THE HEART *Evelyn Garfiel, Ph.D.* 10.00
___ STORY OF ISRAEL IN COINS *Jean & Maurice Gould* 2.00
___ STORY OF ISRAEL IN STAMPS *Maxim & Gabriel Shamir* 1.00
___ TONGUE OF THE PROPHETS *Robert St. John* 10.00

JUST FOR WOMEN

___ COSMOPOLITAN'S GUIDE TO MARVELOUS MEN Foreword by *Helen Gurley Brown* 3.00
___ COSMOPOLITAN'S HANG-UP HANDBOOK Foreword by *Helen Gurley Brown* 4.00
___ COSMOPOLITAN'S LOVE BOOK—A GUIDE TO ECSTASY IN BED 7.00
___ COSMOPOLITAN'S NEW ETIQUETTE GUIDE Foreword by *Helen Gurley Brown* 4.00
___ I AM A COMPLEAT WOMAN *Doris Hagopian & Karen O'Connor Sweeney* 3.00
___ JUST FOR WOMEN—A GUIDE TO THE FEMALE BODY *Richard E. Sand, M.D.* 5.00
___ NEW APPROACHES TO SEX IN MARRIAGE *John E. Eichenlaub, M.D.* 3.00
___ SEXUALLY ADEQUATE FEMALE *Frank S. Caprio, M.D.* 3.00
___ SEXUALLY FULFILLED WOMAN *Dr. Rachel Copelan* 5.00

MARRIAGE, SEX & PARENTHOOD

___ ABILITY TO LOVE *Dr. Allan Fromme* 7.00
___ GUIDE TO SUCCESSFUL MARRIAGE *Drs. Albert Ellis & Robert Harper* 7.00
___ HOW TO RAISE AN EMOTIONALLY HEALTHY, HAPPY CHILD *Albert Ellis, Ph.D.* 10.00
___ PARENT SURVIVAL TRAINING *Marvin Silverman, Ed.D. & David Lustig, Ph.D.* 10.00
___ SEX WITHOUT GUILT *Albert Ellis, Ph.D.* 5.00
___ SEXUALLY ADEQUATE MALE *Frank S. Caprio, M.D.* 3.00
___ SEXUALLY FULFILLED MAN *Dr. Rachel Copelan* 5.00
___ STAYING IN LOVE *Dr. Norton F. Kristy* 7.00

MELVIN POWERS' MAIL ORDER LIBRARY

___ HOW TO GET RICH IN MAIL ORDER *Melvin Powers* 20.00
___ HOW TO SELF-PUBLISH YOUR BOOK & MAKE IT A BEST SELLER *Melvin Powers* 20.00
___ HOW TO WRITE A GOOD ADVERTISEMENT *Victor O. Schwab* 20.00
___ MAIL ORDER MADE EASY *J. Frank Brumbaugh* 20.00

METAPHYSICS & OCCULT

___ CONCENTRATION—A GUIDE TO MENTAL MASTERY *Mouni Sadhu* 7.00
___ EXTRA-TERRESTRIAL INTELLIGENCE—THE FIRST ENCOUNTER 6.00
___ FORTUNE TELLING WITH CARDS *P. Foli* 5.00
___ HOW TO INTERPRET DREAMS, OMENS & FORTUNE TELLING SIGNS *Gettings* 5.00
___ HOW TO UNDERSTAND YOUR DREAMS *Geoffrey A. Dudley* 5.00
___ IN DAYS OF GREAT PEACE *Mouni Sadhu* 3.00
___ MAGICIAN—HIS TRAINING AND WORK *W. E. Butler* 7.00
___ MEDITATION *Mouni Sadhu* 10.00
___ MODERN NUMEROLOGY *Morris C. Goodman* 5.00
___ NUMEROLOGY—ITS FACTS AND SECRETS *Ariel Yvon Taylor* 5.00
___ NUMEROLOGY MADE EASY *W. Mykian* 5.00
___ PALMISTRY MADE EASY *Fred Gettings* 5.00
___ PALMISTRY MADE PRACTICAL *Elizabeth Daniels Squire* 7.00
___ PROPHECY IN OUR TIME *Martin Ebon* 2.50
___ SUPERSTITION—ARE YOU SUPERSTITIOUS? *Eric Maple* 2.00
___ TAROT *Mouni Sadhu* 10.00
___ TAROT OF THE BOHEMIANS *Papus* 7.00
___ WAYS TO SELF-REALIZATION *Mouni Sadhu* 7.00
___ WITCHCRAFT, MAGIC & OCCULTISM—A FASCINATING HISTORY *W. B. Crow* 10.00
___ WITCHCRAFT—THE SIXTH SENSE *Justine Glass* 7.00

RECOVERY

___ KNIGHT IN RUSTY ARMOR Robert Fisher 5.00
___ KNIGHT IN RUSTY ARMOR Robert Fisher *(Hard cover edition)* 10.00

SELF-HELP & INSPIRATIONAL

___ CHARISMA—HOW TO GET "THAT SPECIAL MAGIC" *Marcia Grad* 7.00
___ DAILY POWER FOR JOYFUL LIVING *Dr. Donald Curtis* 7.00
___ DYNAMIC THINKING *Melvin Powers* 5.00
___ GREATEST POWER IN THE UNIVERSE *U. S. Andersen* 7.00
___ GROW RICH WHILE YOU SLEEP *Ben Sweetland* 8.00
___ GROW RICH WITH YOUR MILLION DOLLAR MIND *Brian Adams* 7.00
___ GROWTH THROUGH REASON *Albert Ellis, Ph.D.* 7.00
___ GUIDE TO PERSONAL HAPPINESS *Albert Ellis, Ph.D. & Irving Becker, Ed.D.* 10.00
___ HANDWRITING ANALYSIS MADE EASY *John Marley* 7.00
___ HANDWRITING TELLS *Nadya Olyanova* 7.00
___ HOW TO ATTRACT GOOD LUCK *A.H.Z. Carr* 7.00
___ HOW TO DEVELOP A WINNING PERSONALITY *Martin Panzer* 7.00
___ HOW TO DEVELOP AN EXCEPTIONAL MEMORY *Young & Gibson* 7.00
___ HOW TO LIVE WITH A NEUROTIC *Albert Ellis, Ph.D.* 7.00
___ HOW TO OVERCOME YOUR FEARS *M. P. Leahy, M.D.* 3.00
___ HOW TO SUCCEED *Brian Adams* 7.00